The Philadelphia Association of Sports Trivia Presents:

"WHAT DO YOU KNOW"...

ABOUT PHILADELPHIA SPORTS?

"LEARN FROM THE P.A.S.T."

ISBN 978-0-615-41848-3

Background illustrated artwork on cover by Stan Kotzen
Cover design by Jodi Reilly
Interior design by Jodi Reilly
Edited by The P.A.S.T. Authors

Purchase online at http://www.PhillySportsTrivia.com
P.A.S.T. PUBLISHING (Self Publishing)
304 Greenhill Road
Willow Grove, PA 19090

Visit us on the web!
www.PhillySportsTrivia.com
Facebook.com in the "Search" box type The PAST (Philadelphia
Association of Sports Trivia)
Twitter @PhillyTrivia

Dedicated to Harry Kalas and Joe Frazier

For Harry's grace, his incredible enthusiasm while calling Phillies games, the close connection he held with Philadelphia sports fans and for so many other reasons ... we dedicate this book to a true Hall of Famer -- Harry Kalas!

For Joe who was one of our P.A.S.T. authors and a true Philadelphia icon. His boxing prowess was exceeded only by his humanity and dedication to support the youth of our great city.

CONTENTS

A MESSAGE FROM THE P.A.S.T.   5

ACKNOWLEDGMENTS   6

SPECIAL THANKS   7

MEET THE MEMBERS OF THE P.A.S.T.   8

FOREWORD: BY LARRY KANE   10

PSYCHOLOGY OF PHILLY SPORTS FANS: BY KEVIN WALSH   14

EAGLES TRIVIA   17
    INTRODUCTION BY MERRILL REESE

PHILLIES TRIVIA   55
    INTRODUCTION BY BILL GILES

76ERS TRIVIA   95
    INTRODUCTION BY MARC ZUMOFF

FLYERS TRIVIA   131
    INTRODUCTION BY GARY DORNHOEFER

A's TRIVIA   170
    INTRODUCTION BY TED TAYLOR

BIG 5 TRIVIA   182
    INTRODUCTION BY TOM GOLA

GOLF TRIVIA   205
    G.A.P. HISTORY/INTRODUCTION BY PETER TRENHAM

BOXING TRIVIA   221
    INTRODUCTION BY JOE FRAZIER

MISCELLANEOUS TRIVIA   228

PHILADELPHIA SPORTS HALL OF FAME INDUCTEES   237

ANSWER SECTION   319

PHOTO CREDITS   377

A MESSAGE FROM THE P.A.S.T.

So much in the world of sports (and the world in general) has gone to a better place: underhanded free throws, the single wing formation, the manufacturing of a run with only a walk, stolen base, sacrifice bunt and a sacrifice fly, and even the baseball scorecard. One of the great things about scoring a baseball game is that everybody does it just a little differently, depending on how you were taught (usually by your dad). Take a moment now to reflect on those simpler, saner times. Maybe, just maybe, it will take you back to a time when things weren't quite so hectic: to a time when you were a kid, and you pored over every nuance of a scorecard or a box score like it was your investment portfolio. It may evoke memories of going to a ball game with Dad, be it at Shibe Park, The Vet, or Citizens Bank Park. He always bought you a hot dog and a soda, and sometimes he would even let you score the game (under his watchful eye, of course). Perhaps now you can smell the smells of America: Coca-Cola, freshly popped popcorn, the rich dark soil of the infield, neat's-foot oil, the bitter tang of tobacco juice. And, for a few hours, you could forget about the world at large, sit in the warm sunshine with a loved one, and continue a great American tradition that has survived for more than 125 years.

Are you ready? Then come with us…

- Will Reilly, President   - Joe DeCamara
- Jack Carroll, Vice President   - Bob Herpen
- Cary Beavers, Secretary
- Brendon Crowther, Treasurer

THE PHILADELPHIA ASSOCIATION OF SPORTS TRIVIA

ACKNOWLEDGMENTS

To Jodi Reilly for her tireless work in assembling and categorizing all elements of this book. From the myriad of pictures, its format, the cover design and more, without Jodi's vast talents and dedication this book simply would not exist.

To Ken Avallon, President of the Philadelphia Sports Hall of Fame, for sharing the archives of his great organization with us. We are truly indebted to Ken for his support of our project.

To the players and coaches of the Philadelphia sports teams who have entertained and inspired us throughout our lives.

Special Thanks
To All Of Our Contributing Celebrity Writers
(In order of appearance)

Larry Kane
Legendary Philadelphia TV Newsman

Kevin Walsh
Comcast SportsNet Anchor/ Reporter

Merrill Reese
Philadelphia Eagles Radio Announcer

Bill Giles
Philadelphia Phillies Chairman and Part Owner

Marc Zumoff
Philadelphia 76ers TV Announcer

Gary Dornhoefer
Philadelphia Flyers Two-Time Stanley Cup Champion

Ted Taylor
Past President of The Philadelphia Athletics Historical Society

Tom Gola
LaSalle College National Champion, Philadelphia Warriors NBA
Champion and Basketball Hall of Famer

Peter Trenham
PGA Historian and Lifetime PGA Member

Joe Frazier
Former Heavyweight Champion of the World and
1964 Olympic Boxing Gold Medalist

The Philadelphia Association of Sports Trivia Members

Will Reilly: Will is an avid Philly sports fan. His interests include The NBA and NFL Draft, all Philadelphia sports teams and golf. Will is a member of The Professional Golfers Association and was the Head PGA Professional at Twining Valley Golf and Fitness Club from 1993-2010. In 2011 he accepted the position of PGA of America Junior Development Manager, in Palm Beach Gardens, Florida. Will was the recipient of the PGA of America's 2005 Junior Leader Award for his work in helping to give kids an opportunity to experience the game of golf. In 2007 Will was again honored by the PGA of America when he received The Presidents Plaque Award for his contributions to the growth of golf. Will is a Big 5 fan and a graduate of Villanova University where he had the honor of being the Wildcats Head Golf Coach from 2008-2011. Will resides in Palm Beach County Florida with his wife Jodi. Will is the President of the Philadelphia Association of Sports Trivia.

Jack Carroll: Often referred to as "A fountain of useless knowledge", Jack's unique talents and legendary trivia prowess were perfect for this book. Jack grew up in Boston, but please don't hold that against him. A life-long athlete, Jack has competed against the likes of Tom Glavine and Dana Barros. In 1993 Jack moved to Philadelphia and was immediately swept up in the '93 Phillies pennant race, and ever since has rooted for Philadelphia sports teams with the zeal previously reserved for the Boston sports teams he grew up with. He was overjoyed in 2008 for Philadelphia and all its sports fans when the Phillies finally broke the 25-year championship drought. Jack lives in suburban Philly with his wife, Mary Beth, and daughters Maggie, Betsey and Jackie. Jack is the Vice President of the Philadelphia Association of Sports Trivia.

Cary Beavers: Born in 1968, Cary learned to read by poring over box scores and game stories in the Philadelphia Inquirer and Philadelphia Bulletin. He graduated Temple with a degree in journalism and has served as editor of several Montgomery County newspapers. Cary is a longtime Eagles season ticket holder and was fortunate enough to see the Phillies win it all in 2008 at Citizens Bank Park. He and wife Peg have three children, Zack, Derek and Maggie, each of whom inherited a love of sports and an obsession with trivial sports knowledge. Cary is the Secretary of the Philadelphia Association of Sports Trivia.

Brendon Crowther: Brendon is a lifelong Philadelphia sports fan who was raised in the Somerton section of Northeast Philadelphia. An Eagles season ticket holder from 2000-2005, Brendon has attended many wild games including the devastating loss to Tampa Bay in 2003 and the Eagles victory over Atlanta in 2005 which finally pushed the Birds to the Super Bowl. Brendon considers himself a proud alumni member of section 747 from Veterans Stadium. He is also currently a Phillies season ticket holder and frequent attendee of Villanova basketball games and of Big 5 match ups, and additionally he is a fan of Temple football. Brendon also saw Allen Iverson's 60-point effort versus Orlando at the Wachovia Center. He is very proud of his multiple championships in his uber-competitive fantasy baseball, basketball and football leagues. Brendon is a 1996 graduate of St. Joe's Prep and a 2000 graduate of the University of Hartford. Brendon and his wife Leslie brought twin daughters Morgan and Samantha into the world on October 7th, 2009.

Joe DeCamara: Joe is a lifelong Philly sports fan who is living the dream as a talk show host on 97.5 The Fanatic. He hosts the station's Eagles Pre-Game Show in addition to a variety of other programs. Joe has interviewed a wide-range of notable sports figures such as Randall Cunningham, Cole Hamels, Pat Croce, Roger Goodell, Bernard Hopkins, Dick Vermeil and many others. He has appeared on ESPN-2, Fox-29, FoxSports.com and other outlets. Joe is an original member of the old Sports Talk 950, the pre-cursor of what became 97.5 The Fanatic. He has been instrumental in the creative growth of the Fanatic as its Assistant Program Director. Joe's career in sports broadcasting began a year and a half after he graduated college when he left a job in finance to pursue his passion of sports and "go for it." Joe is a 1996 graduate of St. Joe's Prep and a 2000 graduate of Fairfield University.

Bob Herpen: Bob brings his passionate and encyclopedic knowledge of hockey on all levels to the Philadelphia Association of Sports Trivia. A long-suffering Flyers and Eagles fan (and not-so-long suffering supporter of the Phillies and Boston College), Bob's passion is not limited to the greatest game on ice. Over the last 10 years, he has worked with a variety of well-known local sportscasters such as Merrill Reese and Tim Saunders, worked for MLB Advanced Media, kept statistics for the ECHL and covered the four major sports from high school to the pros for multiple outlets in the region. The 33-year-old Philadelphia native is currently writing for a national sports wire service, and can also be heard as one of the voices for Marple Newtown High School football. Bob's favorite Philly sports memory is sitting with his father in section 626 at the Vet on a bitterly cold New Year's Eve 2000 to see the Eagles crush the Tampa Bay Buccaneers.

Foreword
by Larry Kane

You don't have to travel far, or listen too closely, to get a sense of what moves this city.

It's the roar of the crowd causing ripples of thunder-like noise on the streets. The family sitting around the TV, snacks in one hand, the other nervously twitching, throats sore from screaming, and the butterflies churning throughout the time-honored ritual of giving oneself to the unknown. The puck glides on pristine ice, the baseball soars in a beautiful arc, the basketball hits the rim, catches air for a pregnant moment and bounces through the hoop, the football floats in the air with a perfect spiral as the sea of bodies reach upward.

We watch, and as Philadelphia sports fans, we are engulfed in the two most powerful emotions on the planet: hope and worry. As our teams soar to success, we still pine about days gone by. We are the most enlightened, informed and frustrated sports fans in the world, thinking that the city of champions will let another one get away no matter how the deck is stacked in our favor. Yet despite the incredible odds of going all the way every year in every sport, we have supported winners and losers with our dollars, our hands and in fallow times, qualified support.

After all, we do have all the answers because we are all frustrated coaches, players, managers and fans. We are the Philadelphia faithful and our dreams are littered amongst the great wasteland of ticket stubs. Yet we march on and demand excellence. Winning is not the only thing it is absolutely vital to the collective mood of the region. Losing is a disaster that casts a pall on our lives.

We venerate places like the Palestra, Connie Mack Stadium, the Vet, the Liacouras Center, the Blue Horizon, the Linc, Citizens Bank Park, and the CoreStates/First Union/Wachovia/ and now Wells Fargo Center! Our lives are forever intertwined with the travails of Schilling, Bowa, Schmidt, Randall, McNabb, T.O., Reggie, Smokin' Joe, Gola, Wilt the Stilt, A.I., Sir Charles and the immortal Bobby Clarke.

In more recent years, there was J-Roll as MVP, Cole the Rays slayer, Ryan Howard, Brad Lidge and his perfect season, the ageless Jamie Moyer and now Doc Halladay with the Four Aces. Chase Utley became a household name and not because he committed an error by dropping the F-bomb on TV.

They may not know it, but we own the managers. Charlie Manuel was once universally satirized, but now we celebrate his success with his own bobble-head doll. He is now romanticized in our folklore.

What do we do with all this pent up passion and emotional investment? We take action! We hire the coaches and fire them. We chased Kotite out of town. Those who lost are okay as long as they become one of us by putting in the same effort day in and day out. Ron Jaworski and Bill Bergey never got the big one, but living here when their playing days were over is half the battle. Garry Maddox decided to become a Philadelphian. He will never be in the Hall of Fame, but he's ours. The Tugger lived his final years here, and we love him for that.

John Chaney and Phil Martelli are local heroes. Fran Dunphy is rare class. Dr. J is a superstar, then and now. Win or lose, we know they're just like us. It's always been simple: respect us and we'll respect you.

There are two types of shared experiences in Philadelphia: weather and sports. Bad weather unites us in annoyance. Bad sports unite us in determination. Teams that try hard to win unite us in pride. That pride exploded with emotion as we watched the 2008 Phillies march down Broad Street to end a quarter-century of championship drought.

As an anchor and reporter here for more than 40 years, I've always been excited about the extraordinary obsession with sports of all sorts. It is the common thread that brings all of us together as a community, unless of course you're on the wrong end of a Big Five game.

Think of it: sports is the ultimate distraction in most communities. In our slice of heaven bounded by the Delaware and Schuylkill Rivers, it's bigger than life, overwhelming our emotions. Enjoying local sports in our region is a highlight of our quality of life. And we've got so much of it.

Sports trivia is also a source of great enjoyment as is our Philadelphia Sports Hall of Fame. My memories go back to 1966 when the Eagles played at Franklin Field, the Flyers were just forming, the Sixers were launching a championship squad and the Phillies were still living down 1964. In the Spring of 1967, I covered the Sixers championship party at Pagano's restaurant. Big Wilt shook my hand and I thought he was going to squash it. In 1968 I saw my first hockey game. Back then, I could pick any seat I wanted but as we all know that didn't last too long. One year later, I celebrated a Temple victory at a time when the NIT was still huge. I suffered through the seventies until the Flyers won the Stanley Cup in 1974 and '75.

Then, on my 38th birthday, October 21, 1980, the Phillies finally took the whole thing and George Brett went home to heal his hemorrhoids. Life was indeed improving. The stigma of "The City of Losers" was finally lifted. The roll continued when the Eagles made the Super Bowl in 1981 after shutting down the hated Cowboys on a frigid January afternoon, and Moses helped Doc finally reach the Promised Land in 1983. Ten years later, the Phillies lost the World Series in painful fashion, but forever won the hearts and minds of the fans. Win or lose, it's been nothing short of a roller-coaster ride of epic proportions.

Sometimes I go to bed with the voices of Merrill, Harry, Bill Campbell and others ringing in my ears. When the news of the world turns ugly, I always retreat to sports. And I always feel better. Don't you?

This extraordinary book is about the trivial pursuits of Philadelphia sports that are not so trivial; about the heroes and heroines who left us with memories and still delight us today. I hope you enjoy it as much as the writers enjoyed writing it.

And remember... in Philadelphia sports, teams win and lose, teams rise and choke, sportswriters become the ultimate front runners, but whether the going gets good or bad, the real winners are always the fans of Philadelphia. We are tough. We are unmerciful, but we share the pain and revel in the joy that we are the best sports fans on the globe: miserable losers, magnificent winners, and in between we are proud to say we are from Philadelphia no matter where we are. Who could ask for more and get it like we do?

The Psychology of Philly Sports Fans
by Kevin Walsh

The Phillies World Series win in 2008 helped, but let's not kid ourselves. It was only a matter of time before we'd go back to being miserable. I love Glen Macnow and Anthony Gargano of 610 WIP-AM, but to suggest a lengthy moratorium on booing the Phils made me boo my radio pals. Booing is a measurable. So is cheering. If you didn't care you wouldn't do either. A player always knows where he stands with the fans.

We watch our beloved sports teams as if our viewership really makes a difference in the outcome. Then we watch the highlights of what we just saw on Comcast Sportsnet. The next day we call a talk show under a phony name just trying to stooge our way onto the radio. More often than not we assume a great run by the Eagles, Phillies, Sixers and Flyers won't last—because it usually doesn't. We wallow in our own mire as if it's some kind of twisted badge of honor. Sportscaster Jeff Asch says "It's like we're programmed to lose."

The snowballing of Santa Claus let the world in on our secret—the dysfunction of the Philadelphia sports family. We knew we had problems, but that didn't mean everyone else had to know. And what did we do for an encore? We booed another beloved children's character because, quite frankly, it didn't perform to the standards we'd come to expect.

The Santa story happened in December 1968 at Franklin Field during the Eagles' miserable 2-12 season. The Eagles and Minnesota Vikings were tied at halftime and by that time many fans were pickled. Back then you could bring your own booze in. With a team as bad as the Eagles you could understand that fans would find a way to express themselves badly. Sportscaster Lou Tilley sold programs at Franklin Field that day and remembered Santa appearing out of nowhere to a serenade of boos at halftime. A family friend tells me Santa was a skinny, little guy a crime on the level of being slow to order with a long line standing behind you at a cheesesteak joint.

Inside the Santa suit was 20-year-old Frank Olivo, a last-minute replacement for the real Santa who couldn't make it to the game because of heavy snow. When Olivo ran past the elf-looking Eaglettes to the sound of "Here Comes Santa Claus", there came a barrage of snowballs. When Howard Cosell made mention of the incident on his national sports program it took on a life of its own. Glenn Macnow from 610 WIP-AM wrote a whole chapter about it in "The Great Philadelphia Fan Book".

Then there was the Easter Bunny fiasco in the mid-70's at The Vet orchestrated by Bill Giles and the Phillies. Public Address announcer Dan Baker remembers the day. As part of a marketing gag Giles promised fans they would see the world's highest jumping Easter Bunny. The "jump" was actually a planned flight for the Easter Bunny out of Veterans Stadium and over to New Jersey by way of hot air balloon. Director of Sales Paul Callahan, played the character. Trouble was, it was so windy that day they had to keep the hot air balloon and The Easter Bunny tethered. It was a heavily-promoted act that drew a crowd for something more than baseball. When the fans didn't get what they came to see, they made themselves seen and heard. So, yes, fans booed The Easter Bunny.

These are just for starters and that's just what happened at the stadium. In the late 1970's, Mike Schmidt was the guest of honor at a celebrity golf tournament at Philmont Country Club in Huntingdon Valley. The announcer gave him a rousing introduction to which the gallery applauded warmly. Schmidt suggested he might feel more at home if the gallery booed him. Suddenly the golf course seemed like The Vet.

Then there's The Vet itself which the Phillies and Eagles shared with feral cats, rats, mice, cockroaches and Judge Seamus McCaffery's drunken court. For a place that didn't live and breathe, it sure seemed like it had a demonic life of its own. Its turf cannibalized more ankles and knees than tribes in Papua New Guinea. Its porous walls gave visiting football players a peep show of the cheerleaders, and a safety railing collapsed during the Army/Navy game, injuring dozens of future soldiers.

While we can all probably come up with a story or twelve that just personifies the Philly sports fan mentality, we can only guess at the true psychology behind this collective angst. We know we have issues. We know we shouldn't take sports so seriously. And despite what we know, we can't really help ourselves. But like the words of wise guy wife Karen Hill in the movie Goodfellas, being around so much dysfunction all the time makes it feel "all the more normal."

Introduction To The Eagles
by Merrill Reese

After 36 years of living my dream, I still believe the best is yet to come!

There's nothing – absolutely nothing – that I would rather do than describe Eagles games to a vast audience that covers three states. Actually that's just the broadcast network. Today, through the auspices of Internet and satellite radio that audience is literally world wide, and numbers in the millions.

Eagles fans are the best. They have a passion for this team that in my opinion is unmatched. When the Eagles fell to the New England Patriots in Super Bowl XXXIX you could feel their pain. It was the same after the Super Bowl XV broadcast in New Orleans, where the Eagles went down to the Oakland Raiders. The difference is that Dick Vermeil's 1980 team was never in that game. Andy Reid's 2004 team gave the Patriots all they could handle.

People ask me about my favorite game. Number one occurred on January 11, 1981 - the Eagles over Dallas in the NFC Championship. The conference clincher over Atlanta in January, 2005 was a thrill also but the Falcons will never stir emotions the way the Cowboys do. Also, we expected the Eagles to beat Atlanta while the win over Dallas fit into the upset category.

17

I've also been fortunate to describe some absolutely unbelievable plays. One of my favorites occurred a few Novembers ago in Dallas. Donovan NcNabb rolled right, dodged three tacklers, came back to his left and then launched a missile downfield that Freddie Mitchell stretched out for and hauled in. That reminded me so much of a play pulled off by Randall Cunningham on December 2, 1990 in Buffalo. Randall dropped back into the end zone, narrowly escaped the clutches of ferocious Bruce Smith, fired the ball 50 yards to a leaping Fred Barnett, who did the rest to complete a 95-yard touchdown play.

Who will ever forget November 10, 1985 when Ron Jaworski took a quick drop from the Eagles' one and fired a bullet to Mike Quick who didn't stop until the Eagles had won?

This franchise has had so many great moments. Herman Edwards jaunting into the end zone to finish the "Miracle at the Meadowlands". The Gang Green defense stuffing the Cardinals seven times from the one. Fourth and one, twice to stop Emmitt Smith. The House of Pain game. The Body Bag game. No team names more games than the Eagles. And let's face it, names are what has made this franchise. From Bert Bell to Greasy Neale to Steve Van Buren to Tommy McDonald, Chuck Bednarik, Bill Bergey straight through to Reid, McNabb, Dawkins and Vick.

No Eagles conversation would be complete without a tip of the helmet to Reggie White, a giant of a man who made everyone around him feel larger than life. He left us way too early in 2004. He is missed.

The 1948, 1949 and 1960 championships were great. But those were simpler times with fewer teams, no free agency and no salary cap.

What Andy Reid and his men have achieved over the past decade is remarkable. Andy is the winningest coach in Eagles history. Predicting what will happen is very difficult in a sport where injuries play such a major role. But whether it's next season or some season after that, I'm convinced that the Philadelphia Eagles will complete the job in the near future and reign as Super Bowl Champions.

EAGLES TRIVIA

PASSING QUESTIONS

Answers on page 319

1. Who is the only Eagles QB to throw for 400 yards in a game three times?

2. From 1993 to 2000 the Eagles had eight quarterbacks lead the team in passing yards during a season. Name those eight quarterbacks.

3. What historic NFL defensive end did Randall Cunningham miraculously elude in the end zone moments before launching a 95-yard touchdown pass?

4. Who holds the Eagles record for most career passing yards?

5. Who holds the Eagles record for most TD passes in a game with seven?

6. Who holds the Eagles record for most completions in a game?

7. Who has thrown the most interceptions in Eagles history?

8. Which team did Ron Jaworski suit up for in his last NFL game?

9. In the Eagles 3-13 season of 1998 how many TD passes did Birds QBs throw?

10. What four QBs filled-in as a starter after Randall Cunningham was hurt in 1991?

11. How many quarterbacks threw a touchdown pass for the 1991 Eagles?

12. Which two former Eagles practice squad quarterbacks have thrown an NFL touchdown pass?

13. Did Randall Cunningham win his first NFL start?

14. Who holds the Eagles record for most passing yards in a season?

15. What Eagles QB won his first NFL start in 1996?

16. Who caught Donovan McNabb's first career touchdown pass?

17. Who holds the Eagles record for most passing attempts in a season?

18. Who was the last Eagles player to lead the NFL in touchdown passes in a season?

19. Who holds the Eagles record for most career touchdown passes?

20. Who holds the Eagles record for most passing yards in a game?

21. How many Eagles QBs have thrown for 400 or more yards in a game?

22. Who holds the Eagles record for most touchdown passes in a season?

23. How many NFL teams did Ron Jaworski play for?

24. How many NFL teams did Ty Detmer play for?

25. Was Ron Jaworski the only QB to throw a pass for the Eagles in 1980?

26. Did Jay Fiedler ever attempt a regular season pass as an Eagle?

27. What quarterback did A.J. Feeley back up at the University of Oregon?

28. Who holds the Eagles record for most completions in a season?

29. In 1986, Eagles quarterbacks got batted around as the club set an NFL record by allowing how many sacks in one season?

30. Who was the last Eagles quarterback to lead the NFL in passing yards in a season?

RUSHING QUESTIONS

Answers on page 320

1. Which Eagles running back rushed 35 times for less than 100 yards in a 1991 loss to the Buccaneers?

2. Who holds the Eagles record for most career rushing yards?

3. What Eagles running back threw four touchdown passes in one season?

4. Who holds the record for rushing attempts as an Eagle?

5. Who was the first Eagles running back after Wilbert Montgomery to rush for more than 1,000 yards in a season?

6. Who was the last Eagles player to have a rush of more than 80 yards?

7. What Eagles running back ranks second behind Wilbert Montgomery for most yards rushing in one season?

8. Who was the last Eagles running back to rush for more than 200 yards in a game?

9. Who holds the Eagles record for most rushing touchdowns in a career?

10. Who holds the Eagles rookie record for most rushing yards in a game?

11. With what team did Wilbert Montgomery finish his career?

12. Did Ricky Watters have his highest season total of rushing yards with the 49ers, Eagles or Seahawks?

13. Which two Eagles running backs had over 100 rushing attempts in 1980?

14. Who led the Eagles in rushing yardage in 1985?

15. Which Eagles running back led the 2003 Eagles in regular season rushing yards?
    (This was the "Three Headed Monster" year with Duce Staley, Correll Buckhalter and Brian Westbrook)

16. Who had more regular season rushing touchdowns as an Eagle: Ricky Watters or Randall Cunningham?

17. Who was the last running back to lead the Eagles in scoring for a season?

18. What 27th round draft pick of the Green Bay Packers retired in second place on the Eagles all-time yards rushing list?

19. Who had more 100-yard rushing games as an Eagle: Ricky Watters or Duce Staley?

20. Who was the last Eagles player to lead the NFL in rushing yards in a season?

21. Who is the only Eagles player to rush for a touchdown in eight consecutive games?

22. Who holds the Eagles record for most rushing attempts in a season?

23. Who rushed for more yards as an Eagle: Randall Cunningham or Duce Staley?

24. Who holds the Eagles record for most rushing touchdowns in a season?

25. Who holds the Eagles rookie record for rushing yards in a season?

26. To how many Pro Bowls was Wilbert Montgomery selected?

27. How many seasons did Ricky Watters spend with the Eagles?

28. What Eagles running back, who wore #23 in the early 1990s, was known for having a "low center of gravity?"

29. Who had more 100-yard rushing games as an Eagle: Randall Cunningham or Keith Byars?

30. Who was the primary back-up running back on the 2004 Eagles team that advanced to the Super Bowl?

RECEIVING QUESTIONS

Answers on page 321

1. Who was the last non-kicker to lead the Eagles in scoring for a season?

2. Who holds the Eagles record for receptions in a season?

3. In 1998, two receivers led the Eagles in touchdown receptions with two. Who were they?

4. What wide receiver dropped what would have been a game-clinching catch that cost the Eagles a win in Andy Reid's first game as head coach?

5. Who holds the Eagles record for most career receptions?

6. Who holds the Eagles record for most receptions by a rookie?

7. Who has the most 100-yard receiving games as an Eagle?

8. Who was the last Eagle to have over 200 receiving yards in one game?

9. What two players hold the Eagles record for receptions in a game?

10. Who has more career receptions with the Eagles: Keith Byars or Mike Quick?

11. Who caught a 75-yard touchdown pass from Jeff Garcia in a playoff game versus the New Orleans Saints?

12. With what team did Keith Jackson finish his career?

13. Who holds the Eagles record for most 100-yard receiving games in a season?

14. Who led the Eagles in receiving yards in 1980?

15. Who was the last Eagle to lead the NFL in receiving yards in a season?

16. Who holds the Eagles record for most touchdown receptions in a season?

17. Did Cris Carter ever have more than 10 touchdowns in a season as an Eagle?

18. Which two wide receivers from the 1980 Eagles also played for the Philadelphia Stars in 1983?

19. Who led the Eagles in receiving yards in 1998?

20. Who was the last Eagles receiver to catch four touchdown passes in one game?

21. How many touchdowns did Terrell Owens score in a game in his regular season debut with the Eagles?

22. In 1972 and 1973 two different Eagles led the NFL in receptions. Who were they?

23. What is the highest number of catches Mike Quick recorded in one season?

24. Who was the last Eagle to lead the NFL in receptions?

25. Other than Keith Byars, what other two running backs are in the Eagles top 10 list for receptions in a season?

26. Who holds the Eagles record for most career receiving yards?

27. Who holds the Eagles record for most receiving yards in a game?

28. Did Keith Jackson ever record more than 1,000 receiving yards in a season with the Eagles?

29. Who holds the Eagles record for consecutive 100-yard receiving games?

30. Who led the Eagles in receptions in 2003?

DEFENSE QUESTIONS

Answers on page 322

1. What three defensive tackles have led the Eagles in sacks for a season?

2. Who broke Ernest Givins' nose in the famous "House of Pain" game against the Houston Oilers in 1991?

3. Who is the only Eagle to return two interceptions for a touchdown in one game?

4. Who ranks third on the list of career sacks as an Eagle?

5. What two players combined for the longest interception return in Eagles history?

6. What three players share the Eagles career interceptions record?

7. Who holds the Eagles record for interceptions by a linebacker in one season?

8. What was the last season the Eagles led the league in fewest points allowed?

9. In what season did the Eagles last register a shutout of an opponent?

10. What safety was drafted in 2010 with the pick the Eagles obtained in the Donovan McNabb trade?

11. From what team did the Eagles acquire Bill Bergey?

12. What linebacker from the Eagles 1980 Super Bowl team also played for the Philadelphia Stars in 1983 and 1984?

13. Who led the 2004 Eagles in tackles?

14. What was Reggie White's uniform number in his first season with the Eagles?

15. What Eagle is tied for the NFL record of most interceptions returned for a touchdown in a regular season with four?

16. For what AFC team did Troy Vincent start his career?

17. Which Eagles player led the NFL in sacks during Ray Rhodes first year as head coach?

18. Name the four defensive tackles who have at least 25 sacks in their Eagles career.

19. Which veteran defensive end joined the Eagles in 1980, wearing number 87?

20. Which Eagle is the only player in NFL history to record a sack, an interception, a fumble recovery and a touchdown catch in one game?

21. Which three players have led the Eagles in sacks for three consecutive seasons?

22. Who is the only Eagles defensive player to register four interceptions in one game? This remains an NFL record.

23. Which two Eagles share the team record for sacks in one game?

24. What Temple safety was drafted by the Eagles in 2011?

25. Jevon Kearse led the 2004 Eagles in sacks. Who was second on the team in sacks?

26. For what USFL team did Reggie White suit up?

27. Who led the 1992 Eagles in sacks?

28. For what team did Eric Allen finish his career?

29. Which defensive end set an Eagles record for consecutive games with a sack?

30. Who holds the Eagles record with 11 interceptions in one season?

Answers on page 323

1. Who holds the Eagles record for points in a season?

2. What Giants punter kicked the ball straight to Desean Jackson when Desean won a 2010 game for the Birds with a punt return?

3. Has any Eagle ever made more than 30 field goals in one season?

4. Who holds the Eagles record for longest punt return?

5. Who has kicked two of the three longest punts in Eagles history?

6. Who was named the Eagles Special Teams MVP in 1988 and 1989?

7. Who holds the Eagles record for most career points?

8. The Eagles had two barefoot kickers in the 1980's. Name them.

9. Who knocked down Luis Zendejas in the "Bounty Bowl?"

10. Other than the Eagles, for which NFL teams has Akers scored?

11. Who returned a punt for a touchdown in the Meadowlands versus the Giants in 2003 in what has frequently been described as the play that "saved the Eagles season?"

12. Who was the last place kicker to be traded by the Eagles?

13. During the 2002 season, which Eagle became only the second NFL player to reach 22,000 total yards?

14. Who holds the Eagles record for consecutive extra points made?

15. Who was the last Eagles kicker to lead the league in scoring?

16. Who is the only Eagle to return two kickoffs for a touchdown in one game?

17. Who was the only Eagle to return a kickoff for a touchdown in 2008?

18. Brian Mitchell threw one touchdown pass as an Eagle. Who caught it?

19. Which Eagle has the most career field goals made?

20. Name the place kicker for the underachieving 1994 Eagles team.

21. Which Eagles place kicker would have attempted the field goal against Dallas in that infamous 1997 Monday Night Football game had Tommy Hutton been able to hold the snap?

22. Which New York Giant player was waiting to return the punt that turned out to be Randall Cunningham's 91-yard punt in December 1989?

23. At the end of the 2003 season David Akers ranked second in NFL history for field goal accuracy. Who held first place?

24. In 1988, who scored the winning touchdown versus the Giants in a game at the Meadowlands by catching a blocked field goal behind the line of scrimmage and rumbling in for the winning score in overtime?

25. Who kicked the longest field goal ever against the Eagles?

26. Who is the last Eagles player to return two kickoffs for a touchdown in one season?

27. Who kicked the longest field goal in Eagles history?

28. Which three players hold the Eagles team record with two punt return touchdowns in one season?

29. Who holds the Eagles record for consecutive field goals made?

30. Who holds the Eagles record for most field goals made in one game?

COACHING QUESTIONS

Answers on page 324

1. Who was the head coach the last time the Eagles went undefeated at home?

2. How many seasons did Rich Kotite coach the Eagles?

3. Did Ray Rhodes win fewer than 30 regular season games as head coach of the Eagles?

4. Who won more playoff games as head coach of the Eagles: Buddy Ryan or Rich Kotite?

5. Who was the last Eagles coach to be replaced during the season?

6. Not including the strike season, how many times did Buddy Ryan lose to the Dallas Cowboys as head coach of the Eagles?

7. Rich Kotite's coaching career with the Eagles ended with seven straight losses. What team beat the Eagles in the last one?

8. What team did the Eagles beat in Andy Reid's first win as head coach?

9. What Eagles head coach was nicknamed "The Swamp Fox"?

10. Who coached the Eagles for one and only one game between 1980 and 2008?

11. What was Ray Rhodes' record in the playoffs as coach of the Eagles?

12. Who did the Eagles play in Dick Vermeil's last playoff game with the team?

13. Who was Reggie White's first NFL head coach?

14. Which university did Dick Vermeil leave to coach the Eagles?

15. What Eagles defensive coordinator and future NFL head coach was not awarded the Eagles head coaching vacancy when Buddy Ryan was fired?

16. What head coach ran off the field with a few seconds still on the clock in an Eagles playoff loss?

17. Who was Ray Rhodes' much-maligned special teams coach for most of his tenure as head coach of the Eagles?

18. Who was the first head coach in Eagles history?

19. In 1984, the Eagles traded a 9th round pick for what future NFL head coach?

20. Buddy Ryan ended his Eagles coaching career having beaten the Dallas Cowboys how many consecutive times?

21. What two Eagles assistant coaches went on to become head coach of the Vikings?

22. With which NFL team did Andy Reid serve as quarterbacks coach?

23. What team did Rich Kotite coach after he left the Eagles?

24. Where did Andy Reid attend college?

25. What Eagles assistant coach went on to coach the Raiders and Buccaneers?

26. What team was Dick Vermeil coaching when his career ended?

27. Who has won the most playoff games as head coach of the Eagles?

28. Who was the Eagles head coach during the "Pork Chop Bowl?"

29. What coaching position did Jon Gruden hold with the Eagles?

30. What Eagles assistant coach went on to coach the Baltimore Ravens?

Answers on page 325

1. What college did Randall Cunningham attend?

2. Where did Reggie White go to college?

3. Chris Gocong and legendary broadcaster John Madden were both drafted by the Eagles out of what school?

4. Duce Staley and Sheldon Brown both went to what college?

5. Where did Donovan McNabb go to college?

6. What college did Ron Jaworski attend?

7. When the Eagles selected Brian Dawkins what school was he attending?

8. Who did the Eagles draft in the first round out of Boston College in the 1990s?

9. Where did David Akers go to college?

10. Who did the Eagles select in the first round of the 2011 draft?

11. What college did Terrell Owens attend?

12. Name the last Eagles player to be drafted in the first round out of UCLA.

13. Who was the last UCLA Bruin to be drafted by the Eagles?

14. Where did Ike Reese go to college?

15. What number did Brian Westbrook wear at Villanova?

16. Lito Sheppard and Jevon Kearse went to what college?

17. Mike Quick attended what college?

18. What two members of the 2008 Eagles were teammates at Notre Dame?

19. John Runyan and Jason Avant both attended what school?

20. What college did Bill Bergey and Fred Barnett attend?

21. Where did Chris T. Jones go to college?

22. The Eagles drafted Corey Simon out of what school?

23. What college did Michael Lewis attend?

24. Where did Steve Van Buren go to college?

25. Who was the last Eagles wide receiver drafted from Cal?

26. Where did Calvin Williams go to college?

27. Tony Hunt was the last Eagles player drafted out of what college?

28. Who was the last Eagles offensive lineman drafted out of USC?

29. Where did Kevin Kolb go to college?

30. What Eagles great and NFL Hall of Famer never lost a game during his collegiate career at Oklahoma?

Answers on page 326

1. Who did the Eagles select in the first round the last time they made two first round draft picks?

2. The Eagles once went five consecutive years without a first round draft pick. What linebacker represented the end of that streak in 1979?

3. Before Donovan McNabb, who was the last quarterback selected by the Eagles in the first round of the draft?

4. Name the four wide receivers the Eagles have selected in the first round.

5. In 1990, the Eagles drafted Fred Barnett and Calvin Williams. However, neither player was the first wide receiver drafted by the Eagles that year. Who was?

6. The Eagles had ten first round picks in the 1990's. On which position did they use the most picks?

7. Who was the Eagles first round pick in the draft that they selected Eric Allen with their second round pick?

8. What team did the Eagles trade with to move up and draft Antone Davis?

9. What linebacker did the Eagles draft in the second round the year they selected Donovan McNabb?

10. What "bust" did the Eagles draft in the first round the year they selected Randall Cunningham in the second?

11. What two players did the Eagles pick in the second round the last time the club did not make a first round selection in a draft?

12. Who did the Eagles select with the second pick of the 1968 draft? The Birds picked second because they lost a coin flip for the first pick and otherwise would have been able to draft O.J. Simpson.

13. In the second round of the 2009 draft the Eagles selected what running back from Pitt?

14. Who was the last running back taken in the first-round by the Eagles?

15. From 1974-1978 the Eagles did not have a first round pick. What was the earliest round they made a selection in during that five-year span?

16. How was Cris Carter obtained by the Eagles?

17. In 1986, what eventual backfield tandem was drafted in the first and second round by the Eagles?

18. Name the linebacker from Georgia that Ray Rhodes selected four spots before Miami drafted Zach Thomas.

19. Who did the Eagles select number one overall out of the University of Pennsylvania?

20. What linebacker was the Eagles second-round pick in the 2001 draft?

21. Before Jerome McDougle, who was the last first round pick the Eagles traded up to get?

22. Who did the Tampa Bay Buccaneers select with the 12th pick of the 1995 draft, the pick obtained from the Eagles in the Mike Mamula trade?

23. Did the Eagles have the first pick in the very first NFL draft?

24. How many quarterbacks have the Eagles taken with their first pick in a draft?

25. Who were the other four quarterbacks selected in the first round of the 1999 draft, the same draft that produced Donovan McNabb?

26. The Eagles traded which receiver to move up and select Bobby Taylor?

27. In 1988 the Eagles drafted what quarterback from Syracuse?

28. Who was the Eagles first-round draft choice in 1990?

29. In 1991 the Eagles drafted what defensive tackle out of Kent State?

30. In 1992 the Eagles drafted what diminutive cornerback out of Alabama?

MEMORABLE MOMENTS

Answers on page 327

1. Who scored the winning TD in the "Miracle of the Meadowlands?"

2. Against what team did the Eagles lose both their last game at Veterans Stadium and their first regular season game at the Linc?

3. Which two Eagles have been named MVP of the Pro Bowl?

4. What record did Ron Jaworski and Mike Quick combine to set in a 1985 game against the Falcons?

5. In what city was Super Bowl XXXIX played against New England?

6. Whose hit knocked Randall Cunningham out for the 1991 season?

7. In a 1988 Monday Night Football game, Giants linebacker Carl Banks hit Randall Cunningham, almost forcing #12 to the ground. However, Randall was able to brace himself with one hand and straighten up to throw a touchdown pass to what player?

8. What did Jerome Brown famously say while walking off the field after the Eagles beat the Houston Oilers in the "House of Pain Game?"

9. What former Eagles player, who was close with Jerome Brown, announced the tragic news of Jerome's death on 610 WIP?

10. What was the motto of the 1992 Eagles in honor of Jerome Brown?

11. What did the Eagles players drink to keep cool during the 2000 season opener at Dallas?

12. What player injured Terrell Owens late in the 2004 season?

13. Against what team did the Eagles play the "Body Bag Game?"

14. Which two running backs have rushed for the most yards in one game against the Eagles than any other players?

15. Who was the last quarterback to throw five touchdown passes against the Eagles in one game?

16. What Philly native represented the city of Philadelphia to the nation by speaking about the Eagles and Birds fans on the field shortly before Super Bowl XXXIX?

17. What player drpped the ball at the one yard line thinking he had already scored a TD in a 2008 game?

18. After the Dallas Cowboys ran up the score against the Eagles in a 1987 "scab" game, what did Buddy Ryan specifically order to be done late in a game the next time the Eagles played Dallas as a means of getting revenge?

19. Which Hall of Fame running back did Joe Pisarcik intend to hand the ball to when the Miracle of the Meadowlands occurred?

20. What team did the Eagles combine to play with during the 1943 season in the midst of World War II?

21. The horrific day versus Tampa Bay in January 2003 started out so well when this kick returner had a huge run-back to open the game and then what running back scored a touchdown on the second play from scrimmage?

22. In 2002, Donovan McNabb broke his ankle but still threw four touchdown passes against what team?

23. What Eagles player had a truly sensational interception return for a touchdown versus the New York Jets in the same game that Randall Cunningham hurt his leg during the 1993 season? He handed Randall the ball in the back of the end zone after scoring.

24. When the Eagles finally got Terrell Owens, ending the saga of where T.O. would play in 2004, what player did the Birds surrender in the trade?

25. The last time the Eagles played a game (pre-season game) away from the United States was in 1993. In what city was the game played?

26. What FOX reporter had a major issue with Donovan McNabb after she and McNabb had conflicting answers about a conversation they had about #5's future prior to an Eagles game?

27. Who is the only Eagles player to score four touchdowns in a game twice?

28. Who did the Eagles play in the first televised pro football game?

29. What did Chuck Bednarik famously say while standing over Jim Taylor as the clock expired to end the 1960 NFL Championship Game?

30. What NFL record did Don Shula set at Veterans Stadium?

Answers on page 328

1. At the end of the first half of the Eagles blowout playoff win over the Detroit Lions in 1995 the Birds scored on a Hail Mary pass. Who caught it?

2. Who scored the Eagles first touchdown in a Super Bowl?

3. Who missed a potential game-winning field goal in the Eagles 1978 playoff loss to the Atlanta Falcons?

4. What is the Eagles all-time record for points in a playoff game?

5. Who recorded the only safety in Eagles playoff history?

6. Who earned the #1 playoff seed in the NFC for the 1980 regular season?

7. Who holds the Eagles record for most career playoff receptions?

8. Did Keith Jackson ever score a playoff touchdown for the Eagles?

9. Who is the only team to shut out the Eagles in the playoffs?

10. Which franchise recorded its first playoff victory by beating the Eagles in 1979?

11. Who did the Eagles beat to win the franchise's first NFL title in 1948?

12. In 1947, the Eagles recorded the franchise's first playoff victory against what team?

13. What did Buddy Ryan famously order done after the Eagles landed in Chicago as they got set for their 1988 playoff game with the Bears?

14. Who is the only member of the Eagles 1980 Super Bowl team who went on to win a Super Bowl with another team?

15. What member of the Eagles 2004 Super Bowl team was playing in his 13th season of NFL football?

16. How many times have the Eagles played the Cowboys in the playoffs since the NFC Championship Game victory in 1981?

17. What was the score of the Eagles overtime playoff victory over the Green Bay Packers in January of 2004?

18. What quarterback made his last appearance ever for the Eagles in a playoff loss to end the 1995 season?

19. Are the Eagles the only team to beat Vince Lombardi in the playoffs?

20. What two placekickers have played for the Eagles in a Super Bowl?

21. The Eagles had a touchdown called back in the 1980 Super Bowl. Who scored it?

22. Who did the Eagles beat to win the NFL title in 1949?

23. What Eagles safety tore up his knee in the 2001 NFC Championship Game against the St. Louis Rams?

24. Having each joined the team in 1996, who were the three longest-tenured Eagles to play on the 2004 Super Bowl squad?

25. What three teams did the Eagles lose to in Buddy Ryan's three playoff games with the franchise?

26. Who holds the Eagles record for most playoff passing yards in a career?

27. Which Eagle caught a touchdown pass in four consecutive playoff games?

28. Who holds the Eagles record for most passes completed in a playoff game?

29. How many touchdown receptions does Mike Quick have in his playoff career as an Eagle?

30. Who holds the Eagles career record for most playoff rushing yards?

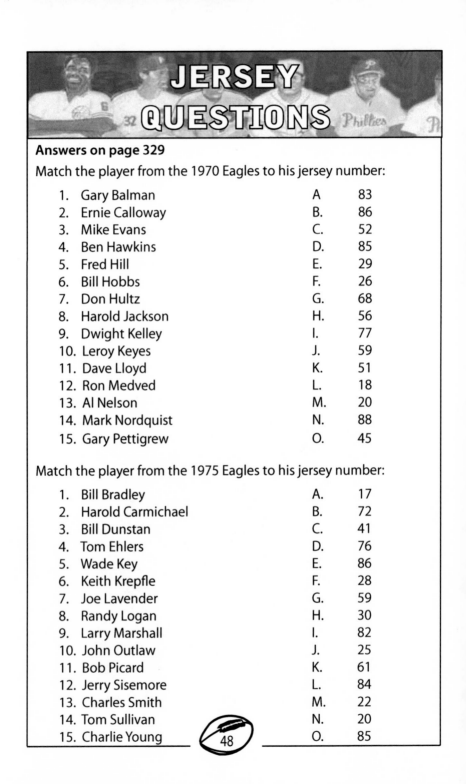

JERSEY QUESTIONS

Answers on page 329

Match the player from the 1970 Eagles to his jersey number:

1.	Gary Balman	A	83
2.	Ernie Calloway	B.	86
3.	Mike Evans	C.	52
4.	Ben Hawkins	D.	85
5.	Fred Hill	E.	29
6.	Bill Hobbs	F.	26
7.	Don Hultz	G.	68
8.	Harold Jackson	H.	56
9.	Dwight Kelley	I.	77
10.	Leroy Keyes	J.	59
11.	Dave Lloyd	K.	51
12.	Ron Medved	L.	18
13.	Al Nelson	M.	20
14.	Mark Nordquist	N.	88
15.	Gary Pettigrew	O.	45

Match the player from the 1975 Eagles to his jersey number:

1.	Bill Bradley	A.	17
2.	Harold Carmichael	B.	72
3.	Bill Dunstan	C.	41
4.	Tom Ehlers	D.	76
5.	Wade Key	E.	86
6.	Keith Krepfle	F.	28
7.	Joe Lavender	G.	59
8.	Randy Logan	H.	30
9.	Larry Marshall	I.	82
10.	John Outlaw	J.	25
11.	Bob Picard	K.	61
12.	Jerry Sisemore	L.	84
13.	Charles Smith	M.	22
14.	Tom Sullivan	N.	20
15.	Charlie Young	O.	85

Match the player from the 1980 Eagles to his jersey number:

1.	Bill Bergey	A.	52
2.	Richard Blackmore	B.	35
3.	John Bunting	C.	37
4.	Lem Burnham	D.	31
5.	Billy Campfield	E.	78
6.	Al Chesley	F.	67
7.	Tony Franklin	G.	55
8.	Louie Giammona	H.	33
9.	Carl Hairston	I.	95
10.	Perry Harrington	J.	89
11.	Dennis Harrison	K.	1
12.	Wally Henry	L.	27
13.	Frank LeMaster	M.	68
14.	Wilbert Montgomery	N.	59
15.	Ray Phillips	O.	66

Match the player from the 1985 Eagles to his jersey number:

1.	Ron Baker	A.	29
2.	Greg Brown	B.	63
3.	Ken Clarke	C.	86
4.	Garry Cobb	D.	98
5.	Herman Edwards	E.	58
6.	Evan Cooper	F.	71
7.	Ray Ellis	G.	26
8.	Elbert Foules	H.	50
9.	Greg Garrity	I.	53
10.	Anthony Griggs	J.	46
11.	Michael Haddix	K.	85
12.	Dwayne Giles	L.	21
13.	Ron Johnson	M.	89
14.	Dave Little	N.	24
15.	Paul McFadden	O.	8

Match the player from the 1990 Eagles to his jersey number:

1.	David Alexander	A.	21
2.	Eric Allen	B.	73
3.	Keith Byars	C.	90
4.	Matt Darwin	D.	78
5.	Robert Drummond	E.	56
6.	Byron Evans	F.	59
7.	Jeff Feagles	G.	46
8.	William Frizzell	H.	72
9.	Mike Golic	I.	5
10.	Britt Hager	J.	88
11.	Ron Heller	K.	34
12.	Terry Hoage	L.	33
13.	Keith Jackson	M.	54
14.	Izel Jenkins	N.	41
15.	Seth Joyner	O.	36

Match the player from the 1995 Eagles to his jersey number:

1.	Fred Barnett	A.	95
2.	Barrett Brooks	B.	79
3.	Mike Chalenski	C.	86
4.	Antone Davis	D.	97
5.	Ronnie Dixon	E.	94
6.	William Fuller	F.	76
7.	Rhett Hall	G.	91
8.	Andy Harmon	H.	82
9.	Lester Holmes	I.	71
10.	Tom Hutton	J.	73
11.	Greg Jefferson	K.	62
12.	Kevin Johnson	L.	78
13.	Chris T. Jones	M.	4
14.	Guy McIntyre	N.	63
15.	Raleigh McKenzie	O.	90

Match the player from the 2000 Eagles to his jersey number:

1.	David Akers	A.	7
2.	Luther Broughton	B.	82
3.	Na Brown	C.	85
4.	Doug Brzezinski	D.	45
5.	Mike Caldwell	E.	10
6.	Rashard Cook	F.	84
7.	James Darling	G.	31
8.	Koy Detmer	H.	57
9.	Damaene Douglass	I.	2
10.	Hugh Douglas	J.	52
11.	Carlos Emmons	K.	53
12.	Barry Gardner	L.	56
13.	Al Harris	M.	51
14.	Tim Hauck	N.	42
15.	Sean Landeta	O.	74

Match the player from the 2005 Eagles to his jersey number:

1.	Keith Adams	A.	86
2.	Shawn Andrews	B.	63
3.	Mike Bartrum	C.	57
4.	Reggie Brown	D.	8
5.	Correll Buckhalter	E.	94
6.	Hank Fraley	F.	32
7.	Paul Grasmanis	G.	88
8.	Todd Herremans	H.	73
9.	Artis Hicks	I.	96
10.	Roderick Hood	J.	79
11.	Dirk Johnson	K.	28
12.	N.D. Kalu	L.	93
13.	Jevon Kearse	M.	89
14.	Chad Lewis	N.	77
15.	Michael Lewis	O.	29

- Chuck Bednarik (1967) - 1949-1962
- Bert Bell (1963) - 1933-1940
- Bob Brown (2004) - 1964-1968
- Mike Ditka (1988) - 1967-1968
- Bill Hewitt (1971) - 1937-1939
- Sonny Jurgensen (1983) - 1957-1963
- James Lofton (2003) - 1993
- John Madden (2007) - Drafted in 1958, never played in a game due to training camp injury
- Ollie Matson (1972) - 1964-1966
- Tommy McDonald (1998) - 1957-1963
- James Arthur "Art" Monk (2008) -1995
- Earle "Greasy" Neale (1969) - 1941-1950
- Pete Pihos (1970) - 1947-1955
- Jim Ringo (1981) - 1964-1967
- Norm Van Brocklin (1971) - 1958-1960
- Steve Van Buren (1965) - 1944-1951
- Reggie White (2006) - 1985-1992
- Alex Wojciechowicz (1968) - 1946-1950

Retired numbers
- #15 Steve Van Buren, HB/S, 1944–51
- #40 Tom Brookshier, DB, 1953–61
- #44 Pete Retzlaff, RB/WR/TE, 1956–66
- #60 Chuck Bednarik, C/LB, 1949–62
- #70 Al Wistert, OT, 1943–51
- #92 Reggie White, DE, 1985–92
- #99 Jerome Brown, DT, 1987–91

HONOR ROLL

In 1987, the Eagles Honor Roll was established. Each Eagle player who had by then been elected into the Pro Football Hall of Fame was among the inaugural induction class.

Current Eagles Honor Roll members include:

- #60 Chuck Bednarik, C-LB, 1949–62, inducted 1987

- Bert Bell, founder-owner, 1933–40, inducted 1987

- #17 Harold Carmichael, WR, 1971–83, inducted 1987

- #56 Bill Hewitt, TE-DE, 1936–39 and 1943, inducted 1987

- #9 Sonny Jurgensen, QB, 1957–63, inducted 1987

- #31 Wilbert Montgomery, RB, 1977–84, inducted 1987

- Earle "Greasy" Neale, Head Coach, 1941–50, inducted 1987

- #35 Pete Pihos, TE-DE, 1947–55, inducted 1987

- #33 Ollie Matson, RB, 1964–66, inducted 1987

- #54 Jim Ringo, C, 1964–67, inducted 1987

- #11 Norm Van Brocklin, QB, 1958–60, inducted 1987

- #15 Steve Van Buren, RB-S, 1944–51, inducted 1987

- #53 Alex Wojciechowicz, C-DT, 1946–50, inducted 1987

- #66 Bill Bergey, LB, 1974–80, inducted 1988

- #25 Tommy McDonald, WR, 1957–63, inducted 1988

- #40 Tom Brookshier, CB, 1954–61, inducted 1989

- #44 Pete Retzlaff, TE, 1956–66, inducted 1989

- #22 Timmy Brown, RB, 1960–67, inducted 1990

- #76 Jerry Sisemore, OT, 1973–84, inducted 1991

- #75 Stan Walters, OT, 1975–83, inducted 1991

- #7 Ron Jaworski, QB, 1977–86, inducted 1992

- #28 Bill Bradley, S-P, 1969–76, inducted 1993

- Dick Vermeil, Head Coach, 1976-82, inducted 1994

- Jim Gallagher, team executive, 1949-95, inducted 1995

- #82 Mike Quick, WR, 1982-90, inducted 1995

- #99 Jerome Brown, DT, 1987-91, inducted 1996

- Otho Davis, head trainer, 1973-95, inducted 1999

- #92 Reggie White, DE, 1987-92, inducted 2006

- #12 Randall Cunningham, QB, 1985-1995, inducted 2009

- Al Wistert, OT, 1943-1951, inducted 2009

- Eric Allen, CB, 1988-1994, inducted in 2011

- Jim Johnson, Defensive Coordinator,1999-2008, inducted 2011

Introduction To The Phillies
by Bill Giles

The Phillies have been playing baseball since the late 1800s. Since then there have been enough highs and lows to fill many books. To truly appreciate the value of a franchise – in the hearts, minds and emotions of all connected – the scope of the focus needs to be wide.

Of course, in this business we're all judged by wins and losses. But what of the players, the managers and, most importantly, the memories? Having been intimately involved with the Philadelphia Phillies for more than 40 years, I know hundreds of players, many managers and have countless moments to reflect upon.

Still fresh in my mind, and yours, are the night of October 29 and the day of October 31, 2008. The celebration after the final out was clearly a joyous eruption, a release of a quarter-century of pent-up frustration. Less than 48 hours later, a veritable Red Sea of fandom was parted down Broad Street, as the players and fans saluted each other during the long, sweet parade through South Philadelphia. The calendar said Halloween, but it really was our city's version of Thanksgiving.

That entire postseason experience brought images of our first World Series title of 1980 rushing back. The numeric reversal of the years '80 and '08 was not lost on me, and proved to be a positive omen for millions of the faithful. I envisioned Tug McGraw reaching for the heavens after the final out in the same way Brad Lidge dropped to his knees. You can't deny the serendipity of both victories ending with a strikeout, the tying

55

run looming on base. Nothing's ever been easy for the franchise – except the ability to draw out the passions of our rabid fan base.

Never was that passion more on display than during the 1993 season, when the most colorful and fun-loving team I've ever been around went from worst to first. The fans jumped on that bandwagon after their season-opening sweep and never got off. Through the 20-inning affair against the Dodgers, Wild Thing's game-winning base hit at 4:40 a.m. against the Padres, the scintillating six-game win over the Braves, right down to Joe Carter – the fans came out in droves and stayed with us all year long.

Those are the moments that linger forever. But even more memorable are the people. At the head of the list have to be Harry and Whitey – no last names needed. Theirs was a broadcast partnership that won't be duplicated in any booth in any era.

Even during the lean years, there have always been players fans could identify with or get fired up about. From Grover Cleveland Alexander to Chuck Klein to Robin Roberts to Richie Allen, to Schmitty, Lefty, Bull and Bowa. From Pete Rose to Sarge to Dutch, Mitchy-Poo and Krukker. From Curt Schilling to the members of the Phils' recent run of success – including The Big Piece, Chase, J-Roll, Doc Halladay and Chooch.

Even the often-mocked Vet is an important part of our past, a symbol of who we are as a franchise. The Hot Pants Patrol, Rip City, the replica Liberty Bell and the infamous turf are part of the building's legend. I could create at least a chapter on classic deliveries of a season's first ball: Kiteman, Benny The Human Bomb, Motorcycle Man, et al. Philadelphia Phil and Phillis were our early attempts at trying to create an image beyond the field – efforts which ultimately led to the creation of one of the most popular mascots in the world. The Phanatic's classic antics over the last 30-plus years obviously warrants a book all their own.

And of course the success in the final years of Veterans Stadium begat Citizens Bank Park, opened in 2004 and now hosting sellout crowds at a clip the franchise has never witnessed before.

There's no question what the Phillies mean to me, to you and to Philadelphia.

PHILLIES TRIVIA

AWARDS QUESTIONS

Answers on page 330

1. Which hurler, who spent his best years in the majors with the Phillies, was elected to the Baseball Hall of Fame in 1976?

2. Name the last Phillie to be named NL Rookie of the Year by the Baseball Writers Association of America.

3. This Phillies pitcher was named Sporting News Comeback Player of the Year in 1983.

4. Name the three Phillies relievers to win the NL Rolaids Relief Man of the Year award.

5. Name the former Phillies announcer who in 1990 received the Ford C. Frick Award for broadcasting achievement.

6. How many Phillies pitchers have won the Silver Slugger Award?

7. How many Gold Gloves did Mike Schmidt win?

58

8. How many Gold Gloves did Garry Maddox win?

9. Who was the first Phillies player selected to the Hall of Fame?

10. Before Roy Halladay, who was the last Phillies pitcher to win the Cy Young Award?

11. Two Phillies pitchers won the National League Cy Young Award in back-to-back years in the 1980's. Name the pitchers and the years they won.

12. Which Phillies reliever on the Whiz Kids team of 1950 won the National League Most Valuable Player Award?

13. Prior to Scott Rolen, who was the last Phillie to win the NL Rookie of the Year Award?

14. Who was selected as MVP of the 1993 National League Championship Series?

15. Which Phillies pitcher did not win a Cy Young Award while with the club in the 1980s?
    a) Steve Carlton   b) Willie Hernandez
    c) Steve Bedrosian   d) John Denny

16. Who was named MVP of the 1980 World Series?
    a) Bake McBride   b) Mike Schmidt
    c) Bob Boone   d) Manny Trillo

17. Who was the MVP of the 1983 League Championship Series?
    a) Tony Perez   b) Steve Carlton
    c) Mike Schmidt   d) Gary Matthews

18. How many Phillies have been named Most Valuable Player in the National League?

ALL-STARS QUESTIONS

Answers on page 330

1. Name the Phillies player who was selected to the most All-Star Games as a member of the team.

2. Who was the last Phillies left fielder to start in the All-Star Game?

3. In 1976, the Phillies had five All-Stars. Name them.

4. Three years later, the Phillies also had five All-Stars. Name them.

5. In the inaugural All-Star Game in 1933, the Phillies placed two starters in the game. Name them.

6. The Phillies began the 2000 season with three 1999 All-Stars in their rotation. Who were they?

7. Which player was the lone representative that the Phillies sent to the 1996 All Star Game, played at the Vet?
   a) Jim Eisenreich
   b) Curt Schilling
   c) Lenny Dykstra
   d) Ricky Bottalico

8. Prior to 1996, when were the last two times Major League Baseball placed the All Star Game in Philadelphia?

9. Who is the last Phillies player to have a hit in the All Star Game?

10. This Phillies slugger was tabbed the Most Valuable Player of the 1964 Mid-Summer Classic.

TWO-BASE ERRORS QUESTIONS

Answers on page 331

1. Which long-time Phillie from the '60s and early '70s ranks in the Top 25 all-time for most games played without a World Series appearance?

2. In 1997, the Phillies selected J.D. Drew with the number two pick in the annual amateur draft. Who was picked third, directly behind Drew?

3. What Hall of Famer claims that the Phillies told him "Don't call us, we'll call you" after a tryout?

4. Tom Qualters never won a game, but was signed instead of this Hall of Famer who starred for the Detroit Tigers.

5. What Boston Red Sox legend did the Phillies refuse to sign because he wanted an extra $10,000 signing bonus?

6. In which decade did the Phillies lose the most games?
    a) 1920's   b) 1930's
    c) 1940's   d) 1950's

7. Which Phillies manager was fired during the middle of a season while the club was in first place?
    a) Pat Corrales   b) Lee Elia
    c) John Felske   d) Nick Leyva

8. What Phillies pitcher from the 1980's was accused during a game of having sandpaper in his glove and tried to get rid of the evidence by tossing the sandpaper away as the umpires came to check out the matter?

    a) Randy Lerch   b) Charlie Hudson

    c) Kevin Gross   d) Don Carman

9. Who did the Phillies pass on to select Jeff Jackson with the 4th pick in the 1990 draft?

    a) Ken Griffey, Jr.   b) Frank Thomas

    c) Roberto Alomar   d) Albert Belle

10. With 12 games remaining in their 1964 season, by how many games were the Phillies leading the St. Louis Cardinals?

    a) 5 ½   b) 6

    c) 6 ½   d) 7

11. Who would have been Greg Luzinski's defensive replacement had Phillies manager Danny Ozark chosen to put him in left field in the 9th inning of Game 3 of the 1977 NLCS against the Dodgers?

12. Which former Phillies pitcher had the worst season of his brief career by going 1-14 in 1992?

13. Which former Phils outfield prospect suffered horrific knee injuries almost one year apart, ending his playing career?

14. Who were the two pitchers that Phillies manager Gene Mauch over-extended down the stretch in the 1964 pennant race?

15. What two teams finished ahead of the Phillies in the National League when the team collapsed down the stretch in 1964?

16. The Phillies set the Major League record for consecutive losses in one season back in 1961. How long did this stretch at futility last?

17. This Hall of Fame starting pitcher and native of Canada was originally, selected by the Phillies but traded away to Chicago after less than two sub-par seasons.

18. In 1915, the Phillies lost the World Series to what team?

19. In 1950, the Phillies lost the World Series to what team?

REGULAR SEASON QUESTIONS

Answers on page 331-332

1. This Phillies pitcher knocked in an amazing seven runs in a single game in 2002.

2. What famous left-handed pitcher once won 15 straight decisions?

3. Who was the only Phillies player in the modern era (post-1900) to register six hits in one game?

4. Who got the win in relief when the Phillies posted their epic 23-22 victory over the Cubs in 1979?

5. Name the Mets batter who made the final out to wrap up Jim Bunning's perfect game.

6. Which NL West team did the '93 Phillies sweep on the road to open the season?
    a) Atlanta   b) Houston
    c) San Diego   d) Los Angeles

7. Who hit the home run against the Brooklyn Dodgers in the 10th inning of the final game of the 1950 regular season to send the Phillies to the World Series?
    a) Johnny Callison   b) Dick Sisler
    c) Richie Ashburn   d) Dick Allen

8. Which player ended an extra-inning tilt in 2000 with an inside-the-park homer?
   a) Scott Rolen
   b) Bobby Dernier
   c) Ron Gant
   d) Bobby Abreu

9. This member of Macho Row hit two home runs in the club's 1993 home opener against the Cubs.
   a) Darren Daulton
   b) John Kruk
   c) Pete Incaviglia
   d) Dave Hollins

10. Who hit a walk-off grand slam to cap a memorable ninth-inning comeback in an August, 1993 game at the Vet?
    a) Mariano Duncan
    b) Pete Incaviglia
    c) John Kruk
    d) Kim Batiste

11. What Phillies infielder made a nice defensive play to record the final out of Terry Mulholland's 1990 no-hitter at Veterans Stadium?
    a) Dickie Thon
    b) Charlie Hayes
    c) Randy Ready
    d) Juan Samuel

12. Which Phillies player fielded the ball that led to the final out of Tommy Greene's no hitter at Olympic Stadium in May, 1991?
    a) Lenny Dykstra
    b) Mickey Morandini
    c) Tommy Greene
    d) Todd Zeile

13. What Phillie hit two home runs in one game off Curt Schilling in 2001 when the Phils faced their former ace?
    a) Scott Rolen
    b) Doug Glanville
    c) Pat Burrell
    d) Bobby Abreu

14. On June 11, 1985 at the Vet, the Phils set a franchise record for runs while crushing the hated Mets. What was the final score of that memorable rout?
    a) 23-5
    b) 26-7
    c) 24-4
    d) 22-3

15. What often-booed player hit two home runs, including a grand slam, in the first inning of that game?
    a) Von Hayes
    b) Mike Schmidt
    c) Juan Samuel
    d) Ozzie Virgil

16. This infielder hit two game-clinching grand slams during the 1993 season, one early and the other late in the regular season.

17. Name the two pitchers who gave up the slams and the teams for which they played.

18. Which Phillies utility player broke up Pirates starter Doug Drabek's no-hit bid with two outs in the ninth inning in 1990?

19. This reserve catcher, who spent two stints with the team, hit a dramatic game-winning, two-run home run in the 13th inning to beat the Boston Red Sox in a June, 2003 game at the Vet.

20. Although he was a bust at bat during his Phillies career, this 1980's shortstop famously hit home runs from both sides of the plate in a single game against the Pirates during the 1989 season.

21. How many consecutive wins did the Phillies reel off in July and August 1991, a streak which pulled them out of the basement of the National League East?

22. Name the two players who made up the right field platoon for the Phillies in 1993.

23. Which pitcher collected the victory, pitching a shutout on Opening Day in 1997 in Los Angeles, the only day the Phillies would be above .500 for that season?

24. Who scored the game-winning run on Mitch Williams' 10th inning single against the Padres in July, 1993, in a game that did not end until 4:41 A.M.?

25. Which two-time Phillies outfielder hit a dramatic three-run, inside-the-park home run to win a game against San Francisco in 1989?

26. Which two players made the final outs in Roy Halladay's two no-hit games in the 2010 season?

Answers on page 332

1. What player was on deck when Mike Schmidt hit his clutch two-run home run in the 11th inning of the NL East clinching game at Montreal, in October, 1980?

2. Which of these players hit the key triple in the eighth inning of Game 5 of the 1980 National League Championship Series at Houston?
   - a) Greg Gross
   - b) Manny Trillo
   - c) Gary Maddux
   - d) Lonnie Smith

3. Which outfielder recorded the final out in that game?

4. Who was the Royals batter that hit the foul pop, which both Bob Boone and Pete Rose played, to record the second out in the ninth inning of Game 6.

5. Who did Tug McGraw strike out for the final out of the 1980 World Series?

6. Name the pitcher who was credited with the victory for Game 6 of the Series.

7. Who did the Phillies beat in the 1983 NLCS to get to the World Series?

8. This burly closer was on the hill for the final out of the NLCS victory.
   - a) Al Holland
   - b) Larry Christensen
   - c) Willie Hernandez
   - d) John Denny

9. What Baltimore Orioles infielder caught the last out of the 1983 World Series?

10. Who was on the mound in 1993 for the final out of the Phillies' NL East-clinching victory at Pittsburgh?
    a) Bobby Thigpen   b) Donn Pall
    c) Mitch Williams   d) Larry Andersen

11. Which Braves starter did the Phillies knock around in Game 6 of the 1993 NLCS?

12. Who was was the winning pitcher in Game 6?

13. Name the Atlanta reserve player that Mitch Williams struck out to end the contest.

14. Which team did the Phillies defeat to clinch the division in both 2007, 2008 and 2010?

FIRSTS, LASTS & MOSTS QUESTIONS

Answers on page 333

1. This knowledgeable but unlucky man managed the Phils for more games than anyone else.

2. Name the last Phillies player to hit for the cycle.

3. Which Phillies player enjoyed the most years of continuous service with the team?

4. This Phillies legend holds the team record for most consecutive games played.

5. This Phillies slugger holds the single season NL record (post-1900) for most assists by an outfielder.

6. The Phillies' club record for most RBI by one player in one season was set with this number, back in 1930.

7. Which Phillies pitcher amassed the most complete games and innings pitched over his tenure with the team?

8. Who was the first – and only – Phillies player to win the Triple Crown?

9. This Phils hurler, who is now better recognized for his life outside the game, was the winning pitcher in the first game played at Veterans Stadium.

10. Who was the last Philadelphia player to get a hit at Veterans Stadium?

11. Who holds the single-season record for most home runs by a Phillie?

12. Which Phillies hurler has absorbed the most career losses for one pitcher in franchise annals?
    a) Chris Short   b) Steve Carlton
    c) Kyle Abbott   d) Robin Roberts

13. Chuck Klein holds the modern day franchise record for most runs scored in a season with this many.
    a) 158   b) 150
    c) 144   d) 141

14. In which decade did the Phillies win the most regular-season games?

15. Name the Phillies infielder who was the last to register 200 hits in a season for the club.

16. This Depression-era player holds the Phillies record for most extra base hits in a season.

17. Who holds the Phillies modern day (post-1900) record for stolen bases in a season?

18. Which two Phillies pitchers have hit the most career home runs?

19. Who collected the first ever hit in any game in Citizens Bank Park, and what was it?

20. In which West Coast city did Mike Schmidt play his last Major League game in 1989?

21. What player had the honor of being the first Phillies player to have his number retired?

22. Who was the last player in franchise history to hit over .400 in a season?

23. Which pitcher holds the club's all-time record for wins in a Phillies uniform?

24. This bespectacled reliever pitched in more games in one season for the Phillies than any other pitcher.

25. Who is the team's all-time leader in saves?

26. Who is the team's all-time single-season leader in saves?

27. This starting pitcher, who never seems to be out of the spot-light, holds the team's single-season record for most strikeouts.

Answers on page 334

1. Mike Schmidt was born and raised in this Southwestern Ohio town.

2. With which team did Steve Carlton end his playing career?

3. How many years did Mike Schmidt play for the Phillies?

4. How many one hitters did Steve Carlton throw with the Phillies?

5. In what now-razed National League stadium did Mike Schmidt hit his 500th home run?

6. How many games did Steve Carlton win with the Cardinals before arriving in Philadelphia?
   a) 67   b) 72
   c) 77   d) 82

7. What was Steve Carlton's ERA in 1972, the year he finished 27-10?
   a) 2.02   b) 1.99
   c) 2.09   d) 1.97

8. How many National League home run titles did Mike Schmidt win during his storied career?
   a) Five   b) Six
   c) Seven   d) Eight

9. What Pirates pitcher (and eventual Phillies reliever) surrendered Mike Schmidt's 500th home run on April 18, 1987?

10. In addition to being a feared pitcher, Steve Carlton could wield a mean bat as well. How many homers did "Lefty" hit in his entire career?

11. Carlton started every opening day for the Phillies from 1972 through 1986 except one. Which starter was the lone exception, in 1976?

12. Although primarily known as a starter, Carlton did see spot duty in the bullpen at the start and end of his career. How many saves did he earn and with what clubs?

13. How many seasons of 10-or-more complete games did Lefty rack up while with the team?
     a) 10   b) 11
     c) 12   d) 13

14. We know Carlton recorded five seasons of 20-or-more wins with the Phillies. How many 20-loss seasons did he suffer?

15. Did Mike Schmidt steal more or less than 180 bases for his career?

Answers on page 334

1. Prior to 1976, how many times had the Phillies made the postseason in the 93-year existence of the franchise?
    a) Two   b) Three
    c) Four   d) Five

2. In 1976, the Phillies lost the NLCS in this many games.

3. In 1977 and 1978, the Phillies lost the NLCS in this many games.

4. In the 1970s the Phillies lost three consecutive National League Championship Series. Which of the following correctly matches the team with the year that they beat the Phillies?
    a) '76 Reds, '77 Dodgers, '78 Astros
    b) '76 Dodgers, '77 Dodgers, '78 Dodgers
    c) '76 Reds, '77 Reds, '78 Dodgers
    d) '76 Reds, '77 Dodgers, '78 Dodgers

5. Perhaps the greatest five-game playoff in baseball history, the 1980 NLCS against Houston, went into extra innings this many times.
    a) Two   b) Three
    c) Four   d) Five

6. Which renowned Phillies slugger from the era hit the only home run for either side during that series?

7. This division rival turned in an upset series victory over the Phillies during the first round of the playoffs during the strike-shortened 1981 season.

8. Curt Schilling set a League Championship Series record by striking out the first five batters he faced in Game 1 of that 1993 set against the Braves. Name at least three of the five who fanned.

9. Which of the following reserves got the game-winning hit in that memorable contest?
   a) Wes Chamberlain   c) Kim Batiste
   b) Tony Longmire   d) Pete Incaviglia

10. Despite wrecking the plans of his starter, this infamous Phillies pitcher got credit for two victories during the six-game triumph over the Braves.

11. This Phillies non-pitcher was the only player to hit better than .300 in the 2007 postseason.

12. Name the infielder who led the club in RBI that series, and the number of runs batted in.

CHAMPIONSHIP SEASONS QUESTIONS

Answers on page 335

1. Who was the manager of the 1980 Phillies?

2. Pete Rose played every regular-season game of that season at this position.

3. Who were the only three members of the 1980 club to have a double-digit home run total?

4. Which Phillies player, saddled with a slippery nickname, led the team in batting that season.

5. What was Tug McGraw's given first name?

6. How many saves did Tugger register in 1980?

7. Who was the only player with more than 300 at bats to hit more than .300 in 1980?

8. Marty Bystrom burst onto the scene in September, 1980 and posted what record for the club?

9. Within three, how many complete games did Steve Carlton hurl in 1980?

10. Which Phillies pitcher with more than 75 innings pitched led the 1980 club in ERA?

11. This Phillies rookie, better known later as a Pittsburgh Pirate, was the winning pitcher for Game 1 of the 1980 World Series.

12. Name the Phillies rookie reliever who knocked George Brett on his behind during the 1980 World Series.

13. What pitcher was second for the 1980 Phillies in wins with 17?

14. What outfielder on the 1980 Phillies eventually made history by playing for the two teams, in the same season, that faced each other in the 1985 World Series?

15. Which Phillies pitcher posted the starting staff's best earned run average in 1993?

16. Who is the only Phillies relief pitcher other than Mitch Williams to record a save in 1993?

17. This former Brooklyn Dodger was the Phillies pitching coach that season.

18. Who was the only Phillies pitcher to hit a home run in 1993, and where did he do it?

19. Which two pitchers led the 1993 Phillies in wins with 16?

20. An untamed fireballer from the start, the young Curt Schilling had the second-highest ERA among starters with this number.

21. Name the five regular members of the 1993 starting rotation.

22. What Phillies reliever finished second on the club in saves in both 1980 and 1983?

23. Mike Schmidt led the 1983 Phils in home runs with 40. Who finished second, with 16?

24. How many saves did Tug McGraw register in 1983?

25. Which player hit a three-run home run in Game 2 of the 1993 World Series
    - a) Mariano Duncan
    - b) Lenny Dykstra
    - c) Jim Eisenreich
    - d) Darren Daulton

26. Who began the 1993 season as the Phillies' regular shortstop?
    - a) Juan Bell
    - b) Kevin Stocker
    - c) Kim Batiste
    - d) Mariano Duncan

27. How many World Series games had the Phillies won prior to their appearance in the 1980 Fall Classic?
    - a) Zero
    - b) One
    - c) Two
    - d) Three

Broad Street Subway to World Series Game

Answers on page 336

1. How many players clubbed more than 30 home runs for the 2008 Phillies?

2. Who was the only hitter to draw more than 100 walks?

3. Who was the only Phillies pitcher to hit a home run, either in the regular season or postseason?

4. Over the entire season how many starting pitchers did the Phillies feature in the rotation?

5. How many pitchers recorded at least one save?

6. How many RBI did Ryan Howard have that year, only three off his career-best total from 2006?

7. How many home runs did Pat Burrell hit as a member of the Phillies?

8. In which year did Ryan Howard hit his first major-league home run?

9. How many home runs did Howard have entering the 2009 season?

10. In what year did Jimmy Rollins make his major-league debut?

11. Who did the Phillies trade to acquire NLCS Game 4 hero Matt Stairs?

12. With which team did Matt Stairs make his major-league debut?

13. Which Phillies infielder holds the major league record with 716 at bats in a single season?

14. Jimmy Rollins has played shortstop for his entire major league career except for one out. At which other position did he appear?

15. At which two positions has Chase Utley played during his major league career?

16. In which season did Jamie Moyer make his major-league debut?

17. For his debut, Moyer pitched for this NL East club against this other NL East team.

18. Charlie Manuel played for which two teams in his American baseball career?

19. How many home runs did Charlie Manuel hit in the major leagues?

20. Manuel played for these two teams while in Japan.

THE 2008 WORLD CHAMPS
POST SEASON QUESTION

Answers on page 336-337

1. This Washington Nationals player hit into the double play that clinched the NL East for the Phillies.

2. What was the Phillies record at home during the 2008 postseason?

3. Who got the Phillies only walk-off hit of the entire playoffs?

4. Against which team did Brett Myers get three hits in a game?

5. Against which Dodgers pitcher did Matt Stairs hit his epic home run in Game 4 of the NLCS?

6. This Dodgers player hit the foul ball responsible for the final out of the NLCS.

7. Who got the Phillies started with a first-inning home run in Game 1 of the 2008 World Series?

8. Who led the Phillies with a .444 batting average in the 2008 World Series (minimum 10 at-bats)?

9. Name the six Phillies to homer in the 2008 World Series.

10. Which Phillies pitcher recorded two wins in the World Series?

11. Who was the only Phillies reliever to give up a run in the Series?

12. How many home runs did the Phillies hit in the 2008 World Series?

13. Two Phillies position players went hitless in the 2008 World Series. Who were they?

14. Which Phillies pitcher was the only one to suffer a loss in the 2008 World Series?

15. Who led off the second part of Game 5 of the 2008 World Series?

16. This Phillies infielder scored the winning run of the 2008 World Series.

17. Brad Lidge fanned this Tampa Bay Ray for the last out of the 2008 World Series.

2009 PHILLIES QUESTIONS

Answers on page 337

1. Harry Kalas' last home run call came in Denver on April 12, when this player launched one into the Coors Field seats.

2. Kalas was taken ill and eventually passed away in this city.

3. The Phils pounded this team for 22 runs in a July 6 victory.
   - a) Pittsburgh
   - b) Chicago Cubs
   - c) San Diego
   - d) Cincinnati

4. Reserve infielder Eric Bruntlett completed this rare feat to end an August 23 contest against the New York Mets.

5. Closer Brad Lidge recorded this many outs in the Phils' NL East clinching contest on September 30.

6. Which bench player recorded the game-winning hit, a home run, in the Phils' regular-season finale on October 4 against Florida?

7. How many regulars posted at least thirty home runs in 2009?

8. Which of these starters posted the highest winning percentage?
   - a) Cliff Lee
   - b) Joe Blanton
   - c) Jamie Moyer
   - d) J.A. Happ

9. Ryan Howard victimized this Rockies pitcher for the game-deciding hit in Game 4 of the NL Division Series.

10. Prior to Cliff Lee's 11-0 victory in Game 3 of the National League Championship Series, which Phillies hurler last failed to allow a run during a playoff start?

11. Name the two players who scored on Jimmy Rollins' game-winning hit in Game 4 of the NLCS.

12. How many Phillies players hit home runs during Game 5 of the NLCS?

13. This infielder set a club record and tied a World Series record with five home runs during the six games.

14. Name the Phillies pitcher who was credited with both of the club's World Series victories.

15. Which player made the last out of the Series?

TRULY TRIVIAL QUESTIONS

Answers on page 338-339

1. Who is the only Phillie ever to be the highest paid player in the major leagues?

2. Who did the Phillies select the only time they had the overall #1 pick in the amateur draft?

3. Which pitcher, not known for his devotion to fitness, was the club's opening day starter in 2006?

4. Who was the last Phillies shortstop to start on opening day before Jimmy Rollins?

5. What players, along with their corresponding numbers, have been retired by the franchise?

6. Name the Phillies regular third baseman in 1972, the year before Mike Schmidt took over.

7. This man was the bench boss for the 1950 Whiz Kids.

8. In 1979, the team trotted out controversial new uniforms dubbed "Saturday Night Specials," which required the players to wear this color from head to toe.

9. Four former Phillies at one time played pro basketball. Can you name them?

10. In the modern era, the Phillies have played two 20-inning games. Against which team did both occur?

11. Seven Phillies have hit for the cycle. Name at least four.

12. In what year did Jim Bunning throw his perfect game?

13. With which team did Jim Bunning pitch from 1955-1963 prior to coming to the Phillies?

14. Terry Mulholland and Kevin Millwood both threw no hitters against this NL West club.

15. Which Phillies second baseman from the 1970's led the NL in double plays turned for three straight years?

16. What fleet-footed Phillies player was born on March 19, 1927 in Tilden, Nebraska?

17. Against what team did Mickey Morandini make his unassisted triple play?

18. An incredible 16 of this pitcher's 33 victories in 1916 came via the shutout.

19. Prior to 1980, who was the only Phillies pitcher to win a World Series game?

20. How did Phillies great Ed Delahanty die?

21. What team did Tug McGraw play for before coming to the Phillies?

22. The Phillies were once involved in the fastest nine-inning game of all time. How long did it take?

23. Who was the first black player to suit up for the Phillies?

24. How many no-hitters have Phillies pitchers thrown in the modern era (post-1900)?

25. On June 10, 1981, Pete Rose tied Stan Musial with his 3,631st hit. How many days later did he break the record?
    a) One   b) Four
    c) Ten   d) Sixty

26. Where was the main entrance to the Baker Bowl located?

27. In what year was ground broken on construction of Veterans Stadium?

28. Who dug the first shovel full of dirt at The Vet's ground breaking ceremony?

29. Robin Roberts enjoyed his best season back in 1952.
How many games did he win that year?
    a) 24   b) 26
    c) 28   d) 30

30. This Phillies outfielder from the 1980s appeared in commercials with a round of bullets draped across his chest.
    a) Von Hayes   b) Gary Redus
    c) Glenn Wilson   d) Randy Ready

31. For which team did Dallas Green leave the Phillies the first time he left the organization?
    a) New York Mets   b) New York Yankees
    c) Chicago Cubs   d) Los Angeles Dodgers

32. How many players did the Phillies trade to the Cleveland Indians to acquire Von Hayes?

33. Who did the Phillies get in return when they traded Larry Bowa and Ryne Sandberg to Chicago?

34. What Hall of Fame pitcher won Game 1 of the 1915 World Series for the Phillies?

35. On what holiday did Jim Bunning throw his perfect game at Shea Stadium?

36. Which of these players launched a grand slam for his first major-league hit?
    a) Ricky Jordan   b) Ron Jones
    c) Keith Moreland   d) Chase Utley

37. What former Phillies player hit the ceremonial device which began the implosion of the Vet?
    a) Mike Schmidt   b) Mitch Williams
    c) Greg Luzinski   d) Darren Daulton

38. This former Phillies catcher, who was a key member of the 1983 pennant squad, tragically died during the faulty installation of a satellite dish.
    a) Johnny Callison   b) Mike Ryan
    c) Bo Diaz

39. What popular former player pulled himself out of a game and retired (as a member of a different club) after hitting a single?
    a) Cookie Rojas   b) John Kruk
    c) Dave Cash   d) Richie Ashburn

40. In 1985, on the road and during the midst of a terrible slump, Mike Schmidt ripped into the Philadelphia fans. Upon returning home, what did he wear during warm-ups to try to alleviate the pressure and joke around with the fans who had been on him?
    a) A dress
    b) Long, dangling earrings
    c) A wig
    d) Flip Flops

41. Which Phillies manager was hired just 13 games into the 1991 season from the broadcast booth?

42. Which power hitter from the 1980's came with Tommy Greene from Atlanta in a 1990 trade?

43. From what Major League ballpark did the Phillies acquire their huge scoreboard at Connie Mack Stadium?
    a) Comiskey Park
    b) Tiger Stadium
    c) Busch Stadium
    d) Yankee Stadium

44. Name the two highly-anticipated free agents the Phillies signed before the 1996 season.

45. Who was the Phillies manager for the 1971 season, the club's first at the Vet?

46. This Phillies pitcher, who formed a solid 1-2 punch with Steve Carlton in the mid 1970's, became a dentist upon retiring from baseball.

47. What color were the 700 level seats at the Vet before the stadium went to all blue?

48. With what team did Greg "The Bull" Luzinski finish his major league career?

49. What number did famous National League hitter Al Oliver wear in his one season with Philadelphia in 1984?

50. For which three teams did Richie Ashburn play in the majors?

51. The Phillies won the NL East in 1976, '77, '78, '80, and '83. Name the division rival who finished second in every year except one.

52. What former Phillies manager, upon his res ignation early in the 1960 season, quipped "I'm 49 years old, and I'd like to live to 50?"

53. At what cross streets was Veterans Stadium located?

54. Begun in the late 1980's, what mid-season Phillies old-timers promotion featured former players engaging in a home-run hitting contest, usually between games of a double header?

55. In 1987, during the celebration of the signing of the Constitution, the Phils placed this slogan to honor the event on the outfield wall.

56. Name the member of the Phillies broadcast team who wrote a weekly column on the Phils for The Evening Bulletin during the mid-to-late 1970's.

57. What is the only other name in the modern era by which the Phillies have been known?

58. In 1964 the Phillies tied a major league record for triple plays turned with this number.

59. In 1980, which fiery player stole second, third and home in one inning?

60. To which team did the Phillies sell Robin Roberts in 1961?

Answers on page 340

Match the Phillies player with the appropriate "Phan Group"

Pat Burrell	People
Jose Mesa	Flotilla
Brandon Duckworth	Pals
Robert Person	Girls
Randy Wolf	Faces
Vicente Padilla	Pond
Chase Utley	Chicks
Sal Fasano	Pack
Cole Hamels	Homies
Chris Coste	Train
Jim Thome	Zombies
Jeremy Giambi	Guard

Answers on page 340

Match the Phillie with the "other" number(s) he wore while with the club.

Ryan Howard	29, 11
Jimmy Rollins	33
Mike Schmidt	39
Pat Burrell	31
Shane Victorino	22
Brett Myers	11, 19
Garry Maddox	28
Mitch Williams	99
John Kruk	29

PHILLIES WALL OF FAME

Honoring Alumni of both the Phillies and the Philadelphia Athletics began in 1978 at Veterans Stadium in a 200-level display originally called the Philadelphia Baseball Hall of Fame.

Enshrined Philadelphia Phillies

Robin Roberts	1978	Sam Thompson	1996
Richie Ashburn	1979	Johnny Callison	1997
Chuck Klein	1980	Greg Luzinski	1998
Grover Alexxander	1981	Tug McGraw	1999
Del Ennis	1982	Gavvy Cravath	2000
Jim Bunning	1984	Garry Maddox	2001
Ed Delahanty	1985	Tony Taylor	2002
Cy Williams	1986	Sherry Magee	2003
Granny Hamner	1987	Billy Hamilton	2004
Paul Owens	1988	Bob Boone	2005
Steve Carlton	1989	Dallas Green	2006
Mike Schmidt	1990	John Vukovich	2007
Larry Bowa	1991	Juan Samuel	2008
Chris Short	1992	Harry Kalas	2009
Curt Simmons	1993	Darren Daulton	2010
Dick Allen	1994	John Kruk	2011
Willie Jones	1995		

Introduction To The 76ers
by Marc Zumoff

This is for all the nerds out there. All the late bloomers. All the people who never excelled in sports when they were kids. All the kids who never got picked to play in a game with their neighborhood buddies.

Once upon a time, I was you.

The memories are still vivid. They hit me almost every time I walk into an NBA arena, saddle up to my courtside broadcast location. They hit me while it's still relatively quiet, while the workers are busy getting the place ready for the game, before the players have changed into their uniforms.

I'm in my 17th season of announcing Philadelphia 76ers basketball on television. And every night, before every game, I think of the kid growing up in Northeast Philly who could only dream of what I'm doing today. The kid who felt the dejection of being left out of the neighborhood baseball "choose-up game" who was left out of the play calling in the touch football game in the street; who went through his adolescent years chubby, pimply-faced and in awe of the jocks who ruled the school and made him feel insignificant and alone.

That was all in my head of course, but in many ways, it was a reality—my reality. And my retreat was into a fantasy world. A world which I'd watch in quiet desperation, eyeing the neighborhood kids from the sidelines or from the stands at the high school basketball game. Left to my own devices, I'd announce the proceedings, whatever they happen to be. From stickball to football, or between two street kids or between high school stars. I'd announce to myself, into a tape recorder or to the person sitting next to me. No, I couldn't/wouldn't/wasn't asked to play in the game, but I could capture it in colorful phrases. The excitement, the emotion, the X's and O's, were usually broadcast to an audience of one.

It's these memories that keep what I do fresh and alive, that allow me to never take what I've accomplished in my life for granted. I am, after all, very lucky. It's like I often tell audiences during speaking engagements: "I sit in the front row of 29 different NBA arenas from October to May, I fly charter jets around the country, I stay in five-star hotels, I'm off from June until September and I get paid for all of it!"

For years, I worked as an anchor/reporter for PRISM, a Philadelphia area channel that showed first-run movies along with professional and college sports. During this time, I so wanted to break into play-by-play announcing, though it appeared an opening would never come.

Then one day in October 1985, a man who was a frequent visitor to The Spectrum approached me. He was an outside salesman who often liked to stop me and talk about sports. Reluctantly, I would listen as he'd talk on and on about his views of the teams, but I was being more kind than interested in what he was saying.

So on this particular day, he stops me outside The Spectrum and asks, "Marc, did you hear about Gene Hart?" He proceeds to tell me that Hart, the legendary Flyers announcer who I grew up listening to and admiring, had suffered a heart attack and would not be able to work for a while.

The wheels started turning.

Somewhere in my collection I had a tape of a Flyers game that I had done while just sitting in the press box, announcing into a recorder. So, I took the tape and gave it to Jay Snider, the son of Ed Snider, the man who invented the Flyers. Jay, who was the team's president then, liked what he heard and agreed to hire me to do the season opener, which was coming up in about a week or so!

When it came time to do the game, I remember the incredible high. Sitting in the upper press box, the sellout crowd taking its seats, the players flying around in warm-ups. I was ready to go. Just then, public address announcer Lou Nolan announced to the crowd that Hart had been hospitalized but would soon be back behind the mic. The place at once arose and roared into a standing ovation. It was then that it hit me. It was like pinch-hitting for Babe Ruth!

Once I started announcing the game, any butterflies, any trepidation, any doubts that I might've had that I belonged in that booth announcing a game in place of an icon vaporized into the cool October night. The cadence of my delivery, the phrases, the timing all came as naturally as breathing. I was no Gene Hart. But I was sitting in his seat, just as I had imagined many years before as a kid, broadcasting a Flyers game. It was no different than doing a game into my tape recorder for the audience of one, only this time, the audience was thousands.

That particular Flyers game was certainly a watershed for me, but by no means was it the only thing that helped to get me to where I am today.

Suffice to say, it has all been great. Sure, arriving at my desired destination has been richly rewarding. But still, from the time I enter the arena on the night of a Sixers game, until the time I take my seat to prepare for my broadcast, I can't help but recount the journey. Rejection letters. Failed auditions. Silly, stupid mistakes. Meetings of happenstance like the one recounted above that led to me subbing for a legend. It's all been one, wonderful trip for the kid from Northeast Philly. The one who couldn't play sports. The one who today announces those sports for the Philadelphia 76ers and gets paid for it.

Not so bad for a nerd.

76ERS TRIVIA

BEFORE THE 76ERS CAME TO TOWN: PHILADELPHIA WARRIORS

Answers on page 341

1. What Warriors great once scored 85 points while playing for Villanova?

2. What Center led the NBA in scoring for three consecutive seasons from the 1952-53 season through the 1955-56 campaign?

3. What rookie guard excelled for the Warriors during the 1956-57 season?

4. What team did the Warriors defeat in 1956 NBA Championship?

5. How many points and rebounds did Wilt Chamberlain average in his rookie season with the Warriors?

6. To which team did the Warriors lose in the 1960 and 1961 playoffs?

7. In what season did Wilt Chamberlain average an all-time best of 50.4 points per game?

8. In what city and against what team did Wilt Chamberlain score 100 points in a game?

9. Who was the radio play-by-play announcer for Wilt Chamberlain's 100-point game?

10. What Boston Celtics player hit the winning shot against the Warriors with two seconds left in Game 7 of the 1962 Eastern Finals?

11. Who sold the Warriors to a San Francisco businessman in 1962?

12. How many NBA seasons went by after the Warriors left Philly, but before the Syracuse Nationals came to town and renamed themselves the Philadelphia 76ers?

Answers on page 341

1. What year were the Syracuse Nationals formed?

2. Who was the founder of the Syracuse Nationals?

3. What season did the Syracuse Nationals win the NBA Championship?

4. What Hall of Famer had the first 50-point game ever for the Syracuse Nationals?

5. What team did the Syracuse Nationals defeat in the 1961 Divisional Finals?

6. What two men purchased the Syracuse Nationals and subsequently moved the franchise to Philadelphia?

76ERS RECORDS QUESTIONS

Answers on page 342

REGULAR SEASON GAME RECORDS

What Sixers player has the highest regular season game record for the following categories:

1. Points scored

2. Rebounds

3. Assists (two players)

4. Steals (three players)

5. Blocked shots (three players)

6. Three-pointers made

REGULAR SEASON SEASON RECORDS

What Sixers player has the highest season total record for the following categories:

1. Scoring average

2. Steals

3. Three-pointers made

4. Most disqualifications

REGULAR SEASON CAREER RECORDS

What Sixers player has the highest career total record for the following categories:

1. Highest scoring average

2. Assists

3. Offensive rebounds

4. Steals

5. Blocked shots

6. Three-pointers made

7. Most turnovers

76ERS DRAFT QUESTIONS

Answers on page 343

1. How many #1 overall draft picks have the Sixers selected? Who were they?

2. In what year and with what pick in the first round did the Sixers select Darryl Dawkins out of Evans High School?

3. Who (other than Charles Barkley) was the Sixers *other* first-round draft pick in the 1984 NBA Draft (the 10th pick overall in the first round)?

4. Who did the Sixers draft and trade to acquire Hersey Hawkins?

5. Who was the club's first-round pick in the 1992 NBA Draft?

6. What guard did the Sixers draft with the third overall pick in the 1995 NBA Draft?

7. What year did the Sixers draft Allen Iverson?

8. From which team did the Sixers acquire John Salmons from on draft night?

Answers on page 343

1. In addition to cash, who did the Sixers trade to acquire Wilt Chamberlain from the San Francisco Warriors in 1965?

2. What three players did the Sixers get in return from the Lakers for Wilt Chamberlain?

3. In what year did the Sixers acquire Julius Erving?

4. In 1986 the 76ers traded the #1 overall draft pick and cash to Cleveland for what player?

5. What forward did the Sixers trade along with Moses Malone and two first-round draft picks to the Bullets in 1986?

6. What three players did the Sixers get from Phoenix in return for Charles Barkley?

7. What two players did the Sixers trade to acquire Theo Ratliff and Aaron McKie?

8. What was the total package that the Sixers acquired when they shipped Allen Iverson to Denver?

9. What did the Sixers get in return when they traded Kyle Korver to Utah?

10. In order to clear cap room to sign Elton Brand, who did the Sixers trade to Minnesota?

76ERS COACHING QUESTIONS

Answers on page 344

1. Who enjoyed the longest tenure as coach in the history of the Sixers?

2. Who was the first coach of the Sixers?

3. Who coached the Sixers from 1973-74 through part of the 1977-78 season?

4. What coach has had the most regular-season wins in franchise history?

5. What coach has had the most regular-season losses?

6. What coach has had the highest regular-season winning percentage?

7. What coach has had the lowest regular-season winning percentage?

8. What coach has had the most playoff wins?

9. What coach has had the most playoff losses?

10. What former St. Joseph's Hawks and Sixers bench boss won an NBA title while coaching against the Sixers?

11. Who replaced Billy Cunningham as head coach of the Sixers?

12. What Sixers coach tried to talk Maurice Cheeks out of retirement while Cheeks was an assistant coach of the team?

13. Who coached Allen Iverson during his rookie season in the NBA?

14. How many seasons did Larry Brown last as Sixers head coach?

15. What two individuals followed Brown as head coach of the Sixers during the 2003-04 season?

76ERS PLAYOFF QUESTIONS

Answers on page 345-346

NAME THE TEAM THE SIXERS LOST TO IN THE PLAYOFFS:

1. 2011 Eastern Conference Quarterfinals

2. 2009 Eastern Conference Quarterfinals

3. 2008 Eastern Conference Quarterfinals

4. 2005 Eastern Conference Quarterfinals

5. 2003 Eastern Conference Semifinals

6. 2002 Eastern Conference Quarterfinals

7. 2001 NBA Finals

8. 2000 Eastern Conference Semifinals

9. 1999 Eastern Conference Semifinals

10. 1991 Eastern Conference Semifinals

11. 1990 Eastern Conference Semifinals

12. 1989 Eastern Conference Quarterfinals

13. 1987 Eastern Conference Quarterfinals

14. 1986 Eastern Conference Semifinals

15. 1985 Eastern Conference Finals

16. 1984 Eastern Conference Quarterfinals

17. 1982 NBA Finals

18. 1981 Eastern Conference Finals

19. 1980 NBA Finals

20. 1979 Eastern Conference Semifinals

21. 1978 Eastern Conference Finals

22. 1977 NBA Finals

23. Which games did the Sixers lose in the 1977 NBA Finals?

24. What was the final score of the Sixers Game 7 loss in the 1986 Eastern Conference Semifinals?

25. What team did the Sixers lose to by one point in Game 7 of the 1965 Eastern Division Final?

26. What is the most historically memorable moment from Game 7 of the 1965 Eastern Division Final? It's not a good memory!

27. How many times have the Sixers reached the NBA Finals? Name the years.

INDIVIDUAL GAME PLAYER PLAYOFF RECORDS

What Sixers player had the most of the following in one playoff game:

1. Points

2. Rebounds

3. Assists

4. Steals

5. Blocked shots

6. Three-pointers made

CAREER PLAYER PLAYOFF RECORDS

What Sixers player has had the most of the following in his career with the Sixers in the playoffs:

1. Games played

2. Points

3. Rebounds

4. Assists

5. Steals

6. Blocked Shots

7. Three-pointers made?

8. Turnovers

9. What was the combined record of the home team in the five games the Sixers and Nets played in the 1984 playoffs?

10. How many games did the Sixers win against the Pacers in the 1999 & 2000 playoffs combined?

11. What Sixers player physically went after Reggie Miller during Game 4 of the 2000 Eastern Conference Semifinals resulting in the ejection and subsequent suspension of both he and Miller?

12. Against which team(s) in the 2001 Playoffs did the Sixers lose to in the first game of a series?

13. What Milwaukee Bucks player, who was a former Sixers, gave Allen Iverson a forearm to the face in Game 6 of the 2001 Eastern Conference Finals resulting in a foul and a subsequent suspension for that player in Game 7 of the series?

14. Who started for the Sixers at small forward in place of the injured George Lynch in Game 7 of the 2001 Eastern Conference Finals versus Milwaukee?

15. Which Sixer' reserve scored an extremely surprising ten points off the bench in the first half of Game 7 of the 2001 Eastern Conference Finals versus Milwaukee?

16. How many points did Allen Iverson score in the Sixers' Game 1 win over the Los Angeles Lakers in the 2001 NBA Finals?

17. As of the conclusion of 2003 playoffs, who were the previous four NBA coaches to defeat the Sixers in a playoff series?

18. How many times did the Sixers make the second round of the playoffs with Iverson?

19. What seed were the Sixers in the 2009 Eastern Conference playoffs?

20. What Sixers player did Orland Magic center Dwight Howard elbow in Game 5 of the 2009 Eastern Conference Quarterfinals resulting in Howard being suspended for Game 6?

CHAMPIONSHIP YEARS QUESTIONS

Answers on page 346

THE CHAMPIONSHIP YEARS: 1967-68 & 1982-83

1. What was the Sixers record during the 1966-67 regular season?

2. Who was the coach of that legendary championship team?

3. How many Sixers averaged double figures in scoring during the 1966-67 season?

4. What team did the Sixers defeat in the 1967 NBA Finals?

5. What was the home arena of the 1966-67 Sixers?

6. Other than a player's number, what else was written on the front of the Sixers jerseys during the 1966-67 season?

7. Who was the general manager of the 1982-83 Sixers?

8. What was the Sixers record during the 1982-83 regular season?

9. Name the typical starting five for the 1982-1983 Sixers championship team.

10. Who were the four players selected from the Sixers for the 1983 Eastern Conference All-Star Team? How many of them started?

11. Who was the only team to defeat the Sixers in a game during the 1983 playoffs?

12. Which team did the Sixers beat in the 1983 NBA Finals?

13. Which two announcers called Game 4 of the 1983 NBA Finals on CBS?

14. What was the final score of Game 4 of the 1983 NBA Finals?

15. In what arena did the 76ers win the 1983 NBA Championship?

16. What was the Sixers playoff record in 1983?

17. Who is the only person to play for the 1966-67 Sixers championship team and later coach the 1982-83 championship squad?

Answers on page 347

1. What seven Sixers players have had their uniform number retired? What are the seven numbers?

2. What four Sixers have won a regular-season MVP?

3. Who is the only Sixers player to have won the NBA Rookie of the Year award?

4. What two Sixers coaches have been named NBA Coach of the Year?

5. Who is the only Sixers player to be named NBA Defensive Player of the Year?

6. What two Sixers players have been named the Sixth Man of the Year?

7. The 2000-01 Sixers became the first team to have four people win separate regular-season NBA awards. Who were these four people and what awards did they win?

8. Which Sixers player has had the most appearances on the First Team All-NBA (while playing for the Sixers)?

9. Which Sixers player made the 1976, 1977, 1978 & 1979 NBA All Star Game?

10. Who was the last Sixers player prior to Allen Iverson to be named to the First Team All NBA?

11. Who are the four Sixers players to be named MVP of the NBA All Star Game?

12. Before Iverson became an NBA All Star who was the most recent Sixers player to do so? This individual is the only Sixers player to make it after Charles Barkley was traded, but before A.I. came to town.

NICKNAME QUESTIONS

Answers on page 347

Name the player for each of the following nicknames:

1. "Chocolate Thunder"

2. "The Round Mound of Rebound"

3. "The Kangaroo Kid"

4. "Thump and Bump" (two players combined for this nickname)

5. "The Hammer"

6. "The Big Dipper"

7. "The Sheriff"

8. "The Boston Strangler"

9. "The G-Man"

10. What three nicknames --- all very similar in origin --- were given to Julius Erving?

UNIFORM NUMBERS QUESTIONS

Answers on page 348

Name who wore the uniform number in the stated season?

1. 0 in 1993-94

2. 00 in 1997-98

3. 1 in 1997-98

4. 3 in 1995-96

5. 4 in 2002-03

6. 8 in 1982-83

7. 9 in 2000-01

8. 11 in 1991-92

9. 17 in 1991-92

10. 20 in 1989-90

11. 21 in 1999-00

12. 23 in 2008-09?

13. 28 in 1993-94

14. 30 in 1976-77

15. 33 in 1974-75

16. 35 in 1992-93

17. 42 in 2000-01

18. 50 in 1999-00

19. 76 in 1993-94

NAME THE COLLEGE
QUESTIONS

Answers on page 348

Name the college or university attended by the following players

1. Hal Greer

2. Billy Cunningham

3. Doug Collins

4. Marvin Barnes

5. Mo Cheeks

6. Earl Cureton

7. Andrew Toney

8. Leo Rautins

9. Charles Barkley

10. Christian Welp

11. Kenny Payne

12. Sharone Wright

13. Larry Hughes

14. Speedy Claxton

15. Thaddeus Young

Answers on page 349

1960's

1. In what year did the Syracuse Nationals move to Philadelphia?

2. How did the new Philadelphia basketball franchise choose the name "76ers?"

3. Who was the first coach of the Sixers?

4. What was the team's regular-season record in their first season in Philadelphia?

5. Who was the Sixers first All Star?

6. What player averaged both the second-most points and second most rebounds in the Sixers inaugural season in Philadelphia?

7. What all-time NBA great player did the Sixers face in the playoffs in their first season in Philadelphia?

8. What year did the Sixers move into the Spectrum?

9. What year did the Sixers acquire Wilt Chamberlain?

10. What was Billy Cunningham's first season with the Sixers?

11. In what season of the 60s did the Sixers have their second-most regular-season wins (trailing only the amount of regular-season wins from the 1966-67 championship campaign)?

12. Who passed the ball that Boston's John Havlicek "stole" to end a playoff series?

13. What future Sixers coach joined the team as a player in the 1966-67 season?

14. What is the historical significance of Chamberlain's game versus the Detroit Pistons in 1967?

15. In what year was "The Stilt" traded to the Lakers?

16. What player averaged the most points for the Sixers in the first season after Chamberlain was traded?

1970's

Answers on page 350

1. What was Steve Mix's first season with the Sixers?

2. Even though the statistic was not yet officially being tracked, which Sixers player had three straight games with a triple-double in 1970?

3. What was Hal Greer's last season with the Sixers?

4. What two members of the 1972 Olympic Basketball Team played at least four seasons for the Sixers?

5. What was the Sixers regular-season record in 1972-73?

6. How many games did the Sixers win on the road during the 1972-73 season?

7. Who was the leading scorer for the 1972-73 Sixers?

8. Who was the second leader scorer for the 1972-73 Sixers?

9. What Sixers player made the 1975 NBA All-Star Game?

10. What was World B. Free's real first name?

11. In the 1970s the Sixers had two players who later had sons who made the NBA All Star Game in the 2000s. Who were these two players?

12. What was Julius Erving's first season with the Sixers?

13. What 76ers player was renowned for breaking backboards on dunks?

14. Who purchased the Sixers in 1976?

15. What was Billy Cunningham's first season as coach of the Sixers?

16. What former Sixers coach was later Michael Jordan's first coach with the Bulls?

17. What five players started the most games for the Sixers in the 1977-78 season?

18. What Sixers player was a First Team All NBA selection for the 1975-76 season?

19. What key reserve on the 1982-83 Sixers championship team joined the Sixers in the 1979-80 season?

1980's

Answers on page 350

1. Who is the only Sixers player to score 50-or-more points during a game in the 1980s?

2. Who bought the Sixers in 1981?

3. What chant arose in the Boston Garden when the Sixers were closing out the Celtics in Game 7 of the 1982 Eastern Conference Finals?

4. What Sixers player led the team in rebounding four straight seasons prior to the arrival of Moses Malone?

5. Who did Julius Erving dunk over when he did his famous windmill slam versus the Lakers at the Spectrum?

6. Which Sixers player was selected to the NBA's All-Defensive First

    Team for four consecutive seasons from 1982-83 through 1986-87?

7. How many seasons did Moses play for the Sixers?

8. What was the name of the saxophonist who frequently performed the national anthem for big games primarily during Erving's time with the Sixers?

9. What legendary member of the Sixers organization died on Christmas Day 1985?

10. What Sixers great was inducted into the Basketball Hall of Fame on May 6, 1986?

11. After the draft day moves of 1986, the Sixers were excited to unveil a new starting frontcourt that included Charles Barkley and what two other players? How many total games did these three players start together?

12. How many seasons did Erving play for the Sixers?

13. What player was informed by Michael Barkann outside the player's home that he had been traded away by the Sixers?

14. What Sixers player once inbounded the basketball and accidentally threw it in the hoop resulting in a turnover?

15. Who is the only non-player in Sixers history to have his name raised to the rafters on a banner similar to how players have their uniform number retired?

16. What Sixers player made the NBA's All-Defensive First Team eight times during his career in the league?

17. Who was the Sixers GM from 1986-1990?

18. What player did the Sixers acquire for Mo Cheeks?

1990's

Answers on page 351

1. Who was the coach of the Sixers Atlantic Division-winning team during the 1989-90 season?

2. Against what team were the 1989-90 Sixers playing when they got into a huge fight near the end of a game on the same night they clinched the Atlantic Division title?

3. What member of the Sixers 1989-1990 Atlantic Division title team died of a heart attack during the 1990s?

4. Who was the Sixers GM from 1990-1992?

5. What former Sixers player shocked and inspired fans when he came out of a five year retirement to play 13 games with the Sixers during the 1991-92 season?

6. What was the final uniform number Charles Barkley wore with the Sixers? Why did he do this?

7. What's the most three-pointers Manute Bol ever made in one game with the Sixers?

8. Who was the last Sixers player prior to Allen Iverson to lead the team in scoring average in a season?

9. How many seasons did Charles Barkley play with the Sixers?

10. Who was the Sixers GM that traded Sir Charles to Phoenix?

11. Who was brought in to coach the Sixers for the 1992-93 season but did such a bad job he was fired after only 55 games?

12. Who stood taller: Manute Bol or Shawn Bradley?

13. Who led the Sixers in scoring the first season after Barkley was traded?

14. Which broadcaster started announcing Sixers games in 1994?

15. Which Sixers player shot .464 percent from three-point land on 425 attempts during the 1994-95 season?

16. Who was the last Sixers player prior to Iverson to score 50-or-more points in a game?

17. What veteran NBA shooting guard did the Sixers turn into their starting point guard for the 1995-96 season?

18. What dubious distinction did the Sixers franchise set at the conclusion of the 1995-96 season?

19. What Sixers GM drafted Iverson?

20. What former top 10 NBA Draft pick played in exactly 20 games for the 1997-98 Sixers?

21. What was the Sixers record in the 50 regular-season games of the lockout-shortened 1999 season?

22. What player tussled with Chuck Daly for the basketball when the ball went out of bounds as the Sixers played the Magic in the 1999 Eastern Conference Quarterfinals?

23. What school has been the Sixers practice home since 1999?

24. What year did the Sixers move into the building currently known as the Wells Fargo Center?

25. Did the Sixers win or lose their first game in the (as it was known then) Core states Center?

26. What is the current seating capacity of the Wells Fargo Center for basketball?

27. What are the other three names that the building currently known as the Wells Fargo has had?

28. Under what three Sixers head coaches was Mo Cheeks an assistant coach?

29. What mascot came into existence early in Pat Croce's tenure with the Sixers? And what mascot did he replace?

30. What Sixers GM from the 1990s did not make one trade during his tenure with the team?

2000's

Answers on page 352

1. What member of the Sixers organization was involved in a serious motorcycle accident in the summer of 2000?

2. What is Tom McGinnis' most well-known pet phrase?

3. How many games in a row did the Sixers win to start the 2000-01 season?

4. What Raptors player missed a shot at the buzzer that would have won the series for Toronto at the end of Game 7 of the 2001 Eastern Conference Semifinals?

5. What Los Angeles Lakers player did Allen Iverson step over after hitting a shot in the corner during overtime of Game 1 of the 2001 NBA Finals in LA?

6. What two announcers called the Sixers – Lakers NBA Finals on NBC?

7. With Eric Snow, Iverson and Aaron McKie all hurt to begin the 2001-02 season, who started at guard in the Sixers first game that season?

8. What member of the Sixers 2000-01 Eastern Conference championship team did the Sixers re-acquire during the 2002-03 season?

9. What member of the 2003-04 Sixers was the two-time Missouri Valley Conference Player of the Year?

10. What three members of the Sixers 2003-04 roster were the #1 overall pick in an NBA draft?

11. Against which team did Iverson score a career-high 60 points in February, 2005?

12. During the 2004-05 season Samuel Dalembert primarily split time at center with what player?

13. What former Sixers player was traded away from Boston when the Celtics acquired Kevin Garnett?

14. What team was Jason Smith drafted by?

15. After Allen Iverson had been traded to Denver, who was the first Sixers player to be named Eastern Conference Player of the Week?

16. What Sixers player averaged a disappointing 13.2 points per game in the 2008 Eastern Conference Quarterfinals against Detroit?

17. The 76ers could not offer Elton Brand more money than some other teams in the summer of 2008. But Brand appreciated the Sixers offering all that they could. What term did Brand, agent David Falk and Ed Stefanski use to describe what the Sixers could offer?

18. What injury was Brand coming off when he signed with the Sixers? He had played a few games to end the previous season with the Clippers but was still working his way back into form from this injury when he signed here.

19. As of September 1, 2008 what Sixers player on the 2008-09 team was exactly 50th all time in franchise history for points scored?

20. During the 2008-09 season what former Sixers player served as the club's "Ambassador of 76ers Basketball?"

21. Which Sixers player won an NCAA championship with the University of Florida?

22. What two front-office titles did Tony DiLeo hold immediately prior to becoming coach of the Sixers?

23. Who made the winning shot for the Sixers in Game 1 of the 2009 Eastern Conference Quarterfinals against Orlando?

24. What player strongly criticized Tony DeLio to the media after the Sixers lost Game 6 of the 2009 Eastern Conference Quarterfinals to the Magic?

PHILADELPHIA 76ERS IN THE HALL OF FAME

Charles Barkley

Wilt Chamberlain

Julius Erving

Bailey Howell

Dolph Schayes.

Al Cervi

Billy Cunningham

Hal Greer

Moses Malone

Former head coaches or assistant coaches Chuck Daly, Alex Hannum, Jack Ramsay, and Larry Brown are in the Hall of Fame. Daniel Biasone, the founding owner of the franchise, is also in the Hall of Fame.

NUMBERS RETIRED BY THE PHILADELPHIA 76ERS

Moses Malone – 2

Maurice Cheeks – 10

Hal Greer – 15

Billy Cunningham – 32

Julius Erving – 6

Wilt Chamberlain – 13

Bobby Jones – 24

Charles Barkley - 34.

A microphone banner hangs with the retired numbers in honor of former public address announcer Dave Zinkoff, who held the position from 1963-1985.

Introduction To The Flyers
by Gary Dornhoefer

If ever a sports team personified the city it represents… well, let's skip the cliché. As unlikely as it may have seemed, the Flyers' birth in 1967 was a resonating event in the collective life of the sports-crazed city of Philadelphia.

Ice hockey was born on the ponds and lakes in small town Canada. The Flyers were born in Philly, a big American city with a small-town feel. And that big city took to them almost immediately. I'm lucky enough to be able to call myself a charter member of the Philadelphia Flyers, a group that includes Bill Sutherland (scored the team's first-ever goal), Ed Hoekstra (first-ever game-winner) and Doug Favell (recorded the team's first-ever shutout).

We enjoyed immediate success, winning the West Division that first year. Although we lost our first playoff series that Spring, I remember feeling right after St. Louis extinguished our hopes that it wasn't the end, but only the beginning.

Flyers management continued to mold the club with mixed results. St. Louis kicked us out again the following year, and Keith Allen left the bench, replaced by Vic Stasiuk for the 1969-70 season. Stasiuk was not the most notable addition that off-season. That distinction belongs to Robert Earle Clarke, known during his playing days as Bobby.

Clarke eventually loaded the team onto his not-so-broad shoulders and, along with Bernie, the Rifle, yours truly, the Hound, Moose and a host of others, brought this city its first professional hockey title. We liked the feeling so much that the next year we decided to do it again. Like any professional sports team, we spent so much time around each other it began to feel like family, or at least a surrogate family when we were away from our homeland to the North.

Along with that feeling came ups and downs. The two Stanley Cups followed by beating the Russians – definite ups. Thirty-five games without a loss – thirty-five ups. Suffering through six failed tries in hockey's final round – six downs. The tragic losses of Barry Ashbee and Pelle Lindbergh were dark days for the franchise the likes of which no win or championship could soothe.

Still, from day one there was that feeling. That unmistakable feeling that whatever it was we were doing, wherever it was we were going, we were doing it and going there together. We played together. We partied together. And we fought together.

Oh how we fought. The mere mention of two words – Broad Street – was enough to intimidate many an opposition before they even took the Spectrum ice. For better or worse, the Bullies will live in hockey lore forever.

Intimidation is but one of many traditions I'm proud to say I've been a part of or have witnessed in my long association with the club. Others include the resulting chills from Kate Smith's timeless renditions of "God Bless America" – and the tradition of melding Kate's voice with Lauren Hart's in the present. Or filing through the Spectrum and the new building's doors on a bone-chilling winter afternoon when the Flyers weren't even playing to attend Flyers Wives Fight for Lives. The annual event raises money to fight leukemia. It was leukemia that took Ashbee away from us at age 37.

Other traditions might not have had the shelf life of the others, but they sure were fun. Flocky Hockey. Long pants. The Guffaw. Crazy Eights. The Legion of Doom. Goalies scoring, goalies fighting, and goalies returning to do the same.

A roll call of Flyers alumni will invigorate the most dormant of memories. From 50-something diehards to those young enough not to remember the early days, it's always about the names. Lacroix. Blackburn. Nolet. Van Impe. Goodenough. Crisp. Flett. Parent. Clarke. Leach. Jim and Joe Watson. Linseman. Holmgren. Marsh. McCrimmon. Howe. Rich and Ron Sutter. Poulin. Propp. Lindbergh. Lindros. Renberg. LeClair. Desjardins. Brind'Amour. Primeau. Roenick.

And now, Giroux, Pronger, Hartnell, Briere, Bryzgalov and even Jagr have added their names to the mighty roll call.

Let's not forget the man whose voice is the soundtrack for so many of these memories. Close your eyes and listen to Gene Hart count down the final seconds from May 19, 1974, thrilling millions by telling them that indeed, "The Flyers win the Stanley Cup! Ladies and Gentlemen the Flyers are going to win the Stanley Cup!"

I'm fortunate enough to still be a part of the Philadelphia Flyers, and hope to be the next time the team hauls home that long-sought after silver chalice. More than 40 years – it's been quite a journey. But each one always leads right back to where it belongs – Philadelphia.

FLYERS TRIVIA

FLYERS DECADE QUESTIONS

1960's

Answers on page 353

1. Name the other five teams, besides the Flyers, which made up the NHL's first major expansion in 1967.

2. Did the Spectrum take more or less than a year to be fully constructed?

3. Ed Snider was already involved with this other sports team before coming in as one of the Flyers' owners.

4. Who was the first captain of the Flyers?

5. In which division did the club play in for the first seven years of its existence?

6. Who was named the team's first head coach?

7. Who was the franchise's first general manager?

8. This team was victimized for the club's first-ever regular-season victory.

9. Philly topped this club for its first-ever home win.

10. The Flyers won the division crown in their first NHL campaign. Did they have a winning or losing record?

11. Which two players manned the crease in the club's first season?

12. Which Flyer posted the club's first hat trick?
    a) Gary Dornhoefer   b) Leon Rochefort
    c) Bill Sutherland   d) Andre Lacroix

13. When the roof of the Spectrum blew off in March, 1968, the Flyers were forced to play their remaining home games on the road, including these two historic arenas located in Manhattan and Toronto.

14. The Flyers lost to this fellow expansion team in seven brutal playoff games in 1968, a series which inspired owner Ed Snider to vow that his team would never be intimidated again.

15. Red Berenson of the Blues cranked home this many goals in an 8-0 shutout win over the Flyers in November, 1968, still the most by any one player against the team.

16. In the 1968-69 season, the Flyers suffered their worst loss ever, at the Spectrum, a 12-0 embarrassment to this Original Six club.

17. Name the two team legends (a goaltender and a defenseman) who were selected to the 1969 All-Star Game.

18. The Flyers were swept in four games in the 1969 playoffs by this fellow expansion club.

19. This man, a former NHL player and teammate of Gordi Howe, took over the team as head coach for the 1969-70 season.

20. General manager Keith Allen used the team's second-round pick in the 1969 draft to select this legendary player.

135

1970's

Answers on page 353-354

1. This man, nicknamed "The Fog," became head coach of the club in 1971.

2. Name the goaltender who suffered a heart attack during a game in the early part of the decade.

3. In a 1972 game at the Spectrum, players from an opposing team went into the stands to brawl with rowdy Flyers fans. Which team was it?

4. The Flyers missed out on the 1971-72 playoffs after Gerry Meehan of this team scored with seconds left in regulation in the club's final regular-season game.
   a) Minnesota North Stars   c) Buffalo Sabres
   b) Los Angeles Kings   d) Vancouver Canucks

5. Who did the Flyers trade to Toronto prior to the 1973-74 season, to re-acquire Bernie Parent?

6. Philadelphia edged out this Original Six team for the 1974 West Division title.

7. The Flyers swept the Atlanta Flames in the opening round of the 1974 playoffs. Which unexpected source of offense provided the winning goal in overtime of the deciding Game 4?
   a) Dave Schultz   b) Ross Lonsberry
   c) Moose Dupont   d) Bruce Cowick

8. Bobby Clarke scored the game winner in overtime of Game 2 of the 1974 Stanley Cup Finals against Boston. Who passed Clarke the puck on that goal?

9. Who scored the lone goal in Game 6 of the 1974 Cup Finals at the Spectrum?

10. What high-scoring Bruins forward did Bernie Parent stop with a right-pad save on a wicked shot from the blue line, with 2 ½ minutes left in that game?

11. From which team did GM Keith Allen acquire Reggie Leach prior to the 1974-75 season?
    a) Kansas City Scouts   b) Toronto Maple Leafs
    c) Atlanta Flames   d) California Golden Seals

12. Who scored the game-winning goal for the Flyers early in the third period of Game 6 of the 1975 Finals against Buffalo?

13. Who scored the second and final goal of that contest?

14. How many shutouts did Bernie record during the 1975 title run, still a Flyers playoff record?

15. The Flyers have only had the top overall selection in the NHL draft one time, in 1975. Which mustachioed player did they select with the pick?

16. Which lesser-known goaltender got the start against the Soviet Red Army team for the memorable contest at the Spectrum on January 11, 1976?

17. What two legendary voices called the action for NBC on that day?

18. Which Flyers defenseman unexpectedly scored a shorthanded goal in that game?

19. This famous line scored a team-record 141 total goals in 1975-76.

20. On May 6, 1976 Leach scored a team-record five goals in a deciding Game 5 of a Stanley Cup Semifinal series against this rival club.

21. After winning two consecutive Stanley Cups in 1974 and 1975, what was the team's slogan, seen on bumper stickers, for the following year?

22. To which team was Dave Schultz dealt prior to the 1976-77 season?

23. This former Flyers firebrand, who retired in 1976, later won a Stanley Cup as head coach of the Calgary Flames.

24. Who holds the Flyers record for most points in his first NHL game, done in the 1976-77 season?

25. During an 11-1 thrashing of the Cleveland Barons on December 11, 1977, this player set an NHL record for points in a game by a defenseman with eight.

26. Rick MacLeish was cut in the neck by this part of a player's equipment during an April, 1978 game in Los Angeles.

27. This original Denver-based team faced the Flyers in a two-game preliminary round series in 1978.

28. How many Hart Trophies as league MVP did Bobby Clarke win in the decade?

29. This Georgia-based team beat the Flyers in the second game of the 1979-80 season, after which the club did not lose until January.

30. Which team did the Flyers defeat on the road to set the all-time NHL record for consecutive games without a loss on December 22, 1979?
    - a) Buffalo
    - b) Minnesota
    - c) Hartford
    - d) Boston

1980's

Answers on page 354

1. On January 7, 1980, the Flyers lost to this club to end their record 35-game unbeaten streak.

2. This brawny forward became the first American-born player to record a hat trick in a Stanley Cup Finals game, in 1980.

3. The Flyers team record for an unbeaten streak to begin a season was set in 1981-82. How many games did the team start off without a loss that year?
   a) Six
   b) Eight
   c) Ten
   d) Twelve

4. This Finnish native scored his first career goal on a penalty shot against the Pittsburgh Penguins in an October, 1981 game.

5. Which goaltender, who was dealt to the Boston Bruins prior to the1982-83 season, eventually came back to the club for two years at the end of his career?

6. Who scored the Flyers' first ever overtime goal, in a game against Pittsburgh, in November, 1983?

7. On November 11, 1984 at the Spectrum, the Flyers topped this team by a 7-5 score, ending their NHL-record 15-game unbeaten streak to start the season.

8. This former Flyer, who spent brief periods of time on the team in the mid-1980's, once was second behind Wayne Gretzky in scoring on a youth hockey team in Brantford, Ontario.

9. In what season did the Flyers set their all-time record for consecutive wins with 13?
   a) 1981-82   b) 1985-86
   c) 1984-85   d) 1996-97

10. Peter Zezel set the Flyers rookie assist mark in 1984-85 with 46. One year later, this Swede and power-play specialist set a new mark with 51.

11. Tim Kerr recorded this many consecutive 50-goal seasons for the team during the decade.

12. Kerr also set an NHL playoff record by scoring four consecutive goals in one period in 1985 against this division rival?

13. This famous captain scored a two-man disadvantage goal in Game 6 of the 1985 Wales Conference Finals against the Quebec Nordiques.

14. What Flyer rookie famously quit hockey in 1985 to try a pro golf career because he couldn't stand to play for Mike Keenan?
   a) Ron Flockhart   b) Ray Allison
   c) Todd Bergen   d) Mark Taylor

15. Name the former Flyers assistant coach who beat the Flyers in a playoff series in 1986 as head coach of the New York Rangers.

16. What was the celebratory hand motion, performed by Brian Propp after he scored a goal from 1986 on, known as?

17. Which former Flyers defenseman of the 1980's currently owns two restaurants in the Ottawa, Ontario area?
   a) Doug Crossman   b) Glen Cochrane
   c) Gordie Murphy   d) Brad Marsh

18. When Wayne Gretzky led the NHL with 62 goals in 1986-87, this Flyer sharpshooter finished second.

19. What Flyer was suspended for the remainder of the 1987 playoffs because he was named the chief instigator in the Flyers-Canadiens brawl in Montreal before Game 6 of the Wales Conference Finals?

20. This Flyer scored the game-winning goal in the third period of that tilt, stunning the crowd at the Montreal Forum.

21. What Flyers defenseman tallied the go-ahead goal in Game 3 of the 1987 Stanley Cup Finals, after the club rallied from an early 3-0 deficit?

22. This player, who only suited up for the club in parts of two seasons, tallied the game-winning goal in Game 6 of that series.

23. Which Edmonton Oiler scored the game-winning goal against the Flyers in the second period during Game 7 of the Finals?
    a) Glenn Anderson   b) Jari Kurri
    c) Mark Messier   d) Marty McSorley

24. What Flyers forward recorded an amazing three hat tricks in a four-game span from February 21-March 1, 1988?
    a) Brian Propp   b) Scott Mellanby
    c) Ilkka Sinisalo   d) Rick Tocchet

25. This infamous agitator, who played for the Nordiques and Capitals, scored an overtime goal to win Game 7 of the 1988 Patrick Division Semifinals for Washington.

26. This Flyers backup goaltender of the late 1980's earned the nickname "Trees" since he had a tree with Flyer symbol leaves painted on his goalie mask.

27. Paul Holmgren's charges beat this Patrick Division winning club in a six-game first-round series in 1989.

28. Name the Flyers backup goaltender who rescued the team by giving up only one goal in Pittsburgh in Game 7 of the 1989 Patrick Division Finals.

29. What Flyer forward, and ex-Penguin, infamously stood on the ice and flipped the bird to Pittsburgh fans after the Flyers won that game 7?

30. In Game 1 of the 1989 Wales Conference Finals, this Montreal Canadiens defenseman viciously elbowed Brian Propp in the head, drawing blood and knocking him unconscious.

1990's

Answers on page 355

1. Who replaced Bob Clarke as Flyers general manager after Clarke was fired following the 1989-90 season?

2. During the latter half of the 1989-90 season, Dave Poulin and Brian Propp were sent to this team, which made the Stanley Cup Finals, in separate deals.

3. Name the father-son, coach-player tandem who worked together with the Flyers from 1991 to 1993.

4. After his acquisition from the St. Louis Blues, this player led Philly in goals, assists and points in 1991-92.

5. Which three players made up the short-lived "Crazy Eights" line for the Flyers in the early 1990's?
   a) Eric Lindros, Josef Beranek, Mark Recchi
   b) Mark Recchi, Eric Lindros, Kevin Dineen
   c) Eric Lindros, Mark Recchi, Brent Fedyk
   d) Mark Recchi, Eric Lindros, Mike Ricci

6. Mario Lemieux made a dramatic return from Hodgkin's Disease treatments, receiving a standing ovation in Philadelphia on March 2, 1993. Did the Flyers win, lose or tie that game?

7. During the "Storm of the Century" on March 13, 1993, the Flyers had an afternoon game postponed at the Spectrum. Which team played the Flyers on that day?

8. What former Czech forward of the Flyers went an unbelievable 28 games without scoring a goal in 1993-94?

9. Who broke Dave Poulin's Flyers record for most goals, points, and assists for a rookie that same year?

10. The Flyers lost the opening game of their lockout-shortened 1995 season against this team, which moved to another city the following year.

11. Name the three players the Orange and Black acquired in the deal which sent Mark Recchi to Montreal in February, 1995.

12. In April, 1995, just two days after clinching their first playoff berth since 1989, the Flyers won the Atlantic Division title with an overtime victory on the road against this division rival.

13. Who memorably scored a fluke overtime game-winner to end Game 1 of the 1995 playoffs against Buffalo?

14. In a February, 1996 Spectrum contest, Montreal's Marc Bureau viciously elbowed this diminutive Flyers defenseman.

15. This long-time NHLer, who was dealt to St. Louis for Dale Hawerchuk in 1996, was the last man in team and league history to play without a helmet.

16. Name the former Flyers goaltender of the mid-to-late 1990's who enjoyed stints with both the Flyers and Phantoms before finishing his NHL career with stops in Winnipeg and Anaheim.

17. Did the Flyers open the CoreStates (now Wells Fargo) Center with a win, loss or tie?

18. What Florida-based team broke the Flyers 17-game unbeaten streak during the 1996-97 season?

19. The Legion of Doom set the all-time record for points from a line in one game with 16 on February 6, 1997. Against which team did they accomplish this feat?

20. Which two goaltenders brawled during the Flyers-Sabres second-round series in 1997?

21. Which player scored the most goals for the team during their 1997 Stanley Cup Finals loss to Detroit?
    a) Rod Brind'Amour   b) John LeClair
    c) Eric Lindros   d) Pat Falloon

22. Name the Flyer brawler from the 1990's who had a special talent for keeping the locker room loose by drawing caricatures and cartoons.

23. What three players comprised the DAN line from 1996-98?

24. John LeClair reached the 50-goal plateau in 1996 and 1997, scoring the landmark tally both years against what team?

25. On December 31, 1997, the Flyers whipped this Western Canadian team by an impressive 8-0 score.

26. Alexandre Daigle recorded a hat trick late in the 1997-98 season against this Western Conference club.

27. Against which dominant goaltender did John LeClair score his 50th goal of the season in 1998, his last time scoring 50 for the team?

28. This conference rival snapped the Flyers' 15-game unbeaten streak in Philadelphia in January, 1999.
    a) Toronto Maple Leafs   b) Ottawa Senators
    c) Boston Bruins   d) Carolina Hurricanes

29. The Flyers also suffered through their longest winless streak ever, later in the 1998-99 campaign, lasting how many games?
    a) Ten
    b) Twelve
    c) Fourteen
    d) Fifteen

30. This defenseman, known better as a Hartford Whaler, scored in overtime to beat Vancouver in the Flyers' final game of the millennium on December 29, 1999.

2000's

Answers on page 355-356

1. The Flyers kicked off the new millennium by defeating this division rival on the road on January 2, 2000.
   - a) New Jersey
   - b) New York Rangers
   - c) New York Islanders
   - d) Pittsburgh

2. Name the two players the Flyers gave up to the Carolina Hurricanes to acquire Keith Primeau in January, 2000.

3. What former defensive specialist took over as head coach for Roger Neilson in February, 2000?

4. What was the score of the contest Keith Primeau ended in five overtimes, in Game 4 of the 2000 Eastern Conference Semi-finals against the Penguins?

5. Who was the goaltender Primeau victimized for that goal?

6. Who scored the only other goal for the Flyers in that game?

7. Which Flyer was the one on the team not to record a shot in the contest?

8. Who was the Flyers netminder that made a spectacular, reverse diving glove stop on New Jersey's Patrik Elias in the 2000 Eastern Conference Finals?

9. Which memorable player, in his second stint with the team, scored the Flyers' lone goal in Game 7 of that fateful series?

10. This former Flyers forward of the late 1990's and widely-regarded bust torched the Orange and Black for a pair of goals in Buffalo's 8-0 victory in Game 6 of a 2001 first-round series.

11. Which skaters recorded the only two goals for the Flyers in their pathetic five-game loss to Ottawa in the first round of the 2002 playoffs?

12. The Flyers participated in a 0-0 tie in San Jose in October, 2003 – the last in franchise history. Who was the Flyer goaltender that blanked the Sharks that night?
    a) Roman Cechmanek
    b) Jeff Hackett
    c) Robert Esche
    d) Sean Burke

13. Name the former Flyers goaltender who won his first NHL game in February, 2004, against the New Jersey Devils.

14. Prior to his game-tying goal in Game 6 of the 2004 Eastern Conference Finals, Primeau in effect passed himself the puck through the goal-mouth with this part of his equipment.

15. Which former Flyer, who tortured the team throughout that series, scored the first Tampa goal in Game 7?

16. Did the Flyers win or lose their first game of the 2005-06 season, at home against the New York Rangers?

17. Did the Flyers win or lose their first-ever shootout, in December, 2005 at Nashville?

18. What forward was hit with a brutal check and given a concussion by Buffalo Sabres defenseman Brian Campbell in a 2006 playoff contest?

19. In an October, 2006 home game, the Flyers and Rangers took this many rounds in a shootout to determine the winner, in a 5-4 decision for New York.

20. Name the four players who came to the team as a result of the Peter Forsberg trade in February, 2007.

21. Name the two forwards who recorded hat tricks in an 8-2 thrashing of the Penguins in December, 2007.

22. When Ron Hextall was inducted into the Flyers Hall of Fame in February, 2008, the team goofed and handed him the wrong one of these.

23. This former Flyer and Phantom was reacquired by the team in a trade-deadline deal in February, 2008.

24. Martin Biron recorded back-to-back shutouts against these two clubs in April, 2008, to ensure a trip to the postseason.

25. This former Flyer, scored the game-winner in overtime in Game 7 against Washington in the first round of the 2008 playoffs.

26. Who led the team in goals during the 2008 postseason?

27. This player, who was signed to a long-term deal in 2007, finished second in playoff goal scoring for the Flyers in 2008.

28. On February 15, 2009 in New York, this Flyer set the NHL record for most career goals scored while skating three-on-five with his breakaway tally against Henrik Lundqvist.

29. Who led the Flyers in goals during the 2008-09 regular season? How many did he score?

30. After not allowing a short-handed goal all regular season, the Flyers gave one up in their 2008-09 season finale against this division foe.

2010 FLYERS QUESTIONS

Answers on page 356

1. Ray Emery posted a shutout in his Flyers' debut, a 2-0 white wash of the Carolina Hurricanes on October 2, 2009. Which goaltender last accomplished that feat, and in what season?
    a) Bernie Parent, 1973-74
    b) Jeff Hackett, 2003-04
    c) Roman Cechmanek, 2000-01
    d) Ron Hextall 86-87

2. This Flyers forward posted the franchise's earliest hat trick in terms of date, in a 6-5 overtime win against Washington on October 6th.
    a) Joffrey Lupul
    b) Jeff Carter
    c) Claude Giroux
    d) Mike Richards

3. The 2010 Winter Classic was contested at this venerable baseball venue.
    a) Wrigley Field
    b) Sportsman's Park
    c) Fenway Park
    d) Comiskey Park

4. Which Boston-area crooner sang the National Anthem that day?
    a) James Taylor
    b) Steven Tyler
    c) Evan Dando
    d) Donnie Wahlberg

5. Which two franchise icons, from the Flyers and Bruins respectively, participated in the ceremonial face-off before the start of the game?

6. The only fight during the contest occurred between these two spirited combatants:
    a) Chris Pronger and Byron Bitz
    b) Dan Carcillo and Shawn Thornton
    c) Dan Carcillo and Zdeno Chara
    d) Ian Laperriere and Shawn Thornton

7. This defenseman posted the club's lone goal in the Classic, his first score of the season.
    a) Randy Jones
    b) Oskars Bartulis
    c) Lasse Kukkonen
    d) Danny Syvret

8. Which former Flyer netted the game-tying goal for Boston late in regulation?

9. Which Bruins player tallied the game-winning goal less than two minutes into overtime?
    a) Mark Recchi
    b) Marc Savard
    c) Marco Sturm
    d) Zdeno Chara

10. This forward posted a career-worst minus-six during a 7-4 loss to Ottawa on January 3, 2010.
    a) Ian Laperriere
    b) Simon Gagne
    c) Claude Giroux
    d) Jeff Carter

11. Flyers goaltender Brian Boucher stopped this now former New York Ranger's shootout chance to win the final regular-season game and push the Orange and Black into the playoffs.

12. This now departed forward scored the game-winning goals in Game 4 and Game 7 of Philadelphia's Eastern Conference Semifinal series victory over the Boston Bruins.

13. With the miraculous recovery from an 0-3 series hole, the Flyers became the first NHL team to win a series when facing such a deficit since this club did it in 1975.
    a) Toronto Maple Leafs
    b) Pittsburgh Penguins
    c) New York Islanders
    d) Colorado Rockies

14. With his shutouts in Games 1 and 2 of the Eastern Conference Finals against the Montreal Canadiens, Michael Leighton became the first Flyers goalie to post consecutive whitewashes in the playoffs since this Hall-of-Famer did so in the first round in 1975 against Toronto.

15. This gritty forward scored a memorable goal to open Game 5 of the Conference Finals, after colliding with Canadiens defenseman Roman Hamrlik and goaltender Jaroslav Halak.

16. Once groomed as an enforcer in the Flyers' farm system, this forward netted the eventual game-winning goal in Game 2 of the Stanley Cup Finals for Chicago.
    - a) Ben Eager
    - b) Jim Vandermeer
    - c) Patrick Sharp
    - d) Brian Campbell

17. This Flyers forward netted the final goal of the season for the Orange and Black, tying Game 6 of the Stanley Cup Finals with 3:59 left in regulation.

18. Ville Leino's 21 points in the playoffs tied him with this sniper of the 1980s and 1990s for the most points in one postseason by a rookie.
    - a) Mike Gartner
    - b) Brendan Shanahan
    - c) Joe Nieuwendyk
    - d) Dino Ciccarelli

19. Danny Briere's 30 playoff points set a new Flyers franchise record, breaking th mark set by this player in the memorable 1987 playoffs.
    - a) Brian Propp
    - b) Tim Kerr
    - c) Dave Poulin
    - d) Rick Tocchet

20. What was the Flyers' overall record in the 2010 postseason?

FLYERS NUMBERS QUESTIONS

Answers on page 357

1. How many jersey numbers have the Flyers raised to the rafters in their history? Provide the number and player for each.

2. The Flyers set the all-time NHL record for ties in one season back in 1969-70, a record which still stands. How many ties did the team collect that year?

3. Rick MacLeish was the first Flyer to do this, in the 1972-73 season.

4. In what season did the Flyers enjoy their best-ever home record at 36-2-2?
   a) 1973-74   b) 1979-80
   c) 1985-86   d) 1975-76

5. In what season did the Flyers set their worst home record ever with a 10-24-7 mark?
   a) 2006-07   b) 1993-94
   c) 1969-70   d) 1989-90

6. In 1974-75, Dave Schultz set the NHL record for penalty minutes in one season with this many.

7. Bill Barber still holds the team record for most career goals by one player with this amount.

8. The Flyers blitzed Pittsburgh and Vancouver roughly seven months apart in 1984 to set a franchise record for goals in one game. How many did they score in each?

9. How many times have the Flyers appeared in the Stanley Cup Finals?
   a) Five   b) Six
   c) Seven   d) Eight

10. Tim Kerr holds the Flyers and NHL record for most power-play goals registered in one season. How many did he tally?
    a) 32
    b) 34
    c) 36
    d) 40

11. In what season did the Flyers last score 10 goals in a game?
    a) 1992-93
    b) 1996-97
    c) 1995-96
    d) 1987-88

12. In what season did the Flyers last allow 10 goals in a game?
    a) 1992-93
    b) 1993-94
    c) 2000-01
    d) 2006-07

13. Mark Recchi holds the Flyers club record for points in a season, with this amount, accomplished in 1992-93.

14. Recchi is famous for wearing the number 8 in his two tenures with the Flyers. What other number did he wear as a Flyer, during his second run with the club?

15. How many times did Eric Lindros record a 100-point season as a Flyer?

16. How many overtime wins did the Flyers accumulate during their 1995 playoff run?

17. On April 26, 1989, in Game 5 of the Patrick Division Finals at Pittsburgh, the Flyers and Penguins engaged in the second-highest-scoring playoff game in league history. What was the score?

18. When Kent Manderville was acquired by the Flyers in 2000, he carried with him a lengthy goal drought that was finally broken during a blowout loss in Pittsburgh in February, 2001. How many games did he go without scoring?

19. Reggie Leach set a franchise record which still stands for total goals in one season including playoffs back in 1975-76. How many did he score?

20. The Flyers have finished an NHL season with the same exact won-loss-tie record on three separate occasions (1995-96, 1996-97, 2002-03). What was the record each time?

21. In 1975-76, the team set a franchise record for most points with this many.

22. In 1983-84, they set a team record for most goals in one season with this number.

23. The Flyers began the 1999-2000 season by going winless in this many games, the longest streak from the start of a season in team annals.
    a) Five   b) Six
    c) Seven   d) Nine

24. How many points did Peter Forsberg score during his brief tenure in Philadelphia?

25. In 2008-09, Mike Richards set a new club record for shorthanded goals by one player in one regular season with this many.

Answers on page 358

1. Bernie Parent wore these two numbers during his two stints with the club.

2. Bobby Clarke wore his iconic Number 16 for the majority of his career, but also had one other number assigned to him. Was it 6, 26, or 36?

3. In 1981-82 and 1982-83, the Flyers bucked a long-standing uniform trend and wore these before the NHL created a rule about standard dress.

4. The Flyers introduced a black third jersey during this season.

5. After their black jerseys became popular, the club issued third jerseys with a predominantly orange color scheme for this campaign.

6. The club made black their primary home color during this season.

7. Since Reggie Leach already wore number 27 when the Flyers acquired Darryl Sittler in 1982, which jersey number was the future Hall-of-Famer issued at that time?

8. Paul Coffey wore this number while a member of the Flyers.

9. If you add up the collective jersey numbers of the Legion of Doom, what number is the sum?

10. What did the Flyers wear on their jerseys to start the 1974-75 season, which were quickly removed after they lost their home-opener to the Los Angeles Kings?

11. This Swedish-born defenseman wore Number 27 immediately after Darryl Sittler and just prior to Ron Hextall.

12. For which full season in the 1980's did the club wear socks with only two stripes?

13. For several years prior to the Flyers' switch to black jerseys, fans, writers and team staff complained that their road colors made the players look like this kind of gourd-like plant.

14. The Number 30 has been worn by how many Flyers goal-tenders in their history?

15. For which holiday in 2001 did the club last wear its orange road uniforms?

16. From 1995 to 1998, the Flyers had three players on their third line whose first letters of their last names are the same as the first letters in the name of a Philadelphia area town. Name these players and the town.

17. Dmitri Tertyshny, who played only one season in Philly before his tragic death in the Summer of 1999, wore this singular digit.

18. Which of these ex-Flyers wore the highest number ever given out by the team?
    a) Donald Brashear   b) Eric Lindros
    c) Mike Comrie   d) Jeremy Roenick

19. While on the same line, Peter Forsberg and Simon Gagne wore these two numbers, mirror images of each other.

20. During the team's 25th anniversary in 1991-92, where did the club place patches commemorating the milestone?

21. All NHL teams, including the Flyers wore this patch to celebrate a centennial event in 1992-93.

22. During their first season, the club's home jerseys were this color, in accordance with league rules of the time.

23. Unlike other teams in Philadelphia, the Flyers declined to wear a patch commemorating this 1976 event.

24. Which company currently manufactures all of the NHL's uniforms including the Flyers?

25. The club wore these jerseys for all home games during the last three postseasons.

PELLE LINDBERGH
QUESTIONS

Answers on page 358

1. What was Pelle's nationality?

2. In which city was he born and raised?

3. Pelle was the only goaltender who did not suffer a loss in the opeining round at the hands of this Gold Medal winning team at the 1980 Winter Games at Lake Placid.

4. What number, which has been unofficially retired by the team, did he wear for his entire career?

5. In what season did he make his Flyers and NHL debut?

6. From what minor-league affiliate was he called up for his first pro start?

7. Which former Flyers goaltender was Pelle's coach, friend and mentor?

8. Who was Pelle's primary net-mate during his Flyers tenure?

9. What former Flyers head coach and General Manager sent Pelle down to the AHL during a rough stretch in his second full season, the only time he spent in the minors after his initial call-up?

10. When Pelle won the Vezina Trophy as the NHL's best goaltender in 1984-85, he also led the league in wins. How many did he have that year?
    - a) 35
    - b) 37
    - c) 39
    - d) 40

11. How many shutouts did Pelle Lindbergh record in the Flyers' 1985 playoff run?

12. Which team did Pelle defeat in his final NHL start?
    a) Boston Bruins   b) Edmonton Oilers
    c) New York Rangers   d) Chicago Blackhawks

13. Which team did the Flyers play on the night before his fatal accident?

14. In which type of car did Pelle suffer his fatal injuries?
    a) Pontiac Trans Am   b) Lamborghini Testarossa
    c) Ford Mustang   d) Porsche Carrera 930

15. Which team did the Flyers host for Pelle's memorial game, only four days after the accident?

16. How did the team honor Pelle for the remainder of the 1985-86 season?

17. What Vezina Trophy winning goaltender, who was mainly responsible for eliminating the Flyers from the playoffs, mentioned Pelle during his acceptance speech?

18. Did Pelle win more or less than 80 games during his brief career?

19. Did he record more or less than 10 shutouts?

20. In what season did the team first award the Pelle Lindbergh Memorial Trophy, given to the player who improves most from one season to the next?

RON HEXTALL QUESTIONS

Answers on page 359

1. For what Western Canadian junior team did Hexy play for?
    a) Regina Pats   b) Portland Winter Hawks
    c) Swift Current Broncos   d) Brandon Wheat Kings

2. For what Flyers farm team did he play, immediately prior to his NHL call-up?

3. Against which team did Hextall record his first NHL win on October 9, 1986?

4. For which two months was he named the league's top rookie in 1986-87?

5. How many penalty minutes did Hexy rack up in his first NHL campaign – more or less than 100?

6. How many wins did Hextall rack up in his initial season?

7. This Edmonton Oiler was on the receiving end of a vicious slash from the fiery netminder during Game 4 of the 1987 Stanley Cup Finals.

8. At the time, Hextall became the fourth man from a losing team (and second Flyer) to win this award as the playoffs' Most Valuable Player in 1987.

9. Hextall scored two goals in his Flyers career, one in the regular season and one in the playoffs. Against which teams did he accomplish those feats?

10. Hextall was suspended during his career twice for incidents in the previous year's playoffs: An eight-game ban to start the 1987-88 season, and a longer one to begin the 1989-90 campaign for attacking Chris Chelios. How many games was this second penalty?

11. Name the two teams for which Hextall played in his only two years he didn't skate for the Flyers.

12. What diminutive Swedish goaltender did the Flyers ship away in 1994 to reacquire Hexy?

13. Which Washington Capitals player did he brawl with in a February, 1995 game?

14. In his second stint with the Flyers, Hexy was the starting goal tender for the first round of the playoffs in which two seasons?
    a) 1994-95 and 1995-96   b) 1995-96 and 1996-97
    c) 1996-97 and 1997-98   d) 1995-96 and 1997-98

15. The pride of Brandon, Manitoba recorded this many shutouts during the 1996-97 regular season, the most he posted in one year as a Flyer.

16. In a February, 1999 game, Hextall allowed a goal from beyond the blue line with one second left in regulation to Jozef Stumpel of this West Coast club.

17. Who eventually took over the starting job for Hextall in the 1998-99 season?

18. Against which long-hated division rival did he start his final NHL game, on April 5, 1999?

19. Did Hextall win more or less than 300 games over his 13-year NHL career?

20. In June, 2006, Hextall was named assistant general manager of this NHL team.

ERIC LINDROS
QUESTIONS

Answers on page 359

1. Which team selected Lindros first overall in the 1991 entry draft?

2. During negotiations to bring Lindros to the Flyers in the summer of 1992, what other team claimed to have worked a deal with the club that drafted him?

3. How many players did the Flyers ship away in order to acquire Lindros? Who were they?

4. What are Eric's parents' names?

5. For which Ontario Hockey League team did the man dubbed The Next One play?
   - a) Sault Ste. Marie Greyhounds
   - b) Niagara Falls Flyers
   - c) Peterborough Petes
   - d) Oshawa Generals

6. Against which club did "The E-Train" score his first NHL goal?
   - a) Pittsburgh
   - b) New Jersey
   - c) Washington
   - d) Tampa Bay

7. Lindros recorded his first career three-goal game against this Canadian-based team which was an expansion entry in 1992-93.

8. How many times did 88 score 40-or-more goals in his first four seasons?

9. Eric suffered an eye injury at the end of the 1995 season against this team when a deflected puck hit him flush in the face.

10. Despite finishing with the same amount of points, which player edged out Eric for the 1995 Art Ross Trophy as scoring champion, on the basis of more goals scored?

11. Lindros beat this Devils goaltender in Game 3 of the 1995 Eastern Conference Finals for his first career playoff overtime score.

12. What did the then 22-year-old do in front of the cameras while accepting his Hart Trophy as league MVP in June, 1995?

13. Against which team did Eric Lindros record an assist to put him over the 100-point plateau back in March, 1996?
    a) New Jersey Devils   b) Toronto Maple Leafs
    c) New York Islanders   d) Hartford Whalers

14. During the ceremony to close out the Spectrum in April, 1996, with which team legend was he paired as the centerpiece of the passing-the-torch portion of the night?

15. With which Tampa Bay Lightning player did Lindros have a memorable feud during the teams' 1996 Eastern Conference Quarterfinal series?
    a) Michel Petit   b) Chris Gratton
    c) Enrico Ciccone   d) Igor Ulanov

16. Number 88 had to contend with this rookie defenseman who gave him fits in the club's 1996 second-round loss to the Florida Panthers.
    a) Paul Laus   b) Robert Svehla
    c) Jesse Belanger   d) Ed Jovanovski

17. The Big E was rumored to have missed a regular-season game in 1997 due to this problem, which led to some contentious times between the organization and the radio personality who broke the story.

18. This hard-hitting defenseman, then with the Pittsburgh Penguins, leveled Lindros with a shoulder which caused a Grade 3 concussion in a March, 1998 game.

19. Following a road game in Nashville on April 1, 1999, Lindros was stricken with this ailment which caused him to miss the remainder of the regular season and all of the playoffs.

20. Which team did the Flyers lose to in Lindros' last regular season game with the team in March, 2000?
    a) Phoenix Coyotes   b) Boston Bruins
    c) New York Islanders   d) Colorado Avalanche

21. Did Eric finish with more or less than 300 goals in his Flyers career?

22. While sitting out the entire 2000-01 season, to which "hometown" team did Lindros demand Bob Clarke trade him?

23. Name the three players that the Flyers acquired from the Rangers for Lindros in August, 2001.

24. Lindros victimized these two goaltenders for a hat trick in a March, 2002 game against the Flyers at Madison Square Garden.

25. For what team did he finish his playing career, with five goals in 49 games during the 2006-07 season?

MINOR LEAGUE QUESTIONS

Answers on page 360

1. The World Hockey Association placed a team in Philadelphia for its inaugural season in 1972-73 called the Blazers. Where were they forced to play their home games?

2. The old Cherry Hill Arena played host to this minor-league club, whose name was an inspiration for a current NHL team.

3. In the late 1970's, Philadelphia hosted an American Hockey League club with this nickname.

4. What was the name of the Flyers' former AHL team which won three Calder Cups in the late 1970's and early 1980's.

5. What was the nickname of the club's AHL farm team immediately before the Phantoms?

6. In what season did the Philadelphia Phantoms begin operations?

7. Which Flyers legend was named their first head coach?

8. When the Flyers transferred their AHL affiliate from Hershey to the Phantoms, what NHL team agreed to make Hershey their farm club?

9. Frank Bialowas, who roamed the ice for the Phantoms from 1996-99, was also known by this fierce nickname.

10. Which journeyman NHL and AHL player from the 1998 Phantoms title-squad is credited with coining the phrase "Legion of Doom" to describe the line of Lindros, LeClair and Renberg?

11. Peter White, an early Phantom standout, is what relation to former Flyers general manager Bob Clarke?

12. What team did the Phantoms defeat to win the Calder Cup Championship in 1998?
    a) St. John's Maple Leafs   b) Saint John Flames
    c) Portland Pirates   d) Albany River Rats

13. Name the goaltending tandem who led Philly to the championship that season.

14. What team did the Phantoms sweep to take their second Calder Cup in 2005?
    a) Portland Pirates   b) Houston Aeros
    c) Manitoba Moose   d) Chicago Wolves

15. Who was the Phantoms' head coach for the second title run?

16. Name the two players, called up from juniors, who stoked the club to their second championship.

17. How many Phantoms from the 2005 championship club played for the Flyers during some point in their NHL careers?

18. Name the Philadelphia native, Boston College product and Phantoms player who was removed from the organization after a rumored fight with an assistant coach during the 2006-07 season.

19. After Craig Berube was promoted to Flyers assistant in 2008, who was named Phantoms head coach?

20. Which long-time rival did the Phantoms beat in the second-to-last game of the 2008-09 season to ensure a playoff berth?

FLYERS COLLEGE QUESTIONS

Answers on page 360

1. Flyers broadcaster Steve Coates attended this university located in Michigan.

2. Flyers color commentator Keith Jones spent four years at this other Michigan-based university.

3. Former Flyers veterans Jeremy Roenick and Tony Amonte both attended this Boston-based school.

4. Flyers forward Darroll Powe may be a third-line grinder, but he put his mind to good use at this nearby Ivy League school.

5. James van Riemsdyk, the club's second-overall pick in the 2007 draft, attended this high-powered New England school.

6. Veteran forward Mike Knuble attended this Big Ten university.

7. John LeClair was a standout at this university, located just south of where he grew up.

8. Former Flyers defenseman and current radio commentator Chris Therien attended this Hockey East school located in Rhode Island.

9. Garth Snow, once the club's battle-ready backup netminder but now the GM of the New York Islanders, played at this university located in the eastern-most state in the U.S.

10. In his college days, was Rod Brind'Amour a Wolverine or a Spartan?

11. Flyers assistant coach Joe Mullen was a star at this school, located just outside the boundaries of Boston, which won national titles in 2001, 2008 and 2010.

12. Dave Poulin attended and later coached this renowned Mid-western university.

13. The Class of 1923 Rink, which served as the Flyers practice facility until the Coliseum was built in the 1980's, is located at this Philadelphia institution.

14. 2008 playoff hero R.J. Umberger, attended this school, now a football rival of Penn State.

15. Defenseman Matt Carle won the Hobey Baker Memorial Award in 2006 as college hockey's top player, for this Colorado-based school.

FLYERS NICKNAMES QUESTIONS

Answers on page 360

The answer and the years played will be provided. Guess the player.

1. Boxcar (1984-85, 1986-87).

2. Rico (1994-06).

3. Hound (1970-80).

4. Styles (2001-04).

5. Crafty (1984-91).

6. Foppa (2005-07).

7. Izzy (1974-77).

8. The Rat (1978-82).

9. Rooster (2006-08).

10. Match the following players with their nickname:

    Brad McCrimmon - 1   Y- "Carts"

    Rich Sutter – 2   L- "Slash"

    Jeff Carter – 3   F- "Beast

    Ron Sutter – 4   S- "Smitty"

    Mark Recchi – 5   E- "Spear"

    Jason Smith – 6   R- "Rex"

PHILADELPHIA FLYERS HALL OF FAME

Inductee	Date of Induction
Bernie Parent	March 1988
Bobby Clarke	March 1988
Keith Allen	March 1989
Bill Barber	March 1989
Ed Snider	March 1989
Rick MacLeish	March 1990
Fred Shero	March 1990
Barry Ashbee	March 1991
Gary Dornhoefer	March 1991
Gene Hart	February 1992
Reggie Leach	February 1992
Joe Scott	April 1993
Ed Van Impe	April 1993
Tim Kerr	March 1994
Joe Watson	February 1996
Brian Propp	March 1999
Mark Howe	April 2001
Dave Poulin	March 2004
Ron Hextall	February 2008
Dave Schultz	November 2009

Introduction To The Philadelphia A'S
by Ted Taylor

There was once a time when Philadelphia had two major league baseball teams. One of them was the dominant team for the first third of the 20th century winning nine pennants and five World Series before 1932. The other one managed but one pennant in its first 50 years. Yet halfway through the 20th century the more successful of the two franchises left town and the other one stayed behind and at this time still has only won two titles. The team that stayed was the Phillies; the team that left was the Athletics, or A's as their devoted fans knew them.

The Athletics made Philadelphia their home for 54 years. They produced a Hall of Fame manager in Connie Mack and nurtured the careers of nine players who were later enshrined in Cooperstown: Frank "Home Run" Baker, Albert "Chief" Bender, Mickey Cochrane, Eddie Collins, Jimmie "Double X" Foxx, Robert "Lefty" Grove, "Gettysburg Eddie" Plank, "Bucketfoot" Al Simmons and George "Rube" Waddell. For at least a brief period, seven other Hall of Famers also played for the A's: Ty Cobb, Stall Coveleski, George Kell, Nelson Fox, Nap Lajoie, Tris Speaker and Zach Wheat. With that kind of talent it is not surprising that the team drew over 25 million fans to Shibe Park and attracted countless others who listened to the players' heroics on the radio or read about them in the newspapers. In short, the A's were a team whose fabric is intimately woven into

170

Philadelphia's sports history, the most successful franchise ever to call the city home. That they have been gone over 50 years, and still have the most championships of any team in this city speaks volumes about what the long-suffering Philadelphia sports fan has had to live with and lives with today.

I find it ironic that many people who consider themselves sports fans know nothing about the A's. I routinely get asked "when did the A's change their name to the Phillies?" The answer, of course, is that they never did!

The 1929-31 A's are considered by many baseball experts to be the best team in the history of major league baseball. That marvelous assemblage of players finished second in 1928 and 1932 and won three straight league titles and two Fall Classics in between.

The depression in the 1930's caused A's manager (and later President) Connie Mack to sell off his star players. Soon Cochrane, then Grove and later Foxx all departed and were replaced by players who had no talent and little future. When the A's were good they were very good, but when they were bad they were dreadful.

Some attribute their demise to Mr. Mack's stubborn desire to continue to manage the team long after most men had comfortably retired. He was 88 years old when he finished his 50th – and final – year as A's manager in 1950. In truth, he should have retired in the late 1930's when illness took him out of the dugout for prolonged periods of time and his son Earle served as manager (ironically, when Mr. Mack stepped down, he was asked if his son Earle would succeed him and he quipped, "no, he's an old man"). Earle was 65 then. Mr. Mack's third baseman from the glory days, Jimmie Dykes, became the second A's skipper – 51 years after the franchise was founded. Conjecture is always easy. But one scenario that might have played out was Mr. Mack stepping down in 1930 – after the club won the

World Series – and turning the reins over to his protégé, future Hall of Famer Eddie Collins. Collins, instead, tired of waiting for Mr. Mack to retire took a job with the Red Sox serving almost two decades as their general manager. Mr. Mack also was on the verge of hiring Babe Ruth as his manager for the 1935 season but lost interest in the Bambino on a trip to the Orient when Mrs. Ruth clearly appeared to be calling all the shots.

Had Collins managed until 1935 and had Ruth followed him as skipper, it is likely that Collins would have moved upstairs as GM, Mr. Mack serving just as President, and whole different scenario might have played itself out into the 1940's and beyond.

As it was the A's teams that played in the post World War II era also struggled with a distorted myth that they were "a bunch of losers who played in a bad ballpark."

While those teams were not as successful as the earlier dynasty of 1929-1931, they still were exciting to follow, being stocked with a solid mix of pedestrian players, stars, near-stars and two future Hall of Famers. In 1948, for example, the A's were in the thick of the pennant race until the very end, losing out, finally, to Cleveland simply because Mr. Mack lost some key players to injuries and couldn't afford to replace them. He also fired relief pitcher Nelson Potter while standing on the steps of the dugout in a bizarre incident. Potter went on to pitch for the Boston Braves that season and was one of their leading hurlers as they won the 1948 NL pennant.

One cannot help but wonder if the A's might have enjoyed one more dynasty had Mr. Mack not traded away George Kell to the Tigers (for outfielder Barney McCosky) and Nellie Fox to the White Sox (for backup catcher Joe Tipton), allowing their Hall of Fame careers to unfold elsewhere. Perhaps the team might have even remained in Philadelphia had Fox and Kell remained in the lineup.

During that last decade in town the A's produced a two time batting champion (Ferris Fain), a Most Valuable Player (Bobby Shantz in 1952), a Rookie of the Year (Harry Byrd, also in 1952), a home run champion (Gus Zernial) and an infield combination (Joost to Suder-to-Fain) that set the American League record for double plays in 1949. That record still stands today.

The A's were eventually sold to Arnold Johnson, an insurance man from Chicago, and owner of the New York Yankees AAA farm club in Kansas City. After a series of "Save the A's" campaigns failed, Mr. Mack's two sons – Roy and Earle – sold the club for peanuts. Mr. Mack's other son, Connie Jr., had left the team in 1950 over a dispute with his older half-brothers and, according to many who knew them, never spoke to either one again.

Many of us who were youngsters at the time felt betrayed when the A's were sold to Kansas City. It was almost as if the Liberty Bell had been sold to Boston. Some reluctantly became Phillies fans, others continued to follow the American League, rooting for the A's from afar, but it was never the same. In 2003 when the Oakland A's returned for an inter-league series with the Phils, one game got rained out and the A's then lost a doubleheader. Some smiled and said "nothing has changed". But it had. Those rooting for the A's at the Vet were in their 60's or older and they were dressed in Philadelphia A's blue and white. The team is gone, but many in the city still love them.

A'S TRIVIA

THE EARLY YEARS QUESTIONS

Answers on page 361

1. What team swept the heavily favored A's in the 1914 World Series?

2. The A's won back to back World Series titles in what years?

3. True or False: Shoeless Joe Jackson played for the A's.

4. Who did the A's defeat in 1910 to win the World Series?

5. The A's won their first pennant the year before the first World Series was played. What year was that pennant won?

6. In 1904 Rube Waddell established a single-season strikeout record that stood for 61 years. How many batters did he fan in that season?

7. In what year did the A's make their first World Series appearance?

8. In 1916 the Athletics put together one of the worst seasons in baseball history. What was their record that year?

9. True or False: The 1916 A's had a worse winning percentage than the 1962 Mets

10. During the 1906 season what A's player hit two inside-the-park home runs in one game?

A'S IN THE 20'S & 30'S QUESTIONS

Answers on page 361

1. What A's players holds the team record for the longest hitting streak?

2. What Hall of Fame A's pitcher led the AL in winning percentage in 1929?

3. What Hall of Fame A's player hit for the cycle twice during his career?

4. The 1929 A's set a team record for most victories in a single season with how many wins?

5. True or False: Ty Cobb played for the A's.

6. What three pitchers won 20-or-more games for the 1931 A's?

7. To which team did the A's trade Jimmy Foxx in 1935?

8. True or False: The A's were the first MLB team to have lights installed at their field.

9. In 1933 the A's had three players hit for the cycle in an amazing 13-day span. Name the three players.

10. For three straight years in the early 1930's an A's player won the AL MVP. One player won it twice and one player won once. Name them?

Answers on page 362

1. In 1946 A's catcher Buddy Rosar had a single-season achievement for catchers that had never been done before and has not been done since in Major League Baseball. What was it?

2. In what year did the A's host their first All-Star Game?

3. Who threw the last no hitter for the A's?

4. What was the final season the A's played in Philadelphia?

5. What Athletic won back-to-back batting titles in 1951 and 1952?

6. What A's hurler won the AL MVP in 1952?

7. During the 1952 all Star Game A's pitcher Bobby Shantz struck out two future Hall of Famers in one inning. Who were these two Hall of Famers?

8. Unforeseen circumstances prevented Shantz from going back out for the sixth inning of that game to try and equal or better Carl Hubbell's All-Star strikeout record. What happened?

9. Who was the first African-American player to play for the A's?

10. What city did the A's move when they left Philadelphia?

ALL-TIME A'S QUESTIONS

Answers on page 362

1. What Hall of Fame player served two tours with the A's and finished his career with 3,312 hits?

2. How many career home runs did A's star Frank "Home Run" Baker hit?

3. What two A's won the Triple Crown?

4. Who holds the team record for most runs scored in a single season?

5. What was "Rube" Waddell's real first name?

6. What A's player won the Rookie of the Year Award?

7. What was Lefty Grove's highest single-season win total?

8. What pitcher won the most games as a member of the A's?

9. What announcer who went on to the Hall of Fame was the A's play-by-play radio announcer from 1938-1954?

10. True or False: Jimmie Foxx was the second player in MLB history to hit 500 career home runs.

MISCELLANEOUS A'S QUESTIONS

Answers on page 362

1. How many years did Connie Mack manage the A's?

2. Other than Connie Mack who were the only other two official managers of the A's?

3. In what year was the first game at Shibe Park played?

4. What was the original measurement to dead center field at Shibe Park?

5. How many numbers were retired by the Philadelphia Athletics?

6. Where was the main entrance to Shibe Park?

7. What was "Lefty" Grove's real first name?

8. How many World Series championships did the A's win in their 54-year history?

9. How old was Connie Mack when he retired from coaching the A's?

10. What was Connie's Mack's real full name?

PHILADELPHIA A'S HALL OF FAMERS

FRANK "HOME RUN" BAKER . . . Born: Trappe, MD . . . B-L, T-R . . . Third baseman in "$100,000 Infield" . . . Played for Athletics, 1908-1914 . . . Won 4 AL home run crowns . . . Elected to Hall of Fame in 1955.

CHARLES ALBERT "CHIEF" BENDER . . . Born: Crow Wing County, MN . . . B-R, T-R . . . Pitched for A's, 1903-14 . . . Won 6 World Series games for Mr. Mack . . . Elected to Hall of Fame in 1953.

GORDON S. "MICKEY" COCHRANE . . . Born: Bridgewater, MA . . . B-R, T-R . . . One of the greatest catchers of all time with .320 lifetime average . . . Played for A's, 1925-33 . . . Elected to Hall of Fame in 1947.

EDWARD T. "EDDIE" COLLINS . . . Born: Millerton, NY . . . B-R, T-R . . . Second baseman with 3,311 lifetime hits, 743 stolen bases, .333 lifetime average . . . A's career: 1906-14, 1927-30 . . . Elected to Hall of Fame in 1939.

JAMES EMORY "JIMMIE" FOXX . . . Born: Sudlersville, MD . . . B-R, T-R . . . First baseman with Athletics, 1925-35 . . . AL MVP, 1932-33 . . . Won Triple Crown in 1933 . . . AL home run leader with A's, 3 times . . . Career: 534 home runs, 1,921 RBI, .325 average . . . Elected to Hall of Fame in 1951.

180

ROBERT MOSES "LEFTY" GROVE . . . Born: Lonaconing, MD . . . B-L, T-L . . . Pitched for A's, 1925-33 . . . 31-4 record with 2.06 ERA in 1931 MVP season . . . Led AL in strikeouts, 7 straight years; ERA leader, 5 times . . . Career: 300-141, 3.06 ERA . . . Elected to Hall of Fame in 1947.

CONNIE MACK . . . Born: East Brookfield, MA . . . B-R, T-R . . . Real name Cornelius McGillicuddy . . . "The Grand Old Man of Baseball". . . Managed the Athletics, 1901-50 . . . Won 9 pennants and 5 World Series . . . Elected to Hall of Fame in 1937.

EDWARD STEWART "EDDIE" PLANK . . . Born: Gettysburg, PA . . . B-L, T-L . . . Went from Gettysburg College to A's; 1901-14 . . . Career: 326-194, 2.35 ERA, 69 shutouts . . . Elected to Hall of Fame in 1946.

ALOYSIUS "AL" SIMMONS . . . Born: Milwaukee, WI . . . B-R, T-R . . . A's outfielder, 1924-32, 1940-41 . . . Two-time AL batting champion . . . Career: .334, 307 HR, 1,827 RBI . . . Elected to Hall of Fame in 1953.

GEORGE EDWARD "RUBE" WADDELL . . . Born: Bradford, PA . . . B-L, T-L . . . Pitched for A's, 1902-07 . . . AL ERA leader, 1905 . . . Led AL in strikeouts each season and averaged over 21 wins a year . . . Elected to Hall of Fame in 1946.

Introduction To The Big Five
by Tom Gola

The Big Five holds great memories for myself, as well as for many Philadelphia college basketball fans. I remember arriving back in Philadelphia after our LaSalle University team won the 1954 NCAA Championship. There were 10,000 screaming fans waiting for us at the airport. It seemed like all of our LaSalle University classmates were there, waiting to celebrate this magical moment. Our team established twelve new NCAA records during the tournament and that same year I was named to the All-American team as a junior.

At the time I knew it was a big moment in my life, but I had no idea how big this event would be to the entire city of Philadelphia. The Big Five is incredibly competitive and the rivalries are intense. So I was a little surprised when the other players, coaches and students of the Big Five schools congratulated us and told us they were behind us the whole way.

 It's that kind of league. We all root for each other when one of the schools is playing great.

There have been many great moments in the storied history of the Big Five. Who can forget that almost surreal April Fools Day at Rupp Arena in 1985, when underdog Villanova shot the lights out to win the NCAA championship against huge favorite Georgetown. Villanova was always one of our biggest rivals, but on that day we were all Wildcats. In 2009, the Wildcats provided another great moment by going to the Final Four before losing to the eventual national champion, North Carolina.

Whenever one of Temple's teams does well in the NCAA tournament I make that metamorphosis from rival to fan. It seems like we all do, and that is what makes the Big Five so unique.

Who will ever be able to forget the 2004 St. Joseph's University team that was on the verge of a perfect season? That year provided us some of the biggest thrills in Big Five history, and the class with which the team carried itself with was merely a reflection of their fine head coach, Phil Martelli.

Even if you didn't go to one of these schools, its certain that you have a favorite amongst them. It's really like a close family. You can fight with your brothers and sisters all day but as soon as someone else tries to start something with them you rush to their defense. Every time I attend a LaSalle home game and enter the arena named in my honor, I remember all of the wonderful moments in the last 60 years and I get goose bumps. Words can never explain the happiness I feel just to have been part of this great tradition that is the Big Five.

BIG FIVE TRIVIA

PENN BIG FIVE TRIVIA QUESTIONS

Answers on page 363

1. What Penn player has scored the most career points?

2. What Penn player has secured the most career rebounds?

3. What Penn player has handed out the most career assists?

4. What Penn player has swatted the most blocked shots?

5. What Penn player has recorded the most career steals?

6. In 1973, who was the first Quaker inducted into the Big 5 Hall of Fame?

7. In 1994, Penn won a game in the NCAA Tournament over Nebraska. What two future NBA players comprised Penn's starting backcourt?

8. Who was the coach of Penn when the Quakers reached the 1979 Final Four?

9. What Penn alum was the first coach of the Charlotte Hornets?

10. What Quaker was a member of the 1976-77 Portland Trailblazers which defeated the 76ers in the NBA Finals?

11. What former Quaker spent three seasons as head coach of the New Jersey Nets starting in 1985-86?

12. Who was the leading scorer of the Penn team that went undefeated during the regular season in 1970-71?

13. What team did Penn lose to in the 1979 Final Four?

14. What Quaker made First Team Big 5 for three straight years starting in 1992-93?

15. How many seasons did Chuck Daly coach Penn?

16. Who coached Penn from 1956-57 – 1965-66?

17. During the 2008-09 season, what duo comprised the Penn radio announcing team?

18. True or False: Fran Dunphy won over 80% of his games at Penn.

19. What Penn player was the Ivy League 10 Player of the Year in both 2005-06 and 2006-07?

20. What Penn player was the Ivy League 10 Freshman of the Year in 1996-97?

21. In the fifteen season stretch from 1992-93 – 2006-07 how many times did Penn make the NCAA Tournament?

22. What team did Penn almost beat in the NCAA Tournament in Fran Dunphy's last game as coach of the Quakers?

23. What Penn player of the mid-1990s averaged over two steals per game for his Quaker career?

24. What player has made the most three-pointers in Penn history?

25. What player from the decade of the 2000s is second in school history in both points scored and blocked shots?

ST. JOSEPH'S BIG FIVE TRIVIA QUESTIONS

Answers on page 364

1. What St. Joe's player has scored the most career points?

2. What St. Joe's player has secured the most career rebounds?

3. What St. Joe's player has handed out the most career assists?

4. What St. Joe's player has swatted the most blocked shots?

5. What St. Joe's player has recorded the most career steals?

6. In 1973 who was the first Hawk inducted into the Big 5 Hall of Fame?

7. St. Joseph's alum Maurice Martin was a first-round pick of what NBA team in 1986?

8. What St. Joe's player made the winning basket against DePaul in the 1981 NCAA Tournament?

9. What St. Joe's player was a member of the 1972 Men's Olympic Basketball Team?

10. Who was the coach of St. Joe's when the Hawks upset #1 ranked DePaul in 1981?

11. What two teams were they only ones to defeat the Hawks in the 2003-04 season?

12. What former Hawks star and one-time UMass head coach now leads the Drexel basketball team?

13. What team selected Jameer Nelson in the first round of the 2004 NBA Draft?

14. What seed was St. Joe's in the 2004 NCAA Tournament?

15. Who was the primary back-up guard off the bench behind Jameer Nelson and Delonte West on the 2003-04 team?

16. Who was the coach of St. Joe's from 1981-82 – 1989-90?

17. What St. Joe's big man was First Team Big 5 in 1987-88?

18. What future Sixers coach was First Team Big 5 in 1965-66?

19. What player scored a spectacular 37 points in a NCAA Tournament loss and also scored 18 points in one minute in a game earlier that season?

20. What freshman backcourt duo raised hopes on Hawk Hill during the 1990-91 season?

21. In the Elite Eight loss in 2004 what Hawk made a shot to put St. Joe's up by a point moments before John Lucas III sank a three-pointer which put St. Joe's down for good?

22. What Hawk was the 2008-09 Big 5 Player of the Year?

23. In 2009, St. Joe's dedicated a new basketball center that bears whose name?

24. Phil Martelli led what school to the NCAA Tournament as a player during the 1970s?

25. In 1997, St. Joe's first made it to the Sweet 16 under Phil Martelli before losing to what perennial power?

TEMPLE BIG FIVE TRIVIA QUESTIONS

Answers on page 365

1. What Temple player has scored the most career points?

2. What Temple player has secured the most career rebounds?

3. What Temple player has handed out the most career assists?

4. What Temple player has swatted the most blocked shots?

5. What Temple player has recorded the most career steals?

6. In 1973 who was the first Owl inducted into the Big 5 Hall of Fame?

7. Name the starting five for the 1987-88 Owls. This team spent a good portion of the season ranked #1 in the nation.

8. What NBA team drafted Tim Perry?

9. What Owl was named the Most Outstanding Player of a Final Four?

10. Who coached Temple from 1952-1973?

11. What former Rhode Island star and current NBA player hit a buzzer-beater to defeat Temple in the 1999 Atlantic-10 Tournament Final?

12. What two teams were they only ones to defeat Temple during the 1987-88 season?

189

13. What former Owl and Indiana Pacers forward made a series of creative dunks using props in the one of the NBA's early Slam Dunk Contests?

14. Where did the Temple play home games before the opening of the Liacouras Center in 1998?

15. What #1 nationally ranked squad did Temple upset in a memorable road game in February, 2000?

16. In what year did Temple last reach the Elite 8 under John Chaney?

17. What duo comprised the famous Temple backcourt of the mid-1950's?

18. What three future NBA players comprised Temple's three-guard offense when John Chaney's squad made the Elite Eight in 1994?

19. In the 1956 Final Four Guy Rodgers scored 48 points against what team in the consolation game?

20. John Chaney led what school to the NCAA Division II championship in 1978?

21. What coach succeeded Harry Litwack at Temple?

22. What NBA team drafted Mark Macon?

23. Duane Causwell was drafted by what NBA team?

24. What rival Atlantic-10 coach did John Chaney threaten to "kill" at a post-game press conference in 1994?

25. What former Owl was traded by the 76ers as part of the deal that brought Dikembe Mutombo to Philly?

LA SALLE TRIVIA QUESTIONS

Answers on page 366

1. What LaSalle player has scored the most career points?

2. What LaSalle player has secured the most career rebounds?

3. What LaSalle player has handed out the most career assists?

4. What LaSalle player has swatted the most blocked shots?

5. What LaSalle player has recorded the most career steals?

6. In 1973, who was the first Explorer inducted into the Big 5 Hall of Fame?

7. What player from LaSalle was named to the First Team Big 5 for three straight years starting in 1981-82?

8. What two LaSalle players have been named a National Player of the Year?

9. What LaSalle alum coached the 1968-69 team to a record of 23-1?

10. What assistant coach from the 1958-59 Explorers was still working in the NBA at the turn of the century?

11. What Explorer was the fifth overall pick in an NBA draft?

12. What LaSalle player scored 1,000 points in the fewest number of games in school history?

13. What was LaSalle's home court prior to Gola Arena?

14. Who was the excellent starting shooting guard on LaSalle's great 1989-90 team which also featured Lionel Simmons and Doug Overton?

15. What NBA team drafted Lionel Simmons?

16. What LaSalle player was First Team Big 5 in 1999-2000?

17. What LaSalle player was First Team Big 5 in 2001-02?

18. Who was the coach of LaSalle in Lionel Simmons' senior year?

19. What Explorer went on to an NBA career that saw him excel as a three-point shooter to the extent, that as of 2009, he held the fourth highest three-point shooting percentage in NBA history?

20. What number did Tom Gola wear at LaSalle?

21. At what school did Dr. John Giannini win a Division II national championship before coming to LaSalle?

22. Who replaced Speedy Morris as coach of LaSalle?

23. Who coached at LaSalle immediately prior to Speedy Morris?

24. What number did Ken Durrett wear at LaSalle?

25. What number did Lionel Simmons wear at LaSalle?

VILLANOVA TRIVIA QUESTIONS

Answers on page 367

1. What Villanova player has scored the most career points?

2. What Villanova player has secured the most career rebounds?

3. What Villanova player has handed out the most career assists?

4. What Villanova player has swatted the most blocked shots?

5. What Villanova player has recorded the most career steals?

6. In 1973 who was the first Wildcat inducted into the Big 5 Hall of Fame?

7. What three players started in the frontcourt in the championship game versus Georgetown?

8. Harold Pressley was a first round pick of what NBA team?

9. What team did John Pinone play for in his one NBA season?

10. What team defeated Villanova in the 1972 NCAA National Championship Game?

11. Who did Villanova beat in the Final Four in 1985 to reach that memorable match-up with Georgetown?

12. What two Villanova players have been named the Final Four's Most Outstanding Player?

13. What Villanova player later coached USC?

193

14. Who is the only Wildcat to score 2,000 points and grab 1,000 rebounds in his college career?

15. What seed was Villanova in the 1985 NCAA Tournament?

16. Where did Villanova play its home games before "The Pavilion" became the Wildcats home court?

17. What Wildcat was punched in the face by Georgetown's Reggie Williams as the first half ended in the 1985 National Championship Game?

18. Prior to a Villanova game at the Spectrum in the mid-1990s what player from an opposing Big East school was chided by the Nova crowd with signs throughout the arena, prompting his coach to tell Villanova officials that his squad would not take the floor unless the signs were removed?

19. What player went 5-for-5 off the bench in the 1985 NCAA Championship Game versus Georgetown?

20. In what city was the 1985 NCAA Championship Game played?

21. Who was the first 'Nova coach to coach in a Big 5 game?

22. What year did Rollie Massimino start coaching Villanova?

23. True or False: Villanova went undefeated in Big 5 play in the championship season of 1984-85.

24. Which college team did Rollie Massamino coach immediately after leaving Villanova?

25. What player scored 40 points in a game as a freshman versus UConn?

MISCELLANEOUS BIG FIVE TRIVIA QUESTIONS

Answers on page 368

1. What former Big 5 coach was the head coach of the 1992 U.S. Olympic Dream Team?

2. What Big 5 player was named captain of the 1980 men's Olympic basketball team? This was the squad that never got to play in the Olympics because of the U.S. boycott of the Moscow Games.

3. What three former Big 5 coaches won championships as NBA head coaches?

4. Name the former 76ers GM who was the first Executive Director of the Big 5.

5. What Big 5 team won the first NIT in Madison Square Garden in 1938?

6. Name the first Big 5 player to score 1,000 points and grab 1,000 career rebounds?

7. What Big 5 coach was elected to the Basketball Hall of Fame in 2001?

8. In what year was the first Big 5 game played?

9. In what venue was the first Big 5 game played?

10. What team won the first Big 5 game?

11. What school went 4-0 in Big 5 play in both 1964-65 and 1965-66?

12. What school went 4-0 in Big 5 play in both 1972-73 and 1973-74?

13. In what season did Big 5 play move from a four-game round-robin for each team to a two-game format for each team?

1984-85 VILLANOVA UNIVERSITY WILDCATS
NCAA NATIONAL CHAMPIONS

14. In what season did Big 5 play move back to a four-game per team round-robin format?

15. Name the five Big 5 coaches for the 1995-96 season.

16. What school went winless in Big 5 play from 1993-94–1996-97?

17. What school went winless in Big 5 play in both 1982-83 and 1984-85?

18. There is only one player in the Big 5 Hall of Fame who has a last name that starts with the letter "I." Who is he?

19. Well before the Big 5 was formed, what year did The Palestra open?

20. As of 2009, what school has won the fewest outright Big 5 season titles?

21. As of 2009, what school had won the most Big 5 titles with 24 but had won only the third most outright titles with 5?

22. What two teams play in what is known as "The Holy War?"

23. What two teams played in the game that created "Goon Gate?"

24. During the 1980s, 1990s and 2000s how many total seasons ended with no Big 5 teams making it to the NCAA Tournament?

25. How many times have all five teams gone 2-2 in Big 5 play in one season?

BIG 5 HALL OF FAME MEMBERS

Since 1973, the Big 5 has been selecting players, coaches, broadcasters, sportswriters and others who have made significant contributions to the Big 5 and its history to become members of the Philadelphia Big 5 Hall of Fame. Each year, inductees are honored at a Luncheon on the Palestra floor, and then enshrined at halftime of a designated Big 5 game.

A

		Played	Inducted
Barbara Albom	Penn	1980-84	1992
Jerome Allen	Penn	1991-95	2009
Cliff Anderson	Saint Joseph's	1964-67	1973
Lisa Angelotti	Villanova	1984-88	1995
Paul Arizin	Villanova	1946-50	2000

B

		Played	Inducted
Dan Baker	Big 5 Executive Secretary		1997
Pam Balogh	Temple	1985-89	1995
Mike Bantom	Saint Joseph's	1970-73	1979
John Baum	Temple	1966-69	1978
Ernie Beck	Penn	1951-53	2000
Kathie Beisel	Villanova	1979-83	1992
Nikki Benedix	Villanova	1987-91	2001
Nancy Bernhardt	Villanova	1980-84	1993
Kathy Bess	La Salle	1978-82	1991
Rashid Bey	Saing Joseph's	1994-98	2011
Bob Bigelow	Penn	1972-75	1989
Steve Bilsky	Penn	1968-71	1988
Debbie Black	Saint Joseph's	1984-88	1995
Norman Black	Saint Joseph's	1975-79	1985

197

Steve Black	La Salle	1981-85	1992
Nate Blackwell	Temple	1983-87	1993
Rodney Blake	Saint Joseph's	1984-88	1994
Lynn Blaszczyk	Temple	1979-83	1990
Bernard Blunt	Saint Joseph's	1991-95	2001
Robyne Bostick	Saint Joseph's	1990-94	2000
Jim Boyle	Saint Joseph's	1962-64	1997
Alex Bradley	Villanova	1977-81	1987
Kirsten Brendel	Penn	1987-91	1984
Clarence Brookins	Temple	1965-68	1984
Michael Brooks	La Salle	1976-80	1986
Trish Brown	Saint Joseph's	1981-85	1992
Rick Brunson	Temple	1991-95	2011
Joe Bryant	La Salle	1973-75	1981

C

Corky Calhoun	Penn	1969-72	1976
Larry Cannon	La Salle	1966-69	1973
Diana Caramanico	Penn	1998-01	2007
Teresa Carmichael	Saint Joseph's	1983-87	1994
Donnie Carr	La Salle	1997-00	2008
Mimi Carroll	Temple	1982-86	1992
Ernie Casale	Temple Athletic Director		1982
Dick Csencsitz	Penn	1954-57	1981
John Chaney	Temple	1982-06	2010
Jeffrey Clark	Saint Joseph's	1978-82	1996
Tim Claxton	Temple	1974-78	1987
Audrey Codner	Saint Joseph's	1991-94	2001
Jenn Cole	La Salle	1989-93	1999
Megan Compain	Saint Joseph's	1994-97	2003
Frank Corace	La Salle	1961-64	1974
Maureen Costello	Saint Joseph's	1994-98	2004
Tony Costner	Saint Joseph's	1980-84	1990
Steve Courtin	Saint Joseph's	1961-64	1980
Jill Crandley	La Salle	1982-86	1993

198

C (continued)

Jim Crawford	La Salle	1970-73	1993
Katie Curry	Saint Joseph's	1989-93	1999
Rap Curry	Saint Joseph's	1991-94	2008

D

Chuck Daly	Penn Coach	1971-77	2001
Denise Dillon	Villanova	1992-96	2004
Chrissie Donahue	La Salle	1994-97	2002
Andy Dougherty	St. Joe's Publicist	1972-83	1989
Bruce Drysdale	Temple	1959-62	1977
Renie Dunne	Saint Joseph's	1978-82	1991
Ken Durrett	La Salle	1968-71	1975

E

Kurt Engelburt	Saint Joseph's	1954-57	1986
John Engels	Penn	1973-76	1995
Howard Evans	Temple	1984-88	1994

F

Bob Fields	La Salle	1969-71	1984
Auretha Fleming	Penn	1980-84	1991
Kim Foley	Saint Joseph's	1985-89	1995
Chris Ford	Villanova	1969-72	1977
Curt Fromal	La Salle	1961-62, 63-65	2009

G

Mary Sue Garrity	Saint Joseph's	1974-78	1989
Tom Gola	La Salle Coach	1968-70	1986
Theresa Govens	Temple	1982-86	1993
Stewart Granger	Villanova	1979-83	1990
Chip Greenberg	La Salle	1982-86	2003
Mel Greenberg	Philadelphia Inquirer		1992

199

G (continued)

Mary Greybush	La Salle	1987-91	1998
Sharon Gross	Penn	1978-82	1990
Matt Guokas	Saint Joseph's	1964-66	1976

H

Ron Haigler	Penn	1972-75	1982
Granger Hall	Temple	1980-85	1991
Phil Hankinson	Penn	1970-73	1980
Claudrena Harold	Temple	1995-97	2008
Dick Harter	Penn Coach	1966-71	1993
Mike Hauer	Saint Joseph's	1967-70	1977
Sandy Hawthorne	Penn	1979-83	1994
Keith Herron	Villanova	1974-78	1984
Linda Hester	La Salle	1982-86	1992
Karen Hiznay	Villanova	1977-81	1990
Dale Hodges	Saint Joseph's	1987-90	1996
Allison Hudson	La Salle	1983-87	1997
Jim Huggard	Villanova	1958-61	1978
Jack Hurd	La Salle	1988-92	1999

I

Tom Ingelsby	Villanova	1970-73	1979

J

Addie Jackson	Temple	1984-88	1994
Harold Jensen	Villanova	1983-87	1995
Olli Johnson	Temple	1969-72	1979
Eddie Jones	Temple	1992-94	2002
Johnny Jones	Villanova	1966-69	1981
Wali Jones	Villanova	1961-64	1973

K

Les Keiter	Big 5 Broadcaster		2003
Dan Kelly	Saint Joseph's	1967-70	1980
Bill Kennedy	Temple	1957-60	1975

200

K (continued)

Donna Kennedy	Temple	1979-83	1991
Mik Kilgore	Temple	1988-92	1998
Kerry Kittles	Villanova	1992-96	2011
Helen Koskinen	Villanova	1986-90	1996
Jack Kraft	Villanova Coach	1961-73	1987
Maureen Kramer	La Salle	1978-81	1989
Carol Kuna	Penn	1977-80	1989

L

Kelly Lane	Temple	1987-90	1996
Faye Lawrence	Temple	1975-79	1989
Jason Lawson	Villanova	1993-97	2004
Hal Lear	Temple	1953-56	1974
Tim Legler	La Salle	1984-88	1995
Alonzo Lewis	La Salle	1954-57	1980
Ralph Lewis	La Salle	1981-85	1991
Harry Litwack	Temple Coach	1952-73	1978
Bob Lojewski	Saint Joseph's	1982-85	1998
Jim Lynam	Saint Joseph's	1960-63	1975

M

Vivian Machinski	Penn	1973-77	1989
Mark Macon	Temple	1987-91	1997
Amy Mallon	Saint Joseph's	1993	2002
Ellen Malone	La Salle	1977-80	1989
Hubie Marshall	La Salle	1964-67	1977
Maurice Martin	Saint Joseph's	1982-86	1992
Rollie Massimino	Villanova	1973-92	2010
John McAdams	Big 5 Announcer		2007
Bob McAteer	La Salle	1959-62	1976
Suzi McCaffrey	La Salle	1982-86	1994
Dwayne McClain	Villanova	1981-85	1993
Jack McCloskey	Penn Coach	1956-66	1994
Keven McDonald	Penn	1975-78	1985
Pat McFarland	Saint Joseph's	1970-73	1984

201

M (continued)

Chrissy McGoldrick	Saint Joseph's	1975-78	1989
Bob McKee	Big 5 Official Scorer		1990
Aaron McKie	Temple	1992-94	2002
Jack McKinney	St. Joseph's Coach	1957-61	1992
Bob McNeill	Saint Joseph's	1957-60	1974
Bill Melchionni	Villanova	1963-66	1974
Al Meltzer	Big 5 TV Play-By-Play		1993
Bill Mlkvy	Temple	1950-52	2000
Bob Mlkvy	Penn	1958-61	1998
Terri Mohr	Saint Joseph's	1984-96	1993
Susan Moran	Saint Joseph's	1998-02	2009
Speedy Morris	LaSalle	1986-2001	2010
Bob Morse	Penn	1969-72	1977

N

John Nash	Big 5 Executive Secretary		1999
Jeff Neuman	Penn	1963-66	1984
Jake Nevin	Villanova Trainer		1985
Hank Nichols	Referee		2004
Jay Norman	Temple	1955-58	1976

O

Jim O'Brien	Saint Joseph's	1971-74	1989
Muffet O'Brien	Saint Joseph's	1973-77	1990
Lisa Ortlip	Villanova	1979-82	1989
Doug Overton	La Salle	1987-91	1997

P

Stan Pawlak	Penn	1963-66	1973
Shelly Pennefather	Villanova	1983-87	1994
Tim Perry	Temple	1984-88	1994
Ed Pinckney	Villanova	1981-85	1991
John Pinone	Villanova	1979-83	1989

P (continued)

Harvey Pollack	Big 5 Statistician		1995
Howard Porter	Villanova	1968-71	1981
Harold Pressley	Villanova	1982-86	1992
Tony Price	Penn	1976-79	1985

R

Jack Ramsay	Saint Joe's Coach	1949-57	1983
Julie Reidenauer	La Salle	1980-84	1990
Guy Rodgers	Temple	1955-58	1973
John Rossiter	Big 5 Business Manager		1975
Margarete Rougier	Temple	1989-93	2000
Cathy Rush	Women's Broadcaster		1995
Ellen Ryan	St. Joe's Asst. AD	1973-	2003
Joe Ryan	Villanova	1956-59	1991

S

James "Booney" Salters	Penn	1978-80	2008
Jack Scheuer	Associated Press		2002
Charles Scott	Penn Assistant AD		1981
George Senesky	St. Joe's Coach	1943-49	2000
Al Severance	Villanova Coach	1936-61	1994
Ellen Shields	Saint Joseph's	1987-90	1997
Al Shrier	Temple Sports Info. Director		1984
Hank Siemiontkowski	Villanova	1969-72	1988
Lionel Simmons	La Salle	1986-90	1996
Tim Smith	Penn	1976-79	1999
Tracey Sneed	La Salle	1985-89	1996
Rory Sparrow	Villanova	1976-80	1986
Joe Spratt	Saint Joseph's	1956-59	1983
June Stambaugh	Penn	1983-86	1998
Terence Stansbury	Temple	1980-84	1990
Beth Stegner	Penn	1979-83	1993
Marilyn Stephens	Temple	1980-84	1989
Kathy Straccia	Villanova	1975-79	1989
Joe Sturgis	Penn	1953-56	1983

T

Bill Taylor	La Salle	1972-75	1989
Roland Taylor	La Salle	1967-69	2004
Lynn Tighe	Villanova	1983-87	1998

V

Stephanie Vanderslice	Villanova	1979-83	1991
Bob Vetrone	Big 5 Broadcaster, Writer		1988
Mike Vreeswyk	Temple	1985-89	1995

W

Bryan Warrick	Saint Joseph's	1978-82	1988
Jim Washington	Villanova	1962-65	1975
Bob Weinhauer	Penn Coach	1977-82	2002
Doug West	Villanova	1985-89	1996
Hubie White	Villanova	1959-62	1976
John Wideman	Penn	1960-63	1974
Alvin Williams	Villanova	1993-97	2003
Bernie Williams	La Salle	1966-69	1982
Boo Williams	Saint Joseph's	1977-81	1987
Jim Williams	Temple	1963-66	1983
Charlie Wise	La Salle	1972-76	1982
Dave Wohl	Penn	1968-71	1975
Randy Woods	La Salle	1989-92	1998
Tom Wynne	Saint Joseph's	1960-63	1978

Z

Jen Zenszer	La Salle	1998-01	2007

204

The Golf Association of Philadelphia

The Golf Association of Philadelphia was founded in 1897 by members of Aronimink Golf Club, Merion Cricket Club, Philadelphia Country Club and Philadelphia Cricket Club. The Association's 134 Member Clubs are spread across parts of four states — Pennsylvania, New Jersey, Delaware and Maryland. GAP encompasses an area that roughly runs from Lancaster to Scranton to Bethlehem to Princeton to Cape May to Wilmington to Rising Sun and back to Lancaster. The purpose of the association is simple: to preserve, protect and promote the game of golf. Every GAP activity is designed to do just that.

A Tribute to Golf in Philadelphia

The following excerpt comes courtesy of "A Centennial Tribute to Golf in Philadelphia" by James W. Finegan.

Rodman E. Griscom, Merion Cricket Club, a founding member of the Golf Association of Philadelphia.

On December 22, 1894, delegates from five clubs – St. Andrews Golf Club, Shinnecock Hills Golf Club, Newport Golf Club, The Country Club (Brookline, MA), and Chicago Golf Club – met at the Calumet Club in Manhattan to form the Amateur Golf Association of the United States (subsequently to change its name, first to The American Golf Association, then to the United States Golf Association). Less than a month afterwards the Essex Country Club and the Philadelphia Country Club were elected to membership, the sixth and seventh on the roll.

A little more than two years later the Golf Association of Philadelphia was founded. It was America's first regional golf association.

Interestingly, once again the Devon Golf Club served as a spur. For it was on this organization's course that the first interclub team match in the Philadelphia area was played. On October 15, 1896 a team representing Philadelphia Cricket Club squared off against Devon's top players. The Cricket Club won 22 to 12. The occasion was so thoroughly enjoyable that the appeal of inter-club matches on a broader scale was discussed and embraced. The obvious outgrowth of such thinking was the formation of an association of local golf clubs to organize and administer these competitions.

On February 5, 1897, seven men gathered at the Market Street National Bank for the express purpose of founding the Golf Association of Philadelphia. Representing the Belmont Golf Association (soon to be reorganized into the Aronimink Golf Club) were Milton C. Work and Dr. Henry Toulmin. From Merion Cricket Club came Rodman E. Griscom and Walter E. Stephenson. Philadelphia Country Club's delegates were George D. Fowle and Isaac T. Starr. Samuel Y. Heebner alone represented Philadelphia Cricket Club, Alan H. Harris being unavoidably absent.

The objective of the fledgling association was simplicity itself: to promote interest in the game of golf and to regulate all competitions between member clubs. In order to join the Association, a club had to be formally organized, have at least nine holes of golf for its exclusive use, and belong to the United States Golf Association. At the outset four clubs - the four founding clubs - were named Associate Members of the Golf Association of Philadelphia. Most clubs which would follow were accepted into the association as Allied Members. The difference was significant: Associate Member clubs had the right to be represented at the annual meeting by two delegates, each with one vote. Allied Members, on the other hand, could send only one delegate to the meeting and he has no vote. Moreover, the Association's three officers-President, Vice-President and Secretary-Treasurer - could be elected from the rosters of Associate Member clubs. The same was true of the other two members of the Executive Committee.

The annual dues were $25 for Associate Member clubs, $10 for Allied Members, the bargain rate doubtless a reflection of the latter category's powerless position in the scheme of things. With the passing of the years, this distinction between the two classes of membership would blur and finally, with a revision of the by-laws, be eliminated.

At an organizational meeting two months later, on April 5, 1897, George D. Fowle, Philadelphia Country Club, was elected the first president of the Golf Association of Philadelphia. Dr. Henry Toulmin, Belmont, was elected Vice President, and Alan Harris, of the Cricket Club, Secretary-Treasurer. Named to join these three on the then five-man Executive Committee (it would become a seven-member body in 1901) were Samuel Heebner, of the Cricket Club, and Louis A. Biddle, of the Country Club and Merion.

Once the officers and Executive Committee were in place, little time was lost in launching the first inter-club team matches. That year the Association's four founding clubs each fielded two teams, six players per team, for a total of 48 players in the "league." Matches were played in both Spring and Fall. When the final tally for the year was in, Merion's 1st team and the Cricket Club's 2nd team were the winners.

The only other competition in the Golf Association's first season was what was then called the Individual Championship Tournament, today known as the Philadelphia Amateur Championship.

Introduction To The Philadelphia Section PGA
by Peter Trenham

The Philadelphia Section PGA has been in business for more than 80 years. However, when the PGA of America was founded in 1916 the golf professionals in the tri-state region of the Delaware Valley were members of the Southeastern Section of the PGA. Many of the golf professionals had been members of the British PGA before emigrating to America and several attempts were made to organize in the early 1900s.

The Wanamaker family who owned the Wanamaker Department Stores was instrumental in finally getting the PGA organized. The Wanamakers imported golf equipment from Great Britain and both sold it at retail to the golfers and wholesale to the golf professionals. By organizing the pros they hoped to expand golf in America and grow their business. In January of 1916, John Wanamaker's son, Rodman, hosted a luncheon at the Taplow Club in New York for some golf professionals, where he offered to put up a purse and a trophy for a PGA Championship. Thus the PGA was born and the PGA Championship winner's name is still engraved on the trophy.

The first president of the PGA was Robert White, a transplant from Scotland, who only two years before had been the pro and green superintendent at the Shawnee Country Club at Shawnee-on-Delaware, Pennsylvania.

The Southeastern Section was one of seven that made up the PGA of America when it was founded. It included Pennsylvania, West Virginia and all of the states on the eastern seaboard south of New Jersey to the Florida border. During that first year James R. Thomson, the professional at the Philadelphia CC, served as a Vice-President of the PGA representing the region. A PGA Championship was planned for that first year at the Sivanoy Country Club in New York. Local qualifying was held in the seven PGA Sections for entry into the starting field of 32 at Sivanoy. In the qualifying, held at the Wilmington CC, Whitemarsh Valley CC professional Jim Barnes won the medal in a playoff with Jock Hutchison. At the PGA Championship in October Barnes and Hutchison met again with Barnes eking out a one-up victory over Hutchison in the finals. Along with having his name on the Wanamaker Trophy, Barnes picked up a check for $500 and a diamond medal.

The pros in the Delaware Valley had had major tournament winners such as Johnny McDermott, Alex Ross and Willie Anderson, but this was an occasion for great pride to have one of their own win the first PGA Championship. McDermott had won the U.S. Open in 1911 and 1912, Ross, the professional at Wilmington CC in 1903, had returned to win the U.S. Open at the Philadelphia Cricket Club in 1907, and Willie Anderson, a four time winner of the U.S. Open, had been the pro at the Philadelphia Cricket Club in 1910. Due to World War I, the PGA wasn't played in 1917 or 1918 but Barnes won it again in 1919, defeating another Southeastern Section member in the finals, Freddie McLeod of the Columbia CC in Washington D.C.

With only seven PGA Sections in the country, the professionals found it difficult to travel to meetings and the PGA Championship qualifying rounds. In 1921 the PGA formed a committee to address the problem. Jack Hobens, the professional at the Huntingdon Valley CC and a Vice-President (later called District Director) of the PGA of America, was a member of the committee. The decision was made to divide the country into 18 Sections rather than the seven that had existed up to that time. One of the 11 new Sections was the Philadelphia Section, which became the only PGA Section in the country named for a city. The new Section's territory was composed of Eastern Pennsylvania, all of Delaware and a few clubs across the Delaware River in New Jersey. The rest of the golf professionals in New Jersey were still in the Metropolitan Section until 1924 when the New Jersey Section was created. At that time, all of the New Jersey golf professionals working south of the 40th parallel, which is near Mt. Holly, were included in the Philadelphia Section.

On Friday December 2nd, 1921, about 30 professionals who were employed in what was now called the Philadelphia Section met in Philadelphia to elect officers and adopt a constitution. The organizing committee was made up of: Tredyffrin CC professional Bob Barnett; James R. Thomson, Overbrook GC, Jack Sawyer, Torresdale CC; Charles Hoffner, Philmont CC; Frank Coltart, Philadelphia CC; Jim Edmundson, Sr., North Hills CC; Bill Byrne, St. Davids GC; Wilfrid Reid, Wilmington CC; Bill Leach, Merchantville CC; Herb Jewson, Roxborough CC; Tony Natale, Lansdowne CC; Joseph Seka, Cedarbrook CC; Jack Hobens, Huntingdon Valley CC; Stanley Hern and Vin O'Donnell.

Many of the region's golf professionals such as Reid, Coltart, and Edmundson had been born in Great Britain and had experience with the British PGA. Another one of those at the meeting was Dave Kirkaldy, the professional at the Aronimink Golf Club and the son of Andra Kirkaldy the golf professional at the St. Andrews Golf Club in Scotland.

The dues were $5 per year, which went to defray the expenses of maintaining the organization, promoting tournaments and other forms of entertainment. The Section was made up of fifty-plus clubs.

They decided to have two classes of membership, active and honorary. The active included all professionals, assistants, caddie-masters and salesmen. The honorary members would be amateurs. They also decided that all their tournaments would be open to all

comers except the Section Championship, which would be open only to PGA members.

On Monday June 12th, the Philadelphia Section held their first Section Championship at the Tredyffrin Country Club in Paoli. The host club put up $230 to enhance the purse, and the Public Ledger newspaper gave a trophy to the Philadelphia Section. It was called the Evening Public Ledger Cup and the Section champion's name was engraved on the cup each year. There were sixty-five entries and the course measured 6,507 yards. At the conclusion of play on a very windy Spring day, Charles Hoffner and Jack Campbell were tied for first with 15-over-par 155 totals. Two days later Hoffner defeated Campbell in an 18-hole playoff and became the first Philadelphia Section champion.

Later that summer the Philadelphia Section had another first, a Pro-Am championship, which was played at the Whitemarsh Valley CC. Hoffner won that event also.

From 1929 to 1951 the greatest playing professionals in the world were associated with the Philadelphia Section.

It seemed to all begin with the arrival of Ed Dudley in 1929 as the professional at the Concord CC. Dudley was a Section member for 19 years and during that time he also served as the professional at the Philadelphia CC and Atlantic City CC. While a Section member, Dudley was president of the Section for seven years, president of the PGA of America for seven years and he played on three Ryder Cup teams. In 1933 Llanerch CC hired Denny Shute as their professional, and that year he won the British Open and played on the Ryder Cup team. Shute went on to win two PGA Championships after leaving Llanerch. The next year Leo Diegel, a two time PGA champion in the late 1920s, arrived in Philadelphia as the pro at the Philmont CC. Henry Picard was the professional at the Hershey CC from 1935 to 1940 and during that time he won the Masters and the PGA Championship. One week after winning the Masters in 1937 Byron Nelson assumed his duties as the professional at the Reading CC and two years later while still the pro at RCC, he won the U.S. Open at the Philadelphia CC.

In 1940 the Shawnee Country Club hired Sam Snead to represent them on the PGA Tour. Two years later Snead became the third Section member to win the PGA Championship while employed in the Section. Snead won the championship at the Seaview CC and two days later he was Seaman First Class Snead in the U.S. Navy. Ben Hogan signed on with the Hershey CC in 1941 and represented the club on the PGA Tour until June of 1951. Three of those years were spent in the Army Air Corps during World War II, and later he missed 11 months after almost losing his life in an automobile accident in 1949. Hogan returned to tournament golf in 1950 and won major tournaments, but from that time on his play was quite limited. During his ten years as Hershey's pro, Hogan won 53 times on the PGA Tour (six were majors) in spite of missing more than four years of tournament golf.

Later on, two homegrown professionals, Art Wall and Jim Furyk, won majors. Wall, who grew up in Northeastern Pennsylvania and represented the Pocono Manor Resort, won the Masters in 1959, and Lancaster County's Furyk won the U.S. Open in 2003.

The Philadelphia Section was the first PGA Section to do several things. In 1924 it held the first pro-lady championship in the country. Under the guidance of two Section presidents, Atlantic City CC's Leo Fraser and Reading CC's Henry Poe, Philadelphia was the first Section to have a caddy scholarship program (1954) and the first to hold their own golf show (1958). Fraser and Poe went on to be presidents of the PGA of America.

The Philadelphia Section has been blessed with strong leadership through the years. Woodcrest CC professional Dick Smith, Sr. was the Section President in the 1970s. He gave the Section another first by creating a Junior PGA Tour in the Philadelphia Section. He went on to

be president of the PGA of America and soon after that Huntingdon Valley CC professional Jack Connelly followed him as the President of our national association for 2001 and 2002. Connelly was the fifth Section member to be elected President of the PGA of America.

In recent years, the Section has had two winners of national awards. Chester Valley CC professional John Poole won for his many years of work in club relations/employment, and Whitford CC professional Harry Hammond was the junior golf leader for his promotion of junior golf through the PGA.

The members of the Philadelphia Section are looking forward to the next opportunity to be the leaders in professional golf in the United States.

GOLF TRIVIA

PHILADELPHIA GOLF QUESTIONS

Courses

Answers on page 369

1. What area course is ranked as the number one course in the world?

2. Since the Philadelphia Amateur Championship began in 1897, what club's members have collected the most championships?

3. In 1989 Big Chris Patton won the US Amateur at what famous golf club?

4. Where is the famous Hoffner Cup held every year?

5. The PGA Tour's SEI Pennsylvania Classic was played for only two years in 2000 and 2002. What course hosted this tournament?

6. What course played host to the PGA Tour's IVB Classic from 1963-1980?

7. In 1985 Pine Valley hosted what famous international competition?

8. The 1960 World Team Championships was hosted by what Ardmore golf club?

9. Name the course that the Bell Atlantic Classic moved to when it was renamed the Instinet Classic in 2000?

10. What area country club has won the most inter-club championships?

11. What three Pennsylvania golf courses hosted the Senior PGA Tour's Bell Atlantic Classic between 1981 and 1999?

12. The AB Thorn Memorial Pro-Am is held at what prestigious venue every year?

13. At what Philadelphia landmark is the Philadelphia Open Amateur held every year?

14. How many courses in the Philadelphia area have hosted a USGA National Championship?
    a.) 4   b.) 9
    c.) 14   d.) 19

Answers on page 370

1. The PGA Championship has been played in the Philadelphia Section 5 times on five different courses. Name the years and the courses.

2. The Senior PGA Championship was played in Philadelphia in 2003. At what course was it held and who was the winner?

3. What golf legend won the 1950 U.S. Open at Merion G.C.? And what club did he famously use to hit his second shot on the 18th hole in the final round of the competition?

4. What was the most famous moment from the 1971 U.S. Open hosted by Merion Golf Club? The memorable scene occurred on the 1st tee before the playoff even began that Monday?

5. Who won that 1971 U.S. Open?

6. Who had the lead at 7-under par, which set a 54-hole U.S. Open record after 3 rounds at Merion?

7. In 1939 the US Open was held at Philadelphia Country Club. What golf legend won the event?

8. Dow Finsterwald captured what Championship at Llanerch C.C.?

9. What local golfer won the 2003 US Open at Olympia Fields?

10. On what famous hole and at what course did Bobby Jones complete his Grand Slam?

11. What Championship did Aleck Ross win at The Philadelphia Cricket Club in 1907?

12. Ironically Bobby Jones played in his first US Open when he was 14 years old at what golf course?

13. What five-time Philadelphia PGA Champion also won the Masters?

THE WINNERS QUESTIONS

Answers on page 370-371

1. What PGA Tour legend collected his 1st Tour victory at the 1976 IVB Classic?

2. Who is the only person to win the IVB Classics three times?

3. What local amateur legend won the 1998 Bell Atlantic Classic?

4. What two players have won the Bell Atlantic Classic twice?

5. What three players have won both the IVB Classic and the Bell Atlantic Classic?

6. What future Philadelphia Section PGA head professional won the U.S. Junior Amateur at Wilmington C.C. in 1965?

7. Who won the SEI Pennsylvania Classic in 2000?

8. What future PGA Tour and Senior PGA Tour winner won the Philadelphia Section PGA Championship three times?

9. What legendary club professional won the Philadelphia PGA Section Championship three years in a row from 1980 to 1982?

10. What great Philadelphia area club professional won the 2004 Senior British Open?

11. Who is the only person to win both the GAP Amateur Championship and the PGA Section Championship?

12. Who won the 1963 IVB Classic at Whitemarsh Country Club?

13. What Villanova resident and Walker Cup Captain won the 2008 USGA Senior Amateur Championship.

14. Who won the 1951 US Amateur at Saucon Valley's Old Course?

15. Besides Jay Sigel, what four Amateurs have won the Philadelphia Open?

16. The 1995 Deposit Guaranty Classic was won by what Chester native?

17. What PGA President won the 1979 Philadelphia Open?

18. What Temple All-American won the Philadelphia Amateur in 1981?

19. Name the only father-son combination to win the Philadelphia Open.

20. What former tour winner won the Philadelphia Open at Stone wall Golf Club in 1996?

21. What Philadelphia Country Club amateur won the 1978 Philadelphia PGA Championship?

22. Which Philadelphia PGA member won the 1947 US Amateur, then played in 16 US Opens, 9 PGA Championships and 11 Masters Tournaments in a row.

23. What PGA Professional won the 2002 Philadelphia Open Championship in a playoff against Laurel Creek's John DiMarco?

24. What local legend and Philadelphia PGA Hall-of-Famer won the Philadelphia Open in 1942 and then again in 1950?

25. What player won the first Tylenol Kids Classic at White Manor Country Club?

LPGA QUESTIONS

Answers on page 371

1. At what Philadelphia club was the U.S. Women's Open played in 1976?

2. The McDonald's LPGA Championship was played at what area course from 1993 to 2004?

3. What four women twice won the McDonald's LPGA Championship when it was played in the area?

4. Louise Suggs won the 1952 U.S. Woman's Open at what Main Line course?

5. What local favorite won the 1983 Senior Women's Amateur at Gulph Mills Golf Course?

6. What LPGA great won the 1976 US Women's Open at Rolling Green Golf Course?

7. Ann Laughlin of Riverton Country Club, arguably the most dominant Philadelphia golfer of all-time, won how many Women's Championships?

Answers on page 371

1. What caused the IVB Classic not to be played in 1981, which led to its eventual demise?

2. What golf legend made his comeback from hip surgery at the 1999 Bell Atlantic Classic?

3. How many USGA National Championships have been held in the Philadelphia area?
   a.) 26   b.) 39
   c.) 52   d.) 68

4. What Philadelphia PGA champion made the cut at the 2002 SEI Pennsylvania Classic?

5. How many Philadelphia Open Championships did Jay Sigel claim?

6. What famous Whitemarsh Valley Country Club member and former GAP President has a scholarship named in his honor?

7. What title did Gordon Brewer of Huntingdon Valley Country Club capture in both 1994 and 1996?

8. Lancaster's Jim Furyk attended what Pac-10 school?

9. Incredibly, there are two families in the Philadelphia area who boast four PGA members. Name those families.

10. What Philadelphia PGA professional who shares his name with a famous television personality won golf tournaments in six different decades?

11. What former area Professional and Villanova University Golf Coach won the Pennsylvania State Putting Championship in 1996 and 1997? The only 2 years it was held.

Introduction To Philadelphia Boxing
by Joe Frazier

Philadelphia has long been at or near the very center of the American boxing universe. Since 1857, when Philadelphian Dominick Bradley claimed the world heavyweight title after defeating Sam Rankin of Baltimore, until this very day, where the likes of Bernard Hopkins carry on the great tradition, Philly has been home to dozens of world champions.

Over the decades, different ethnic groups have come up through the ranks of boxing, as well as the ranks of society. From the Irish fighters of the early 1900's to the Italian fighters of the 30's and 40's, to the great African American boxers of the second half of the twentieth century, Philadelphia has seen it all; brutal knockouts, great title fights, and stunning upsets. I am proud to have been a part of this tradition.

My own personal boxing journey began when I moved to Philly over 50 years ago, at the age of sixteen. I found a job working as a butcher's apprentice in a slaughter house. While working there, I punched sides of beef in a refrigerated room (giving Sylvester Stallone some key inspiration). I first went into a gym in North Philadelphia in December, 1961 with the intention of losing some weight and getting myself into shape. It was a Police Athletic League gym, located at 20th and Columbia. I discovered boxing almost by accident, but became intrigued by the sweet science.

Blessed with a strong jaw and a monster left hook, I did not lose until the Olympic trials of 1964, where I lost by decision to Buster Mathis in the final match. I made plans to turn professional later that year, but I soon got the news that Buster had suffered a hand injury, and would be unable to represent the USA in the Olympics.

I was chosen as Buster's replacement, and traveled to Tokyo with the US Olympic team. I wound up winning all of my fights, and returned home with the Heavyweight Gold Medal.

I turned professional the next year under the tutelage of the great Philadelphia trainer Yank Durham, who shortened my punches, and taught me about balance. I won my first eleven fights easily all by knockout.

Then, on September 21, 1966, I faced my toughest challenge to date against heavyweight contender Oscar Bonavena at Madison Square Garden in New York City. Somehow, I survived to win a 10-round decision, showing the heart and character that would define the remainder of my career.

Less than four years later, after steamrolling the competition, I knocked out Jimmy Ellis in the fifth round of our bout to win the vacant heavyweight crown, and became "the baddest man on the planet". Nonetheless, many still considered Muhammad Ali the rightful champion, even though he had been stripped of his title for refusing induction into the Army in 1967.

When Ali was cleared to fight later that year, it set the stage for one of the most anticipated fights in boxing history.

On March 8, 1971, we finally 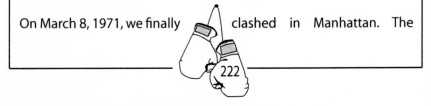 clashed in Manhattan. The build-up to the fight was unparalleled in boxing history; transcending the sport and setting the world on its ear. We were each paid a purse of $2.5 million, an unheard of sum in those days. The sellout crowd witnessed one of the greatest heavyweight battles ever.

The fight raged back and forth, with each man landing power shots. In the 15th and final round, I landed what may be the most famous left hook in the history of boxing, dropping Ali to the canvas with a perfect left to the jaw. He was able to regain his feet, but when the fight went to the judges, I won a unanimous decision, and left the ring as boxing's undisputed champion.

The first Ali fight took a lot out of me, and I did not fight for the rest of that year. In 1972, I defended my title twice, knocking out both opponents. In 1973, I went to Jamaica to fight contender George Foreman. I came out cold, and George took advantage, knocking me down six times in two rounds to take my title by knockout.

I continued to fight for the next three years, including two more classic bouts with Ali, both of which were close losses for me. I also lost to Foreman a second time, getting knocked out in the fifth round on June 15, 1976. I came back for one ill-fated draw in1981, after which I hung up the gloves for good. My professional record was 32-4-1, with 27 knockouts. The only boxers I ever lost to as a professional were Ali and Foreman.

I was the Heavyweight champion of the world from 1970-1973, and looking back, I am proud to say that I left my legacy on the sport, as well as on, my adopted home of Philadelphia.

BOXING TRIVIA

BOXING TRIVIA QUESTIONS

Famous Fights, Fighters and Firsts

Answers on page 372

1. What was the first title bout ever held in Philadelphia?

2. In what year did Jack Dempsey make his Philadelphia boxing debut?

3. On September 23, 1926 Gene Tunney fought Jack Dempsey in Philadelphia for the Heavyweight title. Where did that fight take place?

4. A record crowd watched that fight. Was the attendance more or less than 100,000?

5. The Vice President of the United States attended that fight, sitting on a cushion at ringside. Who was he?

6. What was the outcome of that fight?

7. Philadelphian Billy Fox scored 43 consecutive knockout victories before losing. Who beat him?

8. The year 1952 brought three world title fights to Philly. Can you name who fought in each?

9. Where did all three of these fights take place?

10. In what year did the last major outdoor boxing show in Philadelphia take place?

11. At what venue did that card take place?

12. On July 11, 1949, Sugar Ray Robinson retained his welterweight title at Memorial Stadium (JFK) with a 15-round decision over what fighter?

13. In what round did Rocky Marciano ringup his electrifying knockout of Jersey Joe Walcott, to win the Heavyweight championship at Municipal Stadium (JFK)?

14. This Philly product fought over 225 bouts, between 1921-1940. Name him.

15. Who did Bennie Briscoe fight in Philadelphia on August 24, 1978?

16. What was the outcome of that fight?

17. This Philadelphia-born Heavyweight, who fought such greats as Ali, Foreman, and Norton died in 2005.

18. This Philly fighter lost to Julio Cesar Chavez when the fight was stopped with two seconds left.

19. Joe Frazier won the Heavyweight Crown over what fighter on February 16, 1970?

20. Who defeated Joe Frazier to take his Heavyweight belt on January 23, 1973?

21. How many times was Frazier knocked down in that fight?

22. Joe Walcott (not Jersey Joe) fought in Philadelphia 20 times and never lost. True or false?

23. The great Bob Fitzsimmons defeated what PA Champion at the 1st Regiment Armory on March 27, 1900?

BOXING NICKNAME QUESTIONS

Answers on page 373

1. This popular Heavyweight scored seven knockout victories in Philadelphia, and was nicknamed "Two-Ton."

2. Who was known as "The Philadelphia Bobcat?"

3. What was Philadelphia Light Heavyweight Matt Adgie's nickname?

4. What was the nickname of Joe Harris, the flamboyant Philadelphia fighter?

5. What was Philly fighter Bobby Watts' nickname?

6. What was Willie Monroe's nickname?

7. What was Stanley Hayward's nickname?

8. What is Bernard Hopkins' nickname?

TRAINERS, PROMOTERS & VENUE QUESTIONS

Answers on page 373

1. Perhaps the most famous gym in Philadelphia Boxing history was located in Strawberry Mansion. Can you name it?

2. Where was The Cambria Athletic Club, a venerable Philly boxing venue, located?

3. The National Athletic Club, sight of many early fights, was located where in Philadelphia?

4. What historic venue located in North Philly still holds fights to this day?

5. What is the address of the Blue Horizon?

6. What was the name of promoter Max Hoff's memorable promotion at the old Philadelphia Arena?

7. What was Hoff's repetitive nickname, one which he shared with a Hanna-Barbera cartoon character?

8. Which legendary Philadelphia promoter held that card, 41 years after promoting his first fight at the same venue in 1907?

9. This Philly-born Boxing Hall of Famer was in Muhammad Ali's corner for years, and also tutored the likes of Ray Leonard, Pinklon Thomas, and Michael Nunn.

10. This Philly promoting legend started biweekly boxing at the Blue Horizon in 1969.

11. What was the first main event this legend ever promoted there?

MISCELLANEOUS TRIVIA

MISCELLANEOUS PHILLY SPORTS TRIVIA

Answers on page 374

1. Name the two Philadelphia entries into the World Football League and the USFL.

2. The Philadelphia Wings of the National Lacrosse League have won the most championships of any professional sports team in the city. How many have they won since entering indoor pro lacrosse in 1987?

3. Which long-time punter, who played with the Eagles for several seasons late in his career, played for the Philadelphia USFL franchise?

4. How many titles did the USFL franchise win while playing in Philadelphia?

5. Which former Winter Olympic Speed Skating Champion won the first ever USPRO Cycling event in Philadelphia in 1985?

6. Name the two North American Soccer League teams that called Philadelphia home.

7. Roller Hockey International placed a franchise in Philadelphia in 1994 and 1995. What was the team's nickname?

8. This NFL quarterback who played with the Oakland Raiders graduated with the St. Joseph's Prep class of 1983.

9. What was the original name of the Philadelphia Eagles before the NFL consolidated in the early 1930's?

10. Name the Havertown, PA swimmer who has taken home multiple medals from both the Athens and Beijing Summer Games.

11. Members of the progressive rock group Yes and million-selling artist Peter Frampton had part ownership of this former North American Soccer League team in Philadelphia.

12. For which USBL team did Arthur "Yah" Davis of the 1997 St. Joseph's Hawks NCAA Tournament team play for?

13. Which now-defunct restaurant chain once sponsored Flyers pocket schedules in the 1970's?

14. Name the head coach of the Philadelphia/Baltimore franchise for all three years it played in the USFL.

15. Where did the Philadelphia Charge play their home games?

16. What is the name of the famous crew competition involving colleges and universities called?

17. Who did Mike Tyson fight in Philadelphia at the Spectrum?

18. Name the twin brothers, graduates of Syracuse University, who played for the Wings for a brief period in the early 1990's.

19. The Philadelphia Soul played their first-ever Arena Football League home game against this team.

20. What expansion team of the late 1980's did former Sixer great Billy Cunningham help get off the ground?

Answers on page 375

1. Which small, religiously-affiliated suburban Philadelphia college won three women's basketball titles in the 1970's?

2. Who were the two college teams that squared off in the 1992 NCAA East Regional Final at the Spectrum?

3. What Ivy League school did Eagles tight end of the 1980's John Spagnola attend?

4. How many National Championships has Joe Paterno won as Head Coach of Penn State?

5. Who was the star running back for Temple in 1986?

6. In the 1996 NCAA Tournament, who was the Princeton Tigers center that made the backdoor bounce-pass leading to the winning basket that finally gave the school a tournament victory (Hint: he also played at Penn Charter, almost made the 76ers squad one season, and later played for the Chicago Bulls)?

7. What starting senior forward led Villanova to the Elite Eight in 1988 (not Rodney Taylor)?

8. Who did St. Joseph's lose to in the Elite Eight of the 2004 NCAA Tournament?

9. What player with a Philadelphia basketball connection sank the game-winning shot in that heartbreaking contest?

10. What Temple football coach resigned during the 1996 season, only to take back his resignation, but who was out of a job at the end of 1997 anyway?

231

11. What Penn State running back was drafted in the first round by the Chicago Bears during the 1990's?

12. What college did Temple men's head baseketball coach Fran Dunphy attend?

13. Before John Chaney became head coach of the Temple Owls, he was the head coach at this small university located in the western part of Delaware County.

14. Before Villanova won the 1985 NCAA Tournament, they went to the Final Four on one prior occasion, finishing second to this powerhouse college team in the 1971title game.

15. Prior to officially relocating from Philadelphia to Memphis, the Liberty Bowl was played one time only at this South Jersey venue.

16. What was St. Joseph's record at the end of the 2003-2004 regular season?

17. Name the successful Penn Quaker football coach of the early 1980's, who fared much worse as head coach of Temple in the late 1980's and early 90's.

18. Which school did the Delaware Blue Hens defeat in the 2003 Division I-AA football championship game?

19. What team did Temple surprise and defeat for their last-ever Big East football conference victory?

20. Name the NCAA men's basketball champion the last two times the Final Four was held in Philadelphia.

21. Temple University men's basketball played against Bowling Green on December 28, 2009 in their old arena, named this.

22. St. Joseph's home court morphed from Alumni Memorial Field House into this impressive new venue for the 2009-10 season.

MISCELLANEOUS HIGH SCHOOL SPORTS TRIVIA

Answers on page 376

1. The Philadelphia Catholic League produced two players on the 2004-2005 New York Jets roster. Who were they and what schools did they attend?

2. Name the Philadelphia high school where Rasheed Wallace played.

3. Wilt Chamberlain starred for what Philadelphia high school in the 1950's?

4. From which high school did Hall-of-Fame power hitter Reggie Jackson graduate?

5. Where did Lakers star Kobe Bryant attend high school?

6. What two Philadelphia Catholic League schools has Speedy Morris coached, sandwiching almost two decades at LaSalle University?

7. What two Philadelphia high-school stars went West to play for Paul Westhead's high-scoring Loyola Marymount squad?

8. What high school did ex-Colts wide receiver Marvin Harrison attend?

9. Star of the Fox series "Bones," and son of weatherman Dave Roberts, David Boreanaz played football for this Delaware Valley school. Which plays in the Inter-AC League.

10. DaJuan Wagner, who saw his professional career grind to a halt due to ulcerative colitis, once lit up the court for this South Jersey school.

233

REALLY RANDOM TRIVIA

Answers on page 376

1. What was the original name of John F. Kennedy Stadium when it was completed in 1926?

2. What former Philadelphia athlete was Angelo Cataldi's first on-air partner at WIP?

3. The East River Drive was re-christened Kelly Drive after Jack Kelly, whose family was heavily involved in what sport?

4. What was the name of Smarty Jones' trainer?

5. What was the phrase that Angelo Cataldi made famous with his efforts to lead Eagles fans to pressure team management into signing Herschel Walker prior to the 1992 season?

6. What radio station became Philadelphia's first 24/7 FM sports station when it launched on September 5, 2008?

7. Besides Gene Hart and Jim Jackson, name four other broadcasters who assumed play-by-play duties for the Flyers over the last 42 seasons.

8. What Desperate Housewives actress jumped into Terrell Owens' arms in an ABC promo prior to the Eagles-Cowboys Monday Night Football game in 2004?

9. What PRISM announcer, who called Sixers and Flyers games in the 1980s and who also hosted "Sports Scrapbook," died of cancer in the late 1980s?

10. What horse defeated Smarty Jones to deny him the Triple Crown?

11. Name the two pieces of sports uniforms that were placed on the William Penn statue during Ed Rendell's term as Mayor.

12. In a late 1990's Atlantic 10 basketball contest, the famed St. Joseph's Hawk mixed it up on the court with this other A-10 school mascot.

13. During the rain-soaked first part of Game 5 of the 2008 World Series, what accessory was added to several caps of Phillies and Rays players to keep warm and keep the water away?

14. What nickname was given to Philadelphia's MLS expansion club?

15. What suggestive moniker was applied to Philadelphia's entry into the Lingerie Football League?

16. What creative solution did the city employ to keep rowdy Phillies fans from climbing up light poles in Center City during the 2009 playoff run?

17. Before settling on its current location, which neighborhood near Center City was considered the front-runner to house the new Phillies stadium?

18. Now playing for the Sacramento Kings, 2010 NBA Rookie of the Year Tyreke Evans is a native of this Delaware County, PA town.

19. What were the outfield dimensions (in feet) of Veterans Stadium's baseball configuration?

20. What piece of equipment, located inside the right-field foul pole, did an Alex Rodriguez home run strike during Game 3 of the 2009 World Series?

21. After 13 seasons in Philadelphia, the Phantoms moved to this upstate New York location, which once hosted a Detroit Red Wings minor-league team.

22. During a July 25, 2009 game between the Phillies and St. Louis Cardinals, an unknown fan disrupted play when he used one of these to distract batters and fielders.

23. When the Flyers and Penguins played in Philadelphia early in the 2009-10 season, Philly forward Scott Hartnell allegedly did this to Penguins defenseman Kris Letang during a scrum late in the contest.

Philadelphia

Hall of Fame

THE PHILADELPHIA
SPORTS HALL OF FAME

The Philadelphia Sports Hall of Fame was founded in May 2002. A Pennsylvania 501(c)(3) nonprofit corporation, its mission, in brief, is to preserve and promote the rich history of Philadelphia sports with the ultimate goal of a museum in the city to honor our sports history.

Philadelphia boasts an amazing sports history, dating to the mid-1800's. The story of sports in Philadelphia is a tapestry of people, places, legends and lore. It includes true icons from Connie Mack to Wilt Chamberlain, Steve Van Buren to Joe Frazier, Bill Tilden to Julius Erving. Legendary venues include Baker Bowl and the Palestra, Shibe Park and Boathouse Row, Merion Country Club and Franklin Field. Historic teams such as the 1929 Athletics, the 1960 Eagles, the 1967 Sixers and the Broad Street Bullies dot this history along with landmark events and traditions such as Dempsey-Tunney I, Bobby Jones' Grand Slam at Merion Country Club, the Dad Vail Regatta, the Army-Navy Game, the Big 5 and the Penn Relays.

Until the Philadelphia Sports Hall of Fame was established almost a decade ago, there had been no central organization to preserve and promote this outstanding legacy.

The Philadelphia Sports Hall of Fame's multi-faceted mission extends well beyond honoring the region's sports history.

Using the common bond of sports to help fund its community programs, the foundation helps area youth in numerous of ways. These community programs directly influence the lives of young people in the area. At this grass roots level, local youth are exposed to, and educated about, the tremendous history of sports in Philadelphia. With the fervor of the Philadelphia fan base, this broad-based, mass appeal is the prime directive behind all of the Hall of Fame's programs and initiatives. From youngsters at a Hall of Fame sponsored camp to grandparents reliving their fondest memories at an interactive exhibit, the Philadelphia Sports Hall of Fame, with its multi-generational appeal, is unlike any organization in the area.

The Philadelphia Sports Hall of Fame recognizes the Philadelphia sports fan as its core audience. This robust fan base, combined with key organizational and institutional support, forms the essence of the Foundation's mission. The duality of this approach forms the basis of all Hall of Fame initiatives.

Mission Statement

The Philadelphia Sports Hall of Fame is a not-for-profit association dedicated to honoring those individuals, teams, events, organizations and venues prominent in the history of athletics in Philadelphia and the surrounding area. The Hall recognizes the timeless intertwining of sport into the fabric of everyday life. With this as a credo The Philadelphia Hall of Fame is devoted to honoring those persons, places, organizations and events that have made outstanding contributions through inspiring achievement in both professional and amateur sports while forever enriching the memories fans.
As its mission, the Hall is committed to:

- Through enshrinement, honoring, those individuals who had exceptional careers as participants, coaches, mangers, owners and supporters.

- Memorializing athletic venues of historical import.

- Honoring organizations prominent in the Philadelphia area for contributions to professional or amateur sports.

- Identifying those long-standing establishments that have served to enhance the sporting experience for fans.

- Commemorating defining moments in the history of Philadelphia sport.

- Acquisition, primarily through donation and bequest, of artifacts, memorabilia, works of art, literature, photographs and related materials that focus on the history of sport in Philadelphia and the surrounding area.

- Public edification by establishing a permanent Hall of Fame and Museum in the Delaware Valley.

- Promoting education and training through scholarships, grants and internships to student athletes in the Philadelphia area.

- Establishing Youth Sports and academies in Philadelphia and the surrounding area.

How The Philadelphia Sports Hall of Fame Came About

While sipping a morning coffee while paging through The Philadelphia Inquirer sports section on Friday, May 17, 2002, Ken Avallon looked for his normal fix of Morning Bytes, the often-irreverent musings and observations of Frank Fitzpatrick. As usual, Fitzpatrick's weekly witticisms were rather inclusive with references to Philadelphia's mostly moribund sporting past, over-priced stadium beer, boorish fans, the Flyers and the WWF.

To Ken, however, the final segment was much more than the softly sarcastic observations customary to Morning Bytes. One sentence from Fitzpatrick cut to the heart of what Ken and others have turned into a passion: "Why not a Philadelphia Sports Hall of Fame?"

Fitzpatrick probably never realized the effect these words would have. However, from this brief article, the Philadelphia Sports Hall of Fame was born. Registered as a Pennsylvania nonprofit corporation a few days later, the organization spent the following year in its due-diligence phase, out of the public eye, slowly building its foundation.

This included recruiting like-minded individuals, drafting a constitution and bylaws, establishing federal 501(c)(3) nonprofit status, and developing concepts for community programs. Other steps included membership in relevant organizations such as the Greater Philadelphia Chamber of Commerce, Pennsylvania Association of Nonprofit Organizations, the Maxwell Club and the Mid-Atlantic Association of Museums.

Throughout this time local sportswriters, announcers, broadcasters, athletic directors, authors, coaches and athletes were recruited for the Advisory Panel or simply as support advocates. This group was instrumental in the early going, providing much-needed support and publicity beginning in June 2003. In addition, they were pivotal in lending credibility to the Foundation as they were instrumental in the process of selecting the Charter Class. Though somewhat lost in the bright lights of the opening of a new football stadium, the announcement of the Charter Class garnered a terrific response from the public when announced in September 2003.

The culmination of those first steps was the Charter Class Induction Ceremony, February 9, 2004, kicked off by Governor Ed Rendell, emceed by Pat Williams and attended by new Inductees Chuck Bednarik, Robin Roberts, Steve Van Buren, Joe Frazier, Harry Kalas, Sonny Hill and the late Paul Arizin along with relatives of Wilt Chamberlain, Connie Mack, Richie Ashburn, Jimmie Foxx, Bert Bell and Bill Tilden.

Since 2004, thousands have attended the subsequent inductions with a few notable past attendees including Charles Barkley, Pat Summerall, Tommy Lasorda, Andy Reid, Bernie Parent, Earl Monroe, Vince Papale and Jack Whitaker.

The national reach of the Hall participation from the Pro Football Hall of Fame, NFL Players Association, Green Bay Packers, New

York Giants, Cleveland Browns, Los Angeles Dodgers, New York Knicks, Washington Wizards, Tampa Bay Lightning, University of Tennessee, Penn State University, University of North Carolina, Univeristy of Colorado, Boston University and the University of Illinois.

Paul Arizin - Basketball

In the early days of the NBA a handful of pioneering players laid the groundwork for what would become "modern" basketball. What Ty Cobb, Babe Ruth, and Cy Young were to baseball, these early hoopsters were to the game of basketball. One such player was Paul Arizin. Playing in an era of old-fashioned two-handed set shots and slow-up offenses, Arizin burst into the league in 1950 with a repertoire that included a daring new weapon: the jump shot. By the time Arizin was leading the league in scoring as a second-year player with the Philadelphia Warriors in 1952, only a few other players had mastered the shot.

Richie Ashburn - Baseball

Richie Ashburn was a durable, hustling lead-off hitter and clutch performer with superb knowledge of the strike zone. A fan favorite, "Whitey" batted .308 with nine .300-plus seasons and 2,574 hits in 15 years, winning batting championships in 1955 and 1958. A core player for the 1950 Whiz Kids, the center fielder established major league records for most times leading the league in chances (nine), most years with 500 or more putouts (four) and most seasons with 400 or more putouts (nine). Ashburn spent 35 years broadcasting Phillies games after his playing days, many of them with legendary broadcaster Harry Kalas."

Chuck Bednarik - Football

A two-time All-America at the University of Pennsylvania Chuck Bednarik went on to become the NFL's last "Ironman" as a center and linebacker. A rugged, bulldozing blocker and bone-jarring tackler he missed only three games in 14 NFL seasons. Bednarik was All-NFL seven times and played in eight Pro Bowls, taking the MVP award in the 1954 game. He played 58 minutes and made the game-saving tackle in the 1960 NFL Championship game. "Concrete Charlie" was elected to the Pro Football Hall of Fame in 1967 and named the NFL's all-time center in 1969.

Bert Bell - Football

One of the founders of the National Football League, Bert Bell owned the Eagles from 1933-1940. A graduate of the University of Pennsylvania, he built the NFL's image to unprecedented heights as league commissioner from 1946 to 1959. Bell set up far-sighted television policies, established the NFL draft, implemented strong anti-gambling controls and was first to recognize the NFL Players Association.

Steve Carlton - Baseball

Steve Carlton was an extremely focused competitor with complete dedication to excellence. He thrived on the mound by physically and mentally challenging himself off the field. His out-pitch, a hard, biting slider complemented a great fastball. He won 329 games second only to Warren Spahn among lefties and his 4,136 strikeouts are exceeded only by Nolan Ryan. "Lefty" once notched 19 strikeouts in a game, compiled six 20-win seasons, and was the first pitcher to win four Cy Young Awards.

Wilt Chamberlain - Basketball

He was basketball's unstoppable force, the most awesome offensive force the game has ever seen. Asked to name the greatest players ever to play basketball, most fans and aficionados would put Wilt Chamberlain at or near the top of the list. Dominating the game as few players in any sport ever have, Chamberlain seemed capable of scoring and rebounding at will, despite the double- and triple-teams and constant fouling tactics that opposing teams used to try to shut him down. As Oscar Robertson put it in the Philadelphia Daily News when asked whether Chamberlain was the best ever, "The books don't lie."

Bobby Clarke - Hockey

Bobby Clarke was one of the most hard-nosed competitors to ever play professional ice hockey. As Captain of the Philadelphia Flyers, Clarke centered his "The Broad Street Bullies" to 2 Stanley Cup Championships while securing numerous individual awards, including 2 First Team NHL All-Star berths, 2 Second Team NHL All-Star berths, and 3 Hart Trophies during the early to mid '70s. His leadership, both on and off the ice, helped provide a winning attitude that clearly spread throughout the entire organization. After retiring from playing, Clarke was named General Manager of the Flyers and later worked as General Manager and Vice President of both the Minnesota North Stars and the Florida Panthers. In 1994 Clarke returned to Philadelphia to serve as President and General Manager of the organization.

Billy Cunningham - Basketball

Billy Cunningham played fiercely, coached intensely, and won frequently. And he made it to the Naismith Memorial Basketball Hall of Fame with a career that reads like a how-to book for legends. As a player and then a coach for the Philadelphia 76ers, he was part of two NBA championship teams. Among his numerous career achievements, he was named to the 1966 NBA All-Rookie Team and three All-NBA First Teams. In 1996, he was named to the NBA 50th Anniversary All-Time Team.

Julius Erving - Basketball

Julius Erving, the great and wondrous "Dr. J," was the dominant player of his era, an innovator who changed the way the game was played. He was a wizard with the ball, performing feats never before seen: midair spins and whirls punctuated by powerful slam-dunks. Erving was one of the first players to make extemporaneous individual expression an integral part of the game, setting the style of play that would prevail in the decades to follow. A gracious, dignified, and disciplined man, Erving was the epitome of class and an ideal ambassador for the game.

Jimmie Foxx - Baseball

A fearsome power hitter whose strength earned him the moniker "The Beast," Jimmie Foxx was the anchor of an intimidating Philadelphia Athletics lineup that produced pennant winners from 1929 to 1931. The second batter in history to top 500 home runs, Foxx belted 30 or more homers in a record 12 consecutive seasons and drove in more than 100 runs 13 consecutive years, including a career-best 175 with Boston in 1938. He won back-to-back MVP awards in 1932 and 1933, capturing the Triple Crown the latter year.

Joe Frazier - Boxing

Joe Frazier won the gold medal in the 1964 Olympics as a heavyweight. "Smokin' Joe" was world heavyweight champion from 1970-73. One of the most exciting fighters ever, Frazier fought Muhammad in the "Fight of the Century" on March 8, 1971, the first time in history that two undefeated champions fought for the same title. Frazier sealed the victory with a knockdown in the 15th round and went on to win the decision. Frazier retired with a record of 32 wins, 4 losses and 1 draw, with 27 knockouts. In retirement Frazier continues to train fighters at his gym on Broad Street.

Tom Gola - Basketball

A multi-talented player, Tom Gola starred at LaSalle High and then LaSalle College. In his freshman year, LaSalle won the 1951 National Invitation Tournament with Gola sharing the tournament's MVP award with teammate Norm Grekin. A consensus All-American the next three seasons, Gola was named tournament MVP when LaSalle won the 1954 NCAA championship. The 6-foot-6, 220-pound Gola played all three positions at LaSalle, averaging 20.9 points and 18.7 rebounds a game during his four years as a starter and is still the NCAA's all-time leading rebounder. In 1955, Gola joined the Philadelphia Warriors of the NBA and averaged 10.8 points a game as the Warriors won the league championship. The Warriors moved to San Francisco in 1962 and Gola was traded to the New York Knicks. Gola coached LaSalle to a 23-1 record in 1968-69, when the team was ranked second in the nation.

Jack Kelly, Sr. - Rowing

Jack Kelly was one of America's most renowned rowers, winning three Olympic gold medals but legendarily never rowing at Henley, which is attributed by some to an unlikely claim that he was not an amateur, and by others to the more logical reason of his club Vesper's having a disagreement with Henley. He won two of his three Olympic gold medals 30 minutes apart in 1920, first rowing Brit Jack Beresford to a virtual standstill and a 1-foot verdict in the single sculls, then jumping into the double and doing it all over again.

Connie Mack - Baseball

Connie Mack was once a catcher, but made his mark as a manager. After a stint at the helm of Pittsburgh, he assumed control of the Philadelphia Athletics in 1901 and continued for 50 years until retirement at the age of 88. "The Tall Tactician," best remembered as a dignified, scorecard-waving leader in a business suit, won five World Series crowns and built two dynasties — with four pennants in five years from 1910 to 1914 and three in a row from 1929 to 1931. He holds the mark for most wins (3,776) by a skipper.

Bernie Parent - Hockey

Bernie Parent was the clutch netminder on the Philadelphia Flyers' championship teams in the 1970's. As part of the Flyers' Broad Street Bullies, Parent and his teammates won the Stanley Cup twice in a row, in 1974 and 1975. In both seasons, Parent won the Vezina Trophy as best goalie and the Conn Smythe Trophy as playoff MVP. Parent retired in 1979 and was inducted into the NHL Hall of Fame in 1984.

Robin Roberts - Baseball

Robin Roberts was the ace of the Phillies' staff for most of his brilliant 19-year career. The durable workhorse with a great fastball and pinpoint control won 286 games and compiled six consecutive 20-victory seasons. In 1950, he paced the "Whiz Kids" Phils to their first flag in 35 years with a 20-11 record. A tough competitor, he was a frequent league leader in victories, innings pitched, complete games, shutouts and strikeouts, leading the National League in wins from 1952 to 1955.

Mike Schmidt - Baseball

An unprecedented combination of power and defense made Mike Schmidt one of the game's greatest third basemen. The powerful right-handed hitter slugged 548 home runs, belting 40 or more long balls in three separate seasons and hitting over 30 home runs 10 other times. His 48 homers in 1980 are the most ever in a single season by a third baseman. A three-time National League MVP, he was a 12-time All-Star and won 10 Gold Gloves. Schmidt was named the "Sporting News" Player of the Decade for the 1980s.

Bill Tilden - Tennis

Also known as Big Bill and Gentleman Bill Tilden he was born into a wealthy Philadelphia family and developed late, winning his first major title at Wimbledon in 1920 at the age of 27. He was the first American to win at Wimbledon, and during the 1920s he remained undefeated in any major match for seven years. His ten victories in national men's singles (three at Wimbledon and seven in the US) during 1920 to 1930 set a record until Roy Emerson achieved twelve victories during 1961 to 1967. Bill Tilde's writing in The Art of Tennis is still regarded as authoritative. Tilden was voted the most outstanding athlete of the first half of the twentieth century by the National Sports Writers Association, with ten times the number of votes of the nearest runner-up.

Steve Van Buren - Football

Steve Van Buren was the Eagles No.1 draft pick in 1944. Providing the Eagles with a battering-ram punch, Van Buren won the NFL rushing title four times. He lead the Eagles to consecutive league titles in 1948 and 1949, scoring the only TD 1948 title game and rushing for a then-record 196 yards in the 1949 championship. Van Buren retired as the all-time rushing leader with a career mark of 5860 yards rushing along with 464 points scored. The "Moving Van" was elected to the Pro Football Hall of Fame in 1965.

For integrity, character and exemplary service to the community through sports-related activities. To qualify, individuals must meet any or all of the following qualifications:

- Dedication, leadership and support in advancing community spirit and enhancing the quality of life in the Philadelphia area.

- Longtime history of training, motivating, and inspiring youth in their communities.

- Significant contributions of a lasting nature to promote and develop community programs or events on the local, state or national level.

Sonny Hill - Lifetime Commitment

William R. "Sonny" Hill has been referred to as the "Mayor of Basketball" in Philadelphia. Sonny's influence goes beyond the basketball court having co-founded the Baker League for professionals and the Sonny Hill League for youth as an alternative to the challenges of the street. The Baker League is the oldest and most prestigious professional league in the country and the Sonny Hill League has done more to battle the perils of gangs and drugs and promote life skills than any other program in the city. Sonny was a player, coach, and owner of various teams; he was a color analyst for CBS sports and the Philadelphia 76ers; was featured in the NFL film, "Ten Feet in the Air", and has been honored with over 25 civic awards including Man of the Year.

For outstanding, long-term achievement in contributory, supportive or complementary activities. To qualify, individuals must meet any or all of the following qualifications:

- Broadcaster, announcer or media member.

- Administrator or contributor at the team, collegiate or league level.

- Significant contributions of a lasting nature that enhance the sporting experience for fans.

Harry Kalas - Legacy of Excellence

A native of Naperville, Illinois, Kalas graduated from the University of Iowa in 1959 with a Bachelor of Arts degree in Speech, Radio, and Television. An original member of the Astros broadcast team in 1965, he called games for Houston until 1970. He moved to the Phillies broadcast booth in 1971, where he shared the microphone with Hall of Fame outfielder Richie Ashburn for 26 seasons. Kalas was honored as Pennsylvania Sportscaster of the Year 17 times. He also broadcasted Big Five basketball and Notre Dame football. Kalas, revered for his uncanny ability to connect with his listeners, whether on radio or television, called more than 5,000 Phillies games.

Grover Cleveland Alexander - Baseball

- At retirement, held the #1 Phillies rankings in wins, ERA, strikeouts, games pitched, innings pitched, shutouts, complete games, and winning percentage
- 190-91 won-lost record with the Phillies
- Won 30 or more games three consecutive years (1915-1917)
- Won Pitching Triple Crown in 1915 and 1916 (led the National League in wins, ERA and strikeouts)
- Led the National League in innings pitched seven times in strikeouts, complete games, wins and shutouts five times; and in ERA twice
- Had at least 23 complete games seven years in a row and over 30 complete games in a year five times
- Pitched over 300 innings seven straight seasons and over 350 innings in a year five times
- Lifetime ERA of 2.18 with the Phillies
- Pitched two complete games in the 1915 World Series, going 1-1 with a 1.53 ERA
- Voted to the Baseball Hall of Fame

Eddie Gottlieb - Basketball Pioneer, Owner, Philadelphia Stars, Negro League Baseball

- Highly acclaimed innovator and promoter of the game known as "The Mogul" of basketball
- In 1918, organized and coached a team representing the South Philadelphia Hebrew Association. Known as the SPHAS, Gottlieb's team played 75 to 80 games annually. As part of a special series during the 1925-26 season, the SPHAS defeated both the Original Celtics and the New York Rens
- The SPHAS won 11 championships from the late 1920s to early 1940s, dominating the Eastern and American Leagues
- In 1946, helped establish the Basketball Association of America
- As owner, general manager, coach and chief ticket seller of one of the BAA's original teams, the Philadelphia Warriors, Gottlieb's club captured the league's first championship in 1946-1947
- Very instrumental in the merging of the BAA with the National Basketball League to form the NBA
- Helped organize overseas Harlem Globetrotters tours
- Served as a chairman of the NBA Rules Committee for 25 years
- The trophy named in his honor is awarded annually to the NBA's Rookie of the Year
- Voted to the South Philadelphia High School Sports Hall of Fame, Pennsylvania Sports Hall of Fame, Philadelphia Jewish Sports Hall of Fame and Basketball Hall of Fame
- A successful NBA coach, schedule maker, owner, and a great promoter of honor and integrity, Gottlieb truly was, as former NBA Commissioner Larry O'Brien termed him, "Mr. Basketball"
- Owner of the Negro League Baseball Philadelphia Stars

Lefty Grove - Baseball

- Had 20 or more wins seven consecutive years (1927-1933)
- Led the American League in ERA nine times
- Fourth all-time career winning percentage of .680
- Career ERA of 3.06
- Considered the backbone of the Philadelphia A's dynasty (1929-1931) when he won 79 games
- In 1931 went 31-4 with a 2.06 ERA
- 300-141 career record along with 112 victories in the minors
- Voted to the Baseball Hall of Fame

Pete Pihos - Football

- Fifth-round draft pick (1945)
- 60-minute star on Eagles 1948-1949 title teams, and caught the winning touchdown pass in the 1949 NFL championship
- All-NFL six times in nine seasons including once at defensive end (1952)
- Played in six Pro Bowls
- NFL receiving champ for three consecutive years, 1953-1955
- 373 catches for 5,619 yards, and 378 points scored
- Voted to the Football Hall of Fame

Vic Siexas - Tennis

- Played the US Championships at Forest Hills a record 28 times between 1940 and 1969, winning the singles in 1954 over Rex Hartwig
- Played more Davis Cup matches than any other American until John McEnroe, winning 38 of 55 singles and doubles encounters during his seven years on the team (1951-1957)
- Ranked in the US Top Ten 13 times between 1942-1966, setting an American longevity record of a 24 year span between his first and last entries (later equaled by Pancho Gonzalez, 1948-72)
- In 1953, won the Wimbledon singles title and led the US to the Davis Cup Final
- Won 15 major titles in singles, doubles and mixed, setting a Wimbledon record by winning the mixed four successive years (1953-1955 with Doris Hart, 1956 with Shirley Fry)
- Among his 13 US titles were the Clay Court singles (1953, 1957), the Hard Court doubles (1948), and the Indoor doubles (1955), making Seixas one of the few towin national titles on all four surfaces
- Voted to the International Tennis Hall of Fame

Joe Verdeur - Swimming

- 1948 Olympic Gold medalist
- From 1940-1950 set 19 world records, 21 American records, and participated in the world record medley and freestyle relay teams
- Won 20 AAU National Individual championships, four NCAA National Individual championships, and was part of the AAU national championship team in 1944
- AAU National Individual Medley champion eight consecutive years (1943-1950)
- Renown sportswriter Grantland Rice called Verdeur "the greatest swimmer of the first half of the century"
- Charter member of LaSalle's Hall of Athletes
- Voted to the International Swimming Hall of Fame

Charles Barkley – Basketball

- 76ers first round draft pick in 1984 (5thoverall)
- Played for 76ers 1984-1992
- Voted 1993 NBA MVP
- All-NBA First Team 1988-1991, 1993
- All-NBA Second Team 1986, 1987, 1992, 1994, 1995
- All-NBA Third Team 1996
- 11-time All-Star
- 1991 All-Star Game MVP
- Voted one of 50 Greatest Players in NBA History
- Leading scorer on Olympic Gold Medal winning 1992 "Dream Team" and 1996 Olympic Team
- One of only four players in NBA history to compile 20,000 (23,757) points, 10,000 (12,546) rebounds and 4,000 (4,215) assists
- 13th on all-time NBA scoring list

John Chaney - Basketball

- Philadelphia native played basketball at Benjamin Franklin High School (1948-1951) and was 1951 Philadelphia Public League MVP
- Played in Eastern Professional Basketball League for ten years, twice named MVP
- Coached at Cheney State College for ten years (1972-1982), guiding them to the NCAA Division II Championship in1978, when he was voted Coach of the Year
- Started at Temple in 1982 and made 17 NCAA Tournament appearances including 5 regional finals in (1988, 1991, 1993, 1999, 2001)
- Won eight Atlantic 10 regular season titles and six Atlantic 10 Tournament Championships
- Won or shared thirteen Philadelphia Big 5 Championships
- All time winningest coach at Temple University, compiling 15 20-win seasons (ranking fifth all time in most 20-win seasons)
- Voted 1987 and 1988 USBWA National Coach of the Year
- 1988 Consensus National Coach of the Year, Associated Press Coach of the Year, United Press International Coach of the Year, CNN/USA Today Coach of the Year, Kodak-NABC Coach of the Year, Chevrolet Coach of the Year, and Black Coaches Association Coach of the Year
- Won his 700th game in January 2004 to become the fourth active coach with 700 wins
- Elected to the Basketball Hall of Fame in 2001

James "Jumbo" Elliott - Track & Field

- Spent his early track and field career competing for Villanova in the 220, the 440 and the 880 yard events
- Took over as the team's part time coach after graduation, splitting time between track and selling contracting equipment
- During his tenure as head coach Villanova won eight national titles, three National AAU championships and 39 IC4A indoor, outdoor, and cross country championships
- Athletes he coached won 316 IC4A titles, 82 NCAA crowns, 62 National AAU championships, set 22 outdoor world records, 44 outdoor world records, and won five Olympic Gold medals
- Voted to The National Track and Field Hall of Fame

Guy Rodgers - Basketball

- Philadelphia native led Temple to three third place finishes in postseason play
- Drafted with the first pick by the Philadelphia Warriors in 1958
- Led the NBA in assists twice as play maker and set-up man for NBA greats Wilt Chamberlain and Kareem Abdul-Jabbar
- Recorded 20 assists in Chamberlain's 100-point game in 1962
- Holds the Warriors record for career assists with 4,855
- Four time NBA All Star
- In 24 career playoff games with the Warriors, averaged 14.1 points, 6.1 assists and 40.8 minutes played
- Scored 10,415 career points and recorded 6,917 career assists
- Averaged 11.7 points, 7.8 assists and 4.3 rebounds per game in 12 pro seasons
- Widely considered one of the greatest players not yet voted to the Basketball Hall of Fame

Tommy McDonald - Football

- Won the Maxwell Award in 1956 as college football's Player of the Year
- Six-time Pro Bowl selection (1959-1963,1966)
- Recorded 56 touchdown receptions in 63 games from 1958-1962
- Scored a 35-yard touchdown the 1960 NFL Championship Game
- Led the NFL in receiving yards (1,144) and touchdowns (13) in 1961
- Set Eagles record with seven catches for 237 yards in 1961
- Totaled 495 receptions for 8,410 yards and 84 touchdowns
- Averaged 17 yards per reception during his career
- Inducted as a member of the Eagles Honor Roll in 1987
- Elected to the Football Hall of Fame in 1998

Carl Lewis - Track & Field

- US Amateur Athlete of the Year 1981
- 11½ year winning streak that spanned 65 straight long jump competitions.
- World Athlete of the Year 1982, 1983, 1984
- World Athlete of the Decade 1980's
- Won four Gold medals at 1984 Olympics in Los Angeles (100m, 200m, long jump and 4x100m relay)
- Won two Gold medals and a Silver medal at the 1988 Olympics in Seoul
- In 1991 set a new world record in the 100 meters
- Won two Gold medals at 1992 Olympics in Barcelona, anchoring the US team to a world record of 37.40 seconds that still stands
- Won a Gold medal in long jump at the 1996 Olympics in Atlanta

Cathy Rush - Basketball

- As head coach, Immaculata College won three consecutive National AIAW Champion ships (1972-1974), finished second twice and won five Eastern AIAW Championships
- Voted Coach of the Year in 1973 and 1974
- Career coaching record of 149 wins and 15 losses for an astounding 91% winning percentage
- Coached the US Women's basketball team to the gold medal at the 1975 Pan American Games
- Widely acknowledged for her role in bringing national atten tion and scholarship money to women's sports
- Started Future Stars Camps to help girls in sports and encour age scholarship opportunities
- Received the United States Basketball Writers Association (USBWA) Pioneer Award in 1994
- Voted to the Pennsylvania Sports Hall of Fame
- Voted to the Women's Basketball Hall of Fame
- One of only six "outsiders" inducted into the Philadelphia Big 5 Hall of Fame

Jay Sigel - Golf

- Two-time US Amateur Champion (1982,1983)
- British Amateur Champion (1979)
- Other amateur victories include the US Mid-Amateur (1983, 1985, 1987), Sunnehanna Amateur (1976, 1978,1988), and Northeastern Amateur (1984, 1985, 1991)
- Won the prestigious Porter Cup Championship three times (1975, 1981, 1987)
- Dominant in Philadelphia area, winning three Philadelphia Amateurs, six Philadelphia Opens and five Patterson Cups
- Nine straight Walker Cups (1977-1993) including serving as captain twice (1983, 1985)
- Eight victories on the Senior Tour after turning pro in 1993
- Winner of the Bob Jones Award, the Ben Hogan Award and the Dunlop Award
- President of the Greater Philadelphia Scholastic Golf Association and President of the First Tee, Philadelphia Chapter.
- Voted "Most Courageous Athlete" by the Philadelphia Sportswriters Association in 2000
- Named 2002 "Comeback Player of the Year" by GOLF World Magazine.

Harvey Pollack - Legacy of Excellence

Since the inception of the NBA in 1946, Pollack's involvement in nearly all facets of the game have stationed him in prime position to witness, record, and recount a myriad of unforgettable moments in basketball history. Pollack currently serves as the Director of Statistical Information for the Philadelphia 76ers.

Pollack, a Northeast Philadelphia native and Temple University graduate, began his storied career in 1946 as assistant public relations director with the Philadelphia Warriors. Pollack would ultimately become director of public relations prior to the 1952-53 season and continued in that position until the franchise moved to San Francisco in 1962.

When Eddie Gottlieb purchased the Syracuse Nationals and relocated them to Philadelphia in 1963, he appointed Pollack as director of public relations for the Sixers. Over the next quarter century, Pollack would diligently perform many tasks, but nothing captivated him as much as tracking statistics.

In a league stocked with great stars such as Bill Russel and Wilt Chamberlain, Pollack fully understood the importance of accurately logging the players' feats. A true pioneer, Pollack introduced numerous new statistical categories (rebounds, blocked shots, et al) that today are considered commonplace for the entire league.

In 1988, after an unprecedented stint of 43 years in public relations, Pollack finally decided to leave that position and assume the responsibility of Director of Statistical Information.

At 80, Pollack remains active. Each year he produces his Statistical Yearbook (an annual publication he started in 1968), a book many journalists, coaches, and basketball lifers consult for a wide variety of odd facts and trivial information.

Pollack has been courtside for many memorable sports events, including four NBA titles, Chamberlain's 100-point and 55-rebound games, and has seen almost every player in NBA history. He has won the Marc Splaver Award as the NBA's top public relations person and has been honored by the NBA to mark his 25th, 30th, 40th and 50th year in the league.

Pollack is a true legend in sports and a Philadelphia product who has changed the way we look at basketball.

Bill Campbell - Legacy of Excellence

Bill Campbell, known to all sports fans as "The Dean," is a sports analyst and commentator on KYW News Radio. He began his broadcasting career in 1940 as a spot and general announcer at WFPG Radio in Atlantic City, New Jersey. The following year found him in Lancaster, Pennsylvania doing general radio announcing and covering minor league baseball over WGAL.

He joined WIP Radio in 1942 as a spot and general announcer. In 1946 Bill was named Sports Director at WCAU Radio and WCAU-TV, where he was responsible for producing and broadcasting a daily sports program and for scheduling and negotiating a full calendar of college and professional games. As sports director, he was also a play-by-play broadcaster for the Philadelphia Eagles from 1952 to 1966. In 1962 he became the play-by-play man for the Philadelphia Phillies, a position he held until 1971.

Bill was named Director of Broadcasting for the Philadelphia 76ers in 1972, a post he held until 1981. In addition to play-by-play radio and TV coverage of all 76ers games, Bill was responsible for the administration of the team's broadcasting department. This included personnel, production, announcers, sales and equipment as well as public relations and public appearances. Bill was named Broadcaster of the Year by the National Sports Broadcasters Association in 1961, 1962 and 1963 and received the Philadelphia Sportswriters Award for outstanding service in 1989. He is also a member of the Pennsylvania Sports Halls of Fame.

Bob Levy - Lifetime Commitment

Born, raised and educated in Philadelphia, Mr. Levy graduated from William Penn Charter School and the University of Pennsylvania. He first became involved in sports as a member of the Penn Charter tennis team and continued his career at the University where he played varsity tennis from 1949- 1952.

Mr. Levy was active in many charitable and civic endeavors in Philadelphia. He was an Emeritus Trustee at the University of Pennsylvania where he served actively on the board for over twenty-five years. In 1982, he was appointed chairman of the Philadelphia Sports Congress, which recruits major sporting events for Philadelphia. Under his leadership, the Sports Congress was responsible for attracting major events such as the NBA All Star Game, X Games, Army/Navy Football rivalry, NCAA Women's Final Four, Sr. PGA Championship, International Dragon Boat Races, National Figure Skating Championships, and the US Gymnastic Championships to the Philadelphia region.

In 1953, Mr. Levy founded and coached the Little Quakers, an age specific, all-star football team for boys in the Philadelphia region. The team has become one of the finest boys teams in the nation. Many Little Quakers' graduates have gone on to become successful business and professional leaders in the Philadelphia area. Mr. Levy and the Little Quakers received the John Wanamaker Lifetime Achievement Award.

In the fall of 1985, Mr. Levy served as interim coach for the women's tennis team at Penn. After his tenure as interim coach was over, he was appointed a volunteer assistant due to his popularity with the athletes involved in the program. The University won its first ever Ivy League Championship in the spring of 2001 and repeated that honor in 2002. The team had been nationally ranked over the last several years due in part to Mr. Levy's ongoing support of the women's tennis program.

Over his storied career, Mr. Levy received numerous awards from a variety of institutions. In 2003, he was awarded the John Wanamaker Lifetime

Achievement Award. Mr. Levy was the 24th recipient of the John B. Kelly Award, which is given annually to an individual "who has unselfishly contributed his time directly for the purpose of extending the future of our youth through sports." Other honors include the Philadelphia Police Athletic League's Man of the Year Award, inductee to the William Penn Charter School Sports Hall of Fame, the University of Pennsylvania Hall of Fame and Tennis Hall of Fame, the Philadelphia Jewish Sports Hall of Fame and the Police Athletic League Hall of Fame.

In addition, Pop Warner Little Scholar's Inc. honored Mr. Levy with their Gold Football Award for "distinguished service to youth in community and country." During President Reagan's term in office, Mr. Levy was appointed as a new member to the President's Council on Physical Fitness and Sports. He was also the first recipient of the Service to Youth Award from the Pennsylvania Sports Hall of Fame. Mr. Levy was presented with the Alumni Award of Merit from The University of Pennsylvania and the Penn Charter Alumni Society. He is the recipient of the Distinguished American Award from the Pennsylvania chapter of the National Football Foundation and Hall of Fame.

Ed Snider
Philadelphia Medal

The driving force behind bringing an NHL franchise to Philadelphia, Ed Snider has been a major factor in the city's sports and entertainment business for over 30 years. Snider's undying passion for winning, towering strength, and command of respect have come to symbolize the Flyers on the ice. In his 32 seasons as Flyers sovereign, the team has won two Stanley Cups and appeared in the Finals seven times.

In 1964, Snider, builder Jerry Wolman, and attorney Earl Foreman, who had married Snider's sister, bought the Philadelphia Eagles. Mr. Snider, as he is called by friend and competitor alike, owned seven percent of the team and became its treasurer.

Although he was not an avid hockey fan, Snider became intrigued by the sport while attending a Philadelphia 76ers-Boston Celtics basketball game at the Boston Garden in 1964. A crowd of Bruins fans were lined up to buy the remaining 1,000 tickets for a last-place team. Soon thereafter, he found out that the NHL was planning to expand from six to 12 teams. Snider made plans for a new arena to house a hockey team and the 76ers. He pitched the idea to the NHL and the league awarded Philadelphia a conditional franchise on February 9, 1966. On October 19, 1967, the Flyers played their first game ever at the Spectrum, defeating the Pittsburgh Penguins, 1-0, in front of a crowd of 7,812. Five years later, the Broad Street Bullies became the first expansion team to win the Stanley Cup in 1974 and repeating as champions in 1975.

Snider could not guarantee that an NHL franchise would succeed in Philadelphia, but he liked its chances. "I just had the belief that if you're a regular guy and know what regular guys like, you can't be wrong," he said.

In 1971, Snider assumed control of the Spectrum. Three years later he created Spectacor, a management company to oversee the Flyers and Spectrum. Under his leadership, Spectacor founded or acquired additional businesses, including PRISM, a regional premium cable channel, and WIP radio, which became the country's first all-sports radio station. In 1988, Spectacor began its most ambitious undertaking when Snider decided that the Flyers needed a new home to remain competitive in the NHL. It took eight years from conception to completion, but today the Wachovia Center stands as a tribute to Snider's perseverance and foresight.

Time and age have not tamed Snider's lofty aspirations. In March 1996, he gave up majority ownership of the Flyers by entering into a merger agreement with the Comcast Corporation to create Comcast-Spectacor. Comcast acquired 66 percent of the Flyers, the 76ers, the Philadelphia Phantoms, and the First Union Complex. As chairman of this venture, Snider owns 34 percent of the entire package and oversees the operations of the Flyers and 76ers.

Widely regarded as one of the most influential owners in all of professional sports, fans and peers have recognized Snider's accomplishments. In 1980, he was a co-recipient of the Lester Patrick Trophy for outstanding service to hockey in the United States. He is a member of the Hockey (1988) and Flyers (1989) Hall of Fame. In a 1999 Philadelphia Daily News poll, Snider was selected as the city's greatest sports mover and shaker, beating out legends such as Connie Mack, Sonny Hill, Bert Bell, and Roger Penske.

1954 LaSalle NCAA Mens Basketball Champion
The first team in the Philadelphia area to ever attain ultimate NCAA basketball glory. The team members were: Frank Blatcher, Robert S. Maples, Frank O'Hara (deceased), Tom Gola, Bob Ames (deceased), Charlie Greenberg, Frank O'Malley, Manny Gomez, John Yodsnukis, Charlie Singley, Bob Ptak, Frank Finegan, Gary Holmes, John Moosbrugger (Manager), Ken Loeffler (Coach-deceased),

PHILA SPORTS HALL OF FAME
CLASS III - 2005

Inductee Class III (Does not include Legacy of Excellence, Lifetime Commitment, Team or Venue)

Herb Adderly - Football

- Multi-sport athlete at Northeast High School
- First team for Pennsylvania's All-Century High School football team
- 12-year NFL career with Packers and Cowboys
- 5-Time Pro Bowler.
- Played in 7 NFL championship games from 1961 through 1971, winning al of them with the Packers (5) and Cowboys (2)
- Played in 4 of the first 6 Super Bowls
- 25.7 yard average as kickoff returner
- 48 career interceptions, 7 for TDs
- Elected to the Pennsylvania Sports Hall of Fame in 1992
- Elected to Pro Football Hall of Fame in 1980

Don Bragg - Track & Field

- At Villanova, won NCAA pole vault championship in 1955.
- Six IC4A pole vault titles (indoor and outdoor) 1955-57.
- 6-time AAU champion (indoor & outdoor) 1956; 1958-61
- World record (indoor) 1959
- World record in 1960 Olympic trials
- Gold Medal in 1960 Olympics pole vault
- Wrote 2 books "A Chance to Dare" and "Reflections of Gold"
- Villanova Wall of Honor-1980
- U S Track & Field Hall of Fame 1996

Roy Campanella - Baseball
(Fans' Selection)

- Considered one of the best defensive catchers of his era with a rifle arm and an expert at handling pitchers
- Starred for 9 seasons (1937-42, 1944-45) in the Negro Leagues
- Leader of the 'Boys of Summer' championship Dodgers teams which won 5 pennants from 1949 to 1956.
- Uniform number '39' retired by the Dodgers
- 8-time All Star, catching very inning of every All-Star game for the National League from 1949 through 1953
- Did not enter Majors until 1948 due to segregation and career ended by car accident in 1958
- 3-time National League MVP (1951, '53, '55)
- Voted to the Baseball Hall of Fame in 1969

Del Ennis - Baseball

- Played 11 seasons with the Phillies, plus three with the Cardinals, Reds and White Sox
- Chosen for the Phillies All-Time "Centennial Team"
- 2063 career hits; 288 career home runs
- In 1946, won the original Sporting News Rookie Award batting .313 and finished among the NL top five in BA, HR, slugging and total bases
- Hit over .300 three times, over 30 home runs twice, and 100 RBIs seven times, with a league-leading 126 RBI for the pennant-winning 1950 Phillies
- Hit three home runs in one game
- At time of retirement, held all-time Phillies rankings: #1 HR, #1 games, #2 RBIs, #2 total bases, #2 hits, #2 ABs, #3 extra base hits, #3 doubles

Joe Fulks - Basketball

- One of modern pro-basketball's first scoring sensations, revolutionized shooting by first using a two-handed shot and then gradually switching to one hand
- As a rookie, led the Basketball Association of America in scoring with a 23.2 ppg and led the Warriors to the BAA title
- Considered the BAA's greatest offensive player. Led the league in scoring, with 24 PPG when teams rarely scored over 70 points
- In 1949, the Sporting News called Fulks "the greatest basketball player in the country"
- In 1949, scored an NBA-record 63 points against the Indianapolis Jets
- Three-time All-NBA First Team selection who led the league in scoring in 1947-1948
- Voted to the NBA's 25th Anniversary All-Star team
- Voted to the Basketball Hall of Fame

Hal Greer - Basketball

- Played entire 15-year career for 76ers franchise
- When he retired, he ranked among the top 10 all-time in points scored (21,586), FG attempted (18,811), FG made (8,504)
- Averaged 22 ppg to lead 76ers to NBA Championship (1967)
- Played in 10 consecutive NBA All-Star Games
- NBA All-Star Game MVP (1968)
- Set record for most points scored in a quarter (19) during an All-Star Game (1968)
- Seven-time All-NBA Second Team (1963-69)
- Scored 21,586 career points, including 50 in one game vs. the Boston Celtics
- Scored 1,876 points in 92 playoff games and 120 points in 10 All-Star Games
- Member of the NBA 50th Anniversary Team (1996)
- Uniform #15 retired by 76ers
- Elected to Basketball Hall of Fame – 1982

Reggie Jackson - Baseball

- Four-sport athlete at Cheltenham High School
- Arizona State Sports Hall of Fame - 1966
- 21-year major league career with Athletics, Orioles, Yankees and Angels
- "Mr. October" with 11 post-season appearances
- 4 World Series championships
- 14 All-Star games.
- 1973 American League MVP
- 2-time World Series MVP (1973 & 1977)
- Led league in HRs 4 times
- 563 home runs, 1702 RBIs and 2584 hits for his career
- Bay Area Sports Hall of Fame-1993
- Elected to Baseball Hall of Fame in 1993 Willie Mosconi-Pool/ Billiards

- When pool was front-page sports news, he won the United States pool championship 18 times between 1941 and 1956
- Once ran 526 balls in a row in an exhibition of straight pool; he never missed, he just quit after making the 526th ball
- Served as the technical consultant for the movie The Hustler, which resulted in a worldwide boom in the popularity of pool
- Won 13 World Championships between 1941 and 1955
- Generally considered the greatest pool player of all time
- The Mosconi Cup, an annual pool competition between American and European players, is named in his honor
- Voted to the Billiard Congress of America Hall of Fame-1968

Jack Ramsay - Basketball

- Upper Darby native enjoyed success at every level of coaching winning 1,164 total games (66 high school, 234 collegiate and 864 professional)
- In 1955-56, his first season coaching St. Joseph's, guided the team to a 23-6 record and the school's first Big 5 championship
- Won 7 Big Five championships in his 11 seasons at St. Joe's, leading the Hawks to a 234-72 record
- Overall NBA coaching record of 826-732 (.530)
- Served as 76ers general manager from 1966-1968 (including 1966 championship team) before returning to coaching, leading 76ers to the playoffs in 3 of 4 years
- Guided the Portland Trail Blazers to 49-33 record and an NBA championship in his first season (1977)
- Retired with second most wins among coaches in NBA history, trailing only Red Auerbach
- Overall coaching record (high school, college and professional): 1126-862 (.566)
- Voted to the Basketball Hall of Fame

Helen Sigel Wilson - Golf

- Won more than 350 titles during her 45-year golf career
- Two-time runner-up in US Amateur
- Won Women's Eastern Amateur twice (1952, 1962) and Women's Western Amateur in 1949
- Won US Women's Senior Championship (65-and-over division) in 1967
- Dominant in Philadelphia area, winning 12 Philadelphia Amateur championships and five Pennsylvania Amateur championships
- Three Curtis Cups including serving as captain in 1978
- Set a record low score for an amateur in the 1965 US Women's Open
- Founder of Helen Sigel Wilson Ladies Golf Classic, which has raised money for the Leukemia & Lymphoma Society since 1984

Al Simmons - Baseball

- Philadelphia A's all-time leader in batting (.356), hits (1827), RBI (1178) and total bases (2998)
- Tremendous clutch hitter for championship A's teams of 1929, 1930 and 1931 with 450 RBIs those three years
- Hit over .300 nine straight seasons with the A's
- Drove in over 100 RBIs nine straight seasons with the A's
- League leader in ABs (1929, '32); Runs (1930); Hits (1925, '32); RBI (1929)
- American league batting leader in 1930 (.381) and 1931 (.390)
- Voted to the Baseball Hall of Fame in 1953

Anne Townsend - Multiple sports

- Captained Penn's women's basketball team 1921-1922
- Keyed the growth of field hockey and lacrosse as inter collegiate sports for women at Penn in the early 1920s
- Helped start the US Field Hockey Association, serving as President from 1928-1932
- Captained the US Field Hockey team for 15 years
- Earned All-America honors in lacrosse
- Won state championships in tennis and squash, representing Merion Cricket Club in both sports
- Founded Merestead Sports Camps in 1946 to educate girls about athletic opportunities
- First woman voted into the Pennsylvania Sports Hall of Fame
- Voted to the University of Pennsylvania's Athletic Hall of Fame
- Voted to US Field Hockey Hall of Fame

Beth Anders - Field Hockey

- 4 time All-College selection in Lacrosse and Field Hockey while at Ursinus College (1969-73)
- Played for the U.S. National Field Hockey Team (1969-84)
- Had over 100 international caps for the U.S. while leading the team in scoring each year
- Named U.S. Woman's Field Hockey Athlete of the Year (1981)
- Captain of the 1980 and 1984 U.S. Olympic Field Hockey Team
- Scored 8 of the team's 9 goals in its five games at the 1984 Summer Games in Los Angeles
- Olympic Bronze Medal at the 1984 Summer Games in Los Angeles
- Named Olympic Athlete of the Year (1984)
- Head Coach of the Old Dominion University Field Hockey Team (1980-present)
- led the Lady Monarchs to 9 NCAA D-I Field Hockey Championships (1982-1984, 1988, 1990-1992, 1998, 2000)
- 8 time CAA Field Hockey Coach of the Year
- 2 time National Field Hockey Coaches' Association Coach of the Year (1998, 2000)
- 2nd All Time winningest Coach in Collegiate Field Hockey history
- Inducted into the National Field Hockey Coaches Association Hall of Fame (2000)
- Inducted into the USA Field Hockey Hall of Fame (1989

Walter Bahr - Soccer

- Played for numerous teams in the American Soccer League; under Hall of Fame coach Jimmy Mills, helped the Philadelphia Nationals win four ASL titles and played on almost every ASL All Star Team of the era
- Served as team captain of the 1948 USA Olympic Soccer team
- Served as captain of the 1950 USA World Cup Soccer team, supplying the pass that led to Joe Gaetiens' winning goal against England in one of the biggest upsets in World Cup Soccer history
- Played 19 times for the USA in full international competition
- Became a highly successful coach at Temple University, Penn State University, and for two Philadelphia professional teams
- Widely considered one of the greatest American players of his time
- Inducted into the National Soccer Hall of Fame (1976)
- Inducted into the National Soccer Coaches Association of America Hall of Fame (1995)

Bill Barber - Hockey

- Drafted by the Flyers in the 1st Round, 7th overall (1972)
- Played all 12 seasons of his career with the Flyers as a LW (1972-84)
- Scored 20 or more goals in every season with five seasons of 40 goals or more
- Scored tying goal to force OT against Czechoslovakia in the 1976 Canada Cup, which his team (Canada) won in overtime
- Seven time NHL All-Star (1975-76, 1978-82)
- 1st Team All NHL LW (1975-76), 2nd Team All NHL LW (1978-79, 1980-81)
- All-time leader for Flyers in regular season goals (420) and playoff goals (53)
- Third in Flyers history in assists (463), second in points (883) and second in games played (903)
- Jack Adams award as NHL Coach of the Year (2000-01)
- Flyers retired his number 7
- Inducted into the Flyers Hall of Fame (1989)
- Inducted into the Hockey Hall of Fame (1990)

Mickey Cochrane - Baseball

- Lifetime Batting average of .321 with the A's (4th all-time)
- Considered one of the best defensive catchers of his era
- Fierce, competitive leader, the spark of the A's championship teams 1929-31 (hitting .331)
- Hit over .300 six times with the A's
- Struck out only 157 times in 4097 at bats with the Athletics
- Ranked in top 5 all-time in AVG and OBP for Phily A's
- Ranked in top 10 all-time in Hits, 2B and TB for Philly A's
- Voted 1928 American League MVP
- Inducted into the National Baseball Hall of Fame (1947)

Theresa (Shenk) Grentz - Basketball

- Led Cardinal O'Hara to 3 consecutive Philadelphia Catholic and City League titles
- Star center for the Immaculata Might Macs (1970-74) - career stats of 20.2 ppg, 16.6 rpg 53.2 fg%, and 68.3 ft%
- Immaculata record for most career rebounds (965) and 5th all time in career points (1167)
- 3 time AIAW National Champion (1972-74)
- 3 time 1st Team All American (1972-74)
- AMF Collegiate Player of the Year (1974)
- #12 jersey number retired by Immaculata
- Head Coach of Rutgers University for 19 seasons (1976-95); compiles a 434-150 (.743) record
- First full time woman's basketball head coach in the nation
- 9 consecutive NCAA Tournament appearances (1986-94)
- 1982 AIAW National Champion
- 6 Atlantic 10 Regular Season Titles
- 4 Atlantic 10 Tournament Titles
- 4 time Atlantic 10 Coach of the Year (1986-87, 1987-88, 1992-93, 1993-94)
- Converse National Coach of the Year (1986-87)
- Russell Athletic/WBCA Division I Coach of the Year (1987)
- Metropolitan Woman's Basketball Association Coach of the Year (1992-93)
- Olympic Bronze Medal as Head Coach of the USA Woman's Team (1992)
- Coached the USA Woman's Team to the World Championship (1990)
- Head Coach of the University of Illinois 11 seasons (1995-2007)
- Led the Illinois to the Big 10 Championship (1996-97)
- 2 time Big 10 Coach of the Year (1996-97, 1997-98)
- 10th All Time Winningest Coach in NCAA Division I Women's Basketball history
- Named as a Female Athlete of the Millennium by The Delaware County Times (1999)
- Inducted into the Woman's Basketball Hall of Fame (2001)

Frank "Bucko" Kilroy - Football

- Product of Northeast Catholic High School and Temple University
- All American at Temple University (1941-1942)
- Played 13 seasons with the Philadelphia Eagles (1943-55)
- 1st Team UPI All-Pro (1954)
- 2nd Team AP All-Pro (1952, 1954)
- 2nd Team UPI All-League (1948, 1949, 1950, 1952,1953)
- 2 time NFL Champion with the Philadelphia Eagles (1948, 1949)
- Voted to the Eagles' All-Time 60th Anniversary team as an OG
- Member of NFL 1940's All-Decade Team
- Served in numerous front office positions (Scout, Director of Player Personnel, GM and Vice-President) for over 40 years for various NFL teams including the Washington Redskins, Dallas Cowboys and New England Patriots
- Instrumental in the development modern NFL draft methodology

Chuck Klein - Baseball

- Led the National League in home runs four times with Phillies
- Last player to lead the NL in HR with 38 and Stolen Bases with 20 in one season (1932)
- Holds the single season record for outfield assists with 44 (1930)
- One of only 16 players to win the Triple Crown (1933 - .368 AVG, 28 HR, 120 RBI)
- NL MVP (1932)
- Career statistics of 243 HR, 1705 Hits, .326 AVG with the Phillies
- First NL player to hit four HR in a game in the 20th century (1936)
- Held the following all time Phillies rankings at retirement: #1 HR, #4 Games Played, #2 RBI, #2 Total Bases, #2 Hits, #4 At Bats, #2, Extra Base Hits, #3 Doubles, #2 Runs, #5 Batting AVG
- Inducted into the National Baseball Hall of Fame (1980) Harry Litwack (Basketball) Local
- Played at South Philadelphia High School for four years on the varsity team
- Voted All League three times and MVP twice, leading the team in points and assists twice
- Played three years for Temple University varsity, twice serving as team captain
- Played 7 seasons with the SPHAS (1930-36), with champion ships in both the Eastern and American Basketball Leagues
- Coached Temple's freshman team to a 181-32 record from (1931-51)
- Served as Eddie Gottlieb's assistant coach with the Philadelphia Warriors (1950-51)
- Head coach of Temple Men's Basketball (1947-73) and compiled a 373-193 record
- Directing Temple to 13 post-season tournaments with only one losing season in 21 seasons
- Coached of the NIT Champion Temple Owls (1969)
- Two-time NCAA Basketball Tournament Final Four (1956, 1958)

- Inducted into the Basketball Hall of Fame (1976) Bill Lyon - Legacy of Excellence
- Sports columnist at the Philadelphia Inquirer for over 30 years
- Graduated high school (Western Military Academy in Alton, Illinois) in 1956. Class salutatorian. Went to work full-time the next day for The News-Gazette in Champaign-Urbana, working 48 hours a week to pay his way through the University of Illinois. Took 15 credit hours a semester, graduated with honors in Februrary 1961.
- Served in the 33rd Infantry Division of the Illinois National Guard.
- Married November 6, 1964, still with The News-Gazette. Worked for Evansville (Indiana) Courier and Press for 3 1/2 years, then East St. Louis (Illinois) Journal for a year and a half, then back to News-Gazette as managing editor. Joined Inquirer in summer of 1972.
- Family includes Jim, John (and Sandy), Evan (14) and Josh (12), plus the middle linebacker.
- 6-time Pulitizer Prize nominee.
- Winner of 2 Emmys for TV writing.
- Author of 6 books including "When the Clock Runs Out" and "We Owed You One" (with Pat Williams)
- Winner of the National Headliner Award.
- Inducted into Pennsylvania Sports Hall of Fame (you were there) 1999.
- Winner 8 Keystone Press awards and 9 Associated Press Writing Awards
- 6-time winner of Pennsylvania Sportswriter of the year.
- Covered: More than 2 dozen Super Bowls, more than 2 dozen Masters, more than 2 dozen Final Fours, half a dozen Olympics. All the Triple Crown races, the World Series, Stanley Cup playoffs, more than 30 championship fights, Indy 500, U.S. Opens.

Earl Monroe - Basketball

- Star at Bartram High School (1959-63)
- Tournament MVP for Winston-Salem State NCAA Division II Champion Team
- Division II single season record for most points in a season with 1,326 pts, 41.5 PPG (1967)
- 2-time All-American (1967, 1968)
- NAIA Hall of Fame (1975)
- 13-year NBA career with Baltimore Bullets and New York Knickerbockers (1967-80)
- Named NBA Rookie of the Year and The Sporting News Rookie of the Year (1968)
- 4-time NBA All-Star (1969, 1971, 1975, 1977)
- Member of the Eastern Conference Champion Baltimore Bullets (1971) & New York Knickerbockers (1972)
- Member of the NBA Champions New York Knickerbockers (1973)
- Named to the NBA All-Rookie Team (1967-68)
- 1st Team All-NBA (1968-69)
- Named to the NBA 50th Anniversary All-Time Team
- Inducted into the Basketball Hall of Fame (1990)

Earle "Greasy" Neale - Football

- Eagles head coach for ten years (1941-50)
- 7 straight winning seasons (1943-49)
- Teams finished 1st or 2nd in offense five times
- Teams finished 1st or 2nd in defense five times
- Teams included 4 Pro Football Hall of Famers (Bednarik, Pihos, Van Buren, Wojciechowicz)
- Three straight NFL Championship Games (1947-49)
- Won NFL Championship in 1947 & 1948 both games by shutout
- Inducted into the Pro Football Hall of Fame (1969) Jack Whitaker Legacy of Excellence
- Philadelphia native and graduate of North Catholic and St. Josephs College
- Began broadcasting career on Philadelphia radio in 1947
- Joined WCAU in 1950 as a sportscaster
- Served as a play-by play announcer for both the Philadelphia Eagles and the New York Giants.
- Hosted CBS Sports Spectacular from 1961-81
- Joined ABC in 1982, serving as a reporter for both news and sports divisions covering 1988 Winter Olympics the 1984 Winter and Summer Olympics.
- Reported sports for ABC's "World News Tonight", "ABC News Nightline" and "20/20".
- Covered horseracing's Triple Crown Events, golf's major championships, the Super Bowl, heavyweight championship fights, NASL soccer, AAU track and field champion ships and major league baseball.
- Received the Kentucky Owners and Breeders, Inc. Engelhard Award in 1973
- Named "Best Announcer" by Sports Illustrated in 1976
- Two-time Emmy Award winner (1977, 1991)
- Received Maryland Jockey Club's Hilltop Award for "outstanding coverage of thoroughbred racing for over 20 years (1983)
- Inducted into the American Sportscasters Hall of Fame (1997)
- Inducted into Broadcast Pioneers of Philadelphia Hall of Fame (2003)
- Inducted into Saint Joseph's Athletics Hall of Fame (2005)

Reggie White - Football

- Played 8 seasons as a DI with the Eagles (1985-92)
- 7 time Pro Bowler while with the Eagles (1986-92)
- Recorded at least 11 sacks all eight seasons with the Eagles, leading the team in sacks five times
- Led the NFL in sacks in 1987 (with 21) and 1988 (18)
- Leader of one of the best defenses in Eagles history leading the NFL in rushing, passing and total defense (1991)
- 6 time 1st Team AP All-NFL (1986-91), 2nd Team AP All-NFL (1992)
- 7 time 1st Team UPI All-NFC (1986-92)
- 6 time 1st Team PFWA All-NFL (1987-92)
- AP and Pro Football Weekly NFL Defensive MVP (1987)
- 2 time UP NFC Defensive Player of the Year (1987, 1991)
- Retired as the NFL All Time Sack Leader with 198
- Selected to the NFL 1980's All-Decade Team
- Selected to the NFL 1990's All-Decade Team
- Voted to the NFL's 75th Anniversary Team
- Inducted into the Pro Football Hall of Fame (2006)

Ed Delahanty - Baseball

- Played 13 seasons with the Phillies
- Career batting average of .348 with the Phillies
- Hit over .300 twelve straight years
- Hit over .400 three times
- Hit four home runs in a single game
- 1367 runs scored; 1286 RBI's; 2213 career hits with the Phillies
- At time of retirement, held all-time Phillies rankings: #1 extra base hits, #1 total bases, #1 hits, #1 at bats, #1 games, #1 home runs, #2 batting average, #2 steals
- Inducted into the National Baseball Hall of Fame (1945)

1980 World Champion Phillies

- Won National League East with 91-71 Record
- Won National League Champion Series 3-2 over the Houston Astros
- Won World Series 4-2 over Kansas City Royals for the Phillies first-ever World Championship
- All Stars: Pete Rose, Mike Schmidt, Steve Carlton
- Manny Trillo won 1980 NLCS MVP
- Mike Schmidt won 1980 NL MVP and World Series MVP
- Steve Carlton won 1908 Cy Young

Tommy Loughran - Boxing

- Career record of 94 wins – 23 loses – 9 draws (45 No decisions)
- Fought twelve world champions, ranging from the welterweight to the heavyweight division
- Captured the Light Heavyweight Championship in 1927
- Successful title defenses against Jimmy Slattery, Leo Lomsky, Pete Latzo (twice), middleweight champ Mickey Walker, and future heavyweight champ Jimmy Braddock
- Moved up in weight and beat heavyweights Jack Sharkey, Max Baer and Paolino Uzcudun
- Earned a title fight against heavyweight champion Primo Carnera in 1933
- World Light Heavyweight Champion (12/12/27 – 7/18/29)
- 2 time Ring Magazine Fighter of the Year (1929, 1931)
- Inducted into the International Boxing Hall of Fame (1991)

Dorothy Porter - Golf

- U.S. Amateur Women's Champion which she won at Merion Golf Club (1949)
- 4 time U.S. Senior Women's Amateur Champion (1977, 1980-81, 1983)
- One of only 4 golfers to have captured both the U.S. Amateur and U.S. Senior Amateur titles
- One of only 17 golfers to have won four plus USGA individual titles
- 9 time Philadelphia Women's Champion (1946, 1956, 1959, 1962, 1969-70, 1973, 1983, 1992)
- 3 time Pennsylvania Women's Champion (1946, 1952,1955)
- Won the New Jersey Women's Championship (1967)
- Captured the Eastern Amateur title (1969)
- 3 time Western Amateur Champion (1943-44, 1967)
- Member of the Curtis Cup Champion Team USA (1950)
- Inducted into the Pennsylvania Sports Hall of Fame (1995)

Al Wistert - Football

- Played 9 seasons as a T for the Eagles (1943-51)
- Coach "Greasy" Neale considered him "the greatest offensive tackle I have ever seen"
- Lead blocker for Steve Van Buren's devastating runs
- Served as Eagles captain for five seasons (1946-50)
- Played in the first Pro Bowl (1950)
- 4 time AP 1st Team All-Pro (1944-47)
- 5 time UPI 1st Team All-Pro (1944-48)
- 1 time The Sporting News 1st Team All-NFL (1948)
- 3 time Pro Football Illustrated 1st Team All-NFL (1945, 1946, 1948)
- 1 time Pro Football Illustrated 2nd Team All-NFL (1947)
- 2 time NFL Champion with the Philadelphia Eagles (1948, 1949)
- Member of the NFL's 1940's All-Decade Team
- His #70 was the first number retired by the Eagles

Mickey Vernon - Baseball

- 20 year MLB career as a 1B with the Senators, Indians, Red Sox, Braves and Pirates (1939-60)
- Career stats: .286 AVG, 1196 R, 2495 H, 1311 RBI, 490 2B, .359 OB%
- 7 time AL All-Star (1946, 1948, 1953-56, 1958)
- 2 time AL Batting Champion (1946, 1953)
- Finished in AL Top 5 in Hits two times and Runs scored twice
- 3 time AL leader in doubles (1946, 1953-54)
- Led the AL in Extra Base Hits (1954)
- Lifetime fielding percentage of .990 in 2241 career games
- Current rank on the Twins (Senators) Career Leaders list: 1st in Double Plays [1612]; 2nd in Total Chances [20140]; 2nd in Putouts [15734]; 4th in 2B [391]; 5th in RBI [1026]; 5th in 3B [108]; 7th in Hits [1993]; 7th in TB [2963]; 7th in BB [735] and 8th in Runs [956]
- Holds the MLB record for career Double Plays by a First Baseman with 2041
- Holds the AL record for career Putouts by a First Baseman with 19,754
- Holds the AL record for career Assists by a First Baseman with 1444
- Holds the AL record for career Total Chances by a First Baseman with 21,198

Harold Carmichael - Football

- Played 13 seasons as a WR for the Eagles (1971-83)
- Appeared in more games, caught more passes, and scored more TD than any other player in team history
- Career stats with the Eagles: 590 REC, 8978 REC YDS, 15.2 YDS/REC, 79 RED TD
- 4 time Pro Bowl selection as an Eagle (1973, 1978-80)
- Led the NFL in Receptions (1973)
- Led the NFL in Receiving Yards (1973)

- Led the NFL in Receiving Yards / Game (1973)
- 4 times finished in the NFL Top 5 in Receiving TD
- 2 time AP 2nd Team All-Pro (1973, 1979)
- 1 time PFWA 1st Team All-NFL (1973)
- 2 time UPI 1st Team All-NFC (1978, 1979)
- 4 time UPI 2nd Team All-NFC (1973, 1974, 1977, 1980)
- 2 time The Sporting News 1st Team All-NFC (1978, 1979)
- 3 time Pro Football Weekly 1st Team All-NFC (1973,1978, 1979)
- Current rank on the Eagles Career Leaders list: 1st in REC [589]; 1st in REC YDS [8978]; 1st in REC TD [79]; 1st in TD [79]; 1st in TOTAL YDS [9042] and 4th in Scoring [474]
- Recipient NFL's Man of the Year Award (1980)
- Member of the NFC Champion Philadelphia Eagles (1980)
- Established NFL record for receptions in consecutive games with 127 (1972-80)
- Finished his career ranked 6th on the NFL's all time reception list
- Enshrined in the Eagles Honor Roll (1987)
- Voted to the Eagles 75th Anniversary All-Time Team
- Member of the NFL's 1970's All-Decade Team

Fred Shero - Hockey

- Head Coach of the Flyers (1971-78)
- Overall record of 308-151-95 with the Flyers
- Holds the following team records: Years Coached (7), Wins (308), Winning % (.642), Playoff Wins (48)
- Coached Flyers to 3 straight Conference Championships (1974-76)
- Head Coach of the 2 time Stanley Cup Champion Philadelphia Flyers (1974, 1975)
- Recipient of the Jack Adams Award as NHL Coach of the Year (1974)
- Recipient of the Lester Patrick Award for outstanding contributions to hockey in the USA (1981)
- Inducted into the Flyers Hall of Fame (1991)

Maurice Cheeks - Basketball

- Played 11 seasons at G for the Philadelphia 76ers (1978-89)
- Career stats with the 76ers: 12.1 PPG, 7.3 APG, 2.3 SPG, 528 FG%, .790 FT%
- 4 time NBA All Star (1983, 1986-88)
- 6 times finished in the NBA Top 5 in Steals
- 5 times finished in the NBA Top 5 in Steals Per Game
- Led the 76ers in Assists and Assists Per Game in each of his 11 seasons with the club
- Led the 76ers in Steals and Steals Per Game in 10 of his 11 seasons with the club
- Shares the 76ers single game record for Assists with 21 (10/30/82)
- Shares the 76ers singles game record for Steals with 9 (1/5/87)
- Holds the 76ers single season record for Assists with 753 (1985-86)
- Holds the 76ers single season record for Assists Per Game with 9.2 (1985-86)
- Current rank on the 76ers Career Leaders list: 1st in AST [6212]; 1st in APG [7.3]; 1st in STL [1942]; 2nd in SPG [2.3]; 5th in FG% [.528]; 8th in PTS [10429] and 8th in FG [4192]
- 4 time 1st Team NBA All-Defense, 1 time 2nd Team NBA All-Defense
- Retired as the NBA All Time Steals Leader
- Current rank on the NBA Career Leaders list: 4th in STL [2310] and 9th in AST [7392]
- 3 time NBA Eastern Conference Champion with the 76ers
- Member of the NBA Champion Philadelphia 76ers (1983) His #10 was retired by the 76ers (2/6/95)

Leroy Burrell - Track and Field

- Overcame being legally blind in one eye to become on the most accomplished sprinters of his time
- Won the 100m, 200m, Long Jump and Triple Jump at the PA Class AAA State Track Field Championship (1985)
- Leads Penn Wood High School to the PA Class AAA State Track Field Championship (1985)
- Named high school track and field All-American (1985)
- Named Eastern Track Athlete of the Year (1985)
- 9-time All-American at University of Houston
- Established NCAA outdoor record in the Long Jump at 27'5.50" (1989)
- Part of the team that establishes world record in the 4x200m Relay (1989)
- SWC champion in the 100m and 200m (1990)
- 2 time NCAA Division I Indoor Long Jump Champion (1989. 1990)
- NCAA Division I Outdoor 100m Champion (1990)
- Holds the University of Houston record in the 100m with a time of 9.94 sec. (1989)
- Recipient of the "Jumbo Elliott Award" as the nation's top collegiate track and field athlete (1990)
- U.S. National Indoor 55m Champion (1989)
- U.S. National Indoor 60m Champion (1992)
- 2 time U.S. National Outdoor 100m Champion (1989,1991)
- 3 times had a top 10 world ranking by The Track and Field News in the 200m
- 6 times had a top 10 world ranking by The Track and Field News in the 100m
- Ranked 1st in the world in the 100m for two consecutive years (1990-91)
- Won 19 out of his 22 races over two years (1990-91)
- Part of the team that currently holds the world record in the 4x100m relay with a time of 37.40 (8/8/92 + 8/21/93)
- Part of the team that currently holds the world record in the

4x200m relay with a time of 1:18.68 (4/17/94)
- World Record holder in the 100m (6/4/91-8/25/91 & 7/6/94-7/27/96)
- 2 time IAAF World Championships Gold Medal in the 4x100m Relay (1991, 1993)
- IAAF World Championships Silver Medal in the 100m(1991)
- Olympic Gold Medal in the 4x100m Relay at the Summer Games in Barcelona (1992)
- University of Houston Track and Field Head Coach (1998-present)
- 3 time C-USA Men's Outdoor Track and Field Champions (1999, 2000, 2005)
- 7 time C-USA Men's Indoor Track and Field Champions (1999. 2000, 2003-05, 2007-08)
- 5 time C-USA Women's Outdoor Track and Field Champions (2000. 2002, 2004-06)
- 4 time C-USA Women's Indoor Track and Field Champions (2002-03, 2006-06)
- 2 time C-USA Men's Outdoor Track and Field Coach of the Year (1999, 2000)
- 5 time C-USA Men's Indoor Track and Field Coach of the Year (1999, 2000, 2003-04, 2007)
- 3 time C-USA Women's Outdoor Track and Field Coach of the Year (2000, 2002, 2004)
- 3 time C-USA Women's Indoor Track and Field Coach of the Year (2002, 2003, 2005)
- 2 time NCAA Regional Coach of the Year (2003, 2004)
- Inducted into the University of Houston's Hall of Honor (2000)

Herb Magee - Basketball

- High school basketball star at West Catholic High, leading the Burrs to the 1959 Catholic League Championship
- Philadelphia University Rams All-Time Leading Scorer with 2235 points
- Member of the Rams Eastern Regional Championship team (1963)
- 2 time All-American selection (1961-62 and 1962-63)
- Head Coach of the Philadelphia University Rams (1967-Present)
- Career record of 854-3339 with .716 winning %
- Has taken the Rams to the 22 NCAA Tournaments
- Has won 3 NCAA Regional Championships
- Head Coach of the NCAA Division II Men's Basketball Champion Rams (1970)
- Became NCAA Division II All Time Winningest Coach with 829 victories (2/1/07)
- 5th All Time in NCAA Men's Basketball history for Wins
- Awarded National Association of Basketball Coaches (NABC) Guardian of the Game in 2005
- NABC Milestone in Coaching Award in 2007
- Inducted in to the West Catholic Hall of Fame 1959
- Member of Pennsylvania Sports Hall of Fame

Lionel Simmons - Basketball

- 2-time All-City star Southern High School in 1985 & 1986
- Scored 56 points in a high school game -1986
- One of five players to score 3000 points in his college career
- 4-year starter for the LaSalle University Explorers (1986-90)
- Career stats at LaSalle: 24.6 PPG, 10.9 RPG, .501 FG%, .722 FT%
- Led LaSalle in Scoring and Rebounds in each of his 4 seasons
- 3 times led LaSalle in Steals (1986-89)
- 2 time MAAC Regular Season Champion (1988, 1989)
- MAAC Southern Division Champion (1990)
- 3 time MAAC Tournament Champion (1988-90)
- Led LaSalle to three consecutive NCAA Tournament appearances (1988-90)
- Holds LaSalle single game records for Free Throws (18), Blocks (7)
- Holds LaSalle single season records for Points (908), Points Per Game (28.4), Field Goals (349), Blocks (77)
- Current rank on the Explorers Career Leaders list: 1st in PTS [3217]; 1st in PPG [24.6]; 1st in FG [1244]; 1st in FT [673]; 1st in BLK [248]; 2nd in REB [1429]; 2nd in STL [239]; 3rd in 3-PT% [.415]; 7th in FG% [.501]; 8th in RPG [10.9]
- 3 time Big 5 Player of the Year (1988-90)
- 4 time 1st Team All-Big 5 (1986-90)
- 3 time Metro Atlantic Athletic Conference Player of the Year (1988-90)
- Named UPI 3rd Team All-American (1987-88)
- Named UPI 2nd Team All-American (1988-89)
- Named AP 3rd Team All-American (1988-89)
- Consensus 1st Team All-American (1989-90)
- Consensus Player of the Year honors (1990) - AP / UPI / Basketball Weekly
- 1990 National Player of the Year USBWA Oscar Robertson Trophy, John Wooden Award, Naismith Award

- Big 5's All Time Leading Scorer with 3217 PTS
- Current Rank on the NCAA Career Leaders; 3rd in PTS [3217]; 6th in REB [1429]
- Holds the NCAA Basketball record for most consecutive games scoring in double figures with 115 (1987-90)
- Played 7 seasons at F-G for the Sacramento Kings (1990-97)
- Drafted in the 1st Round (7th Overall) in the NBA Draft (1990)
- Career NBA stats: 12.8 PPG, 6.2 RPG, 3.3 APG, .433 FG%, .771 FT%, 1.1 SPG
- Named to NBA 1st Team All-Rookie (1990-91)
- Inducted into the Philadelphia Big 5 Hall of Fame (1996)
- Inducted into the LaSalle University Hall of Athletes

Larry Bowa - Baseball

- Played 12 seasons at SS with the Phillies (1970-81)
- Career stats with the Phillies: .264 AVG, 816 R, 1798 H, 421 RBI, 206 2B, 81 3B, 288 SB, .301 OB%
- Career Fielding stats with the Phillies: .981 F%, 8129 TC, 2557 PO, 5416 A, 998 DP
- 5 time NL All Star (1974-76, 1978-79)
- 6 times led the NL in Fielding % at SS (1970-72, 1974, 1978-79)
- Currently ranked 1st among Phillies SS in career Total Chances, Assists, and Double Plays
- Established a MLB single season record for Fielding % at SS at .991 which stood for ten years (1979)
- Holds the NL record for career Fielding % at SS at .980
- 2 time NL Gold Glove recipient at SS (1972, 1978)
- Member of the World Series Champion Philadelphia Phillies (1980)
- Enshrined in the Phillies Wall of Fame (1991)
- Voted to the Phillies Centennial Team (1983)
- Spent 4 seasons as manager of the Phillies (2001-04)
- Named BWAA NL Manager of the Year (2001)

John Cappelletti - Football

- Played football at Monsignor Bonner High School
- Named 1st Team All-Delco and 1st Team All-Catholic (1969)
- Played as DB and RB at Penn State University (1971-73)
- Career stats at PSU: 2639 YDS RUSH, 29 TD, 120 YDS/GM, 5.1 YDS/ATT
- Established an NCAA record by rushing for 200+ YDS in three consecutive games (1973)
- Led the Nittany Lions to an undefeated season and a win in the Orange Bowl (1973)
- Consensus 1st Team All-American (1973)
- Named College Football Player of the Year by various groups (1973) ABC / UPI / Washington TD Club / Walter Camp Foundation
- Named Amateur Athlete of the Year by the PSWA (1973)
- Received the Maxwell Award as the Collegiate Football Player of the Year (1973)
- Recipient of the Heisman Trophy (1973)
- Played 9 seasons as a RB in the NFL
- Named to the Pennsylvania Football News 2nd Team high school football All-Century Team
- Inducted into the College Football Hall of Fame (1993)
- Named to the Pennsylvania Football News 2nd Team high school football All-Century Team
- Inducted into the College Football Hall of Fame (1993)

Eddie Collins - Baseball

- Played 13 seasons at 2B for the Athletics (1906-14, 1927-30)
- Career stats with the A's: .337 AVG, 756 R, 1308 H, 496 RBI, 377SB, .407 OB%
- Batted over .300 in six consecutive seasons with the Athletics (1909-14)
- Part of Connie Mack's famous $100,000 infield
- 3 time AL leader in Runs (1912-14)
- Only American League player to steal six bases in a single game, twice in 1912
- His .337 career batting average is 3rd all time in Athletics history
- Shares AL record for most seasons leading the league in Double Plays at 2B with 5
- Holds the AL record for career Putouts at 2B
- Holds the MLB record for career Chances and Assists at 2B
- Named AL MVP (1914)
- 4 time AL Champion with the Athletics (1910-11, 1913-14)
- 3 time World Series Champion with the Athletics (1910-11,1913)
- Inducted into the National Baseball Hall of Fame (1939)

Joey Giardello - Boxing

- Area boxer who fought in the middle weight division
- Career record of 101-26-7 with 33 wins by KO in 135 bouts
- Record of 5-3-1 against boxers inducted into boxing's Hall of Fame
- First title fight for the NBA Middleweight title against Gene Fullmer ended in a draw (4/20/60)
- His 10 round win over Henry Hank chosen as Fight of the Year by Ring Magazine (1/30/62)
- Upset Sugar Ray Robinson by unanimous decision and named #1 challenger to the world middleweight title (6/24/63)
- World Boxing Commission Middleweight Champion (12/7/63 – 10/21/65)
- World Boxing Association Middleweight Champion (12/7/63 – 10/21/65)
- Defeated Dick Tiger to claim the WBC and WBA Middle weight title
- Defended the title with a unanimous decision victory over Rubin "Hurricane" Carter (12/14/64)
- Lost the title by unanimous decision to Dick Tiger
- Inducted into the International Boxing Hall of Fame (1993)

Charlie Jenkins - Track and Field

- Outstanding member of the Villanova Track Team (1955-57)
- Only Villanova University athlete to have won two Olympic Gold Medals
- 1 time AAU 440yd Outdoor Champion (1955)
- 2 time AAU 600yd Indoor Champion (1957, 1958)
- 3 time IC4A 600yd Indoor Champion (1955-57)
- 2 time IC4A 440yd Outdoor Champion (1955, 1957)
- 2 time IC4A Outdoor Mile Relay Champion (1955, 1956)
- Set the World Indoor Record in the 500yd at the NYAC Games (2/18/56)
- Top 5 World Ranking at the 400m for 3 consecutive years (1955-57)
- Olympic Gold Medal winner in the 400m at the Summer Games in Melbourne (1956)
- Olympic Gold Medal winner in the 4 x 400m Relay at the Summer Games in Melbourne (1956)
- Inducted into the U.S. Track and Field Hall of Fame (1992)

1974-75 Stanley Cup Philadelphia Flyers

- The first "expansion team" in the NHL to win the coveted Stanley Cup
- The team included NHL Hall of Famers   Bobby Clarke, Bernie Parent and Bill Barber
- Their tough style of play earned them the name "The Broad Street Bullies"

301

William Julius "Judy" Johnson - Baseball

- Played 11 seasons for the Darby Hilldales as a 3B (1921-29, 1931-32)
- Considered the Negro Leagues' top 3B in the 1920s and 1930s
- Known as a sure handed third baseman with good range and a strong arm
- Described as a line drive clutch hitter who compiled a lifetimebatting average of .349
- Played in the first 2 Negro League World Series (1924, 1925)
- 1924 Negro League World Series leader in batting (.364), hits (16), and RBI (8)
- Considered as the league's most valuable player (1929)
- 3 time Eastern Colored League Champion with the Daisies (1923-25)
- Member of the Negro League World Series Champion Hilldales (1925)
- Inducted into the National Baseball Hall of Fame by the Negro Leagues Committee (1975)

Neil Johnston - Basketball

- Played 8 NBA seasons as a C for the Philadelphia Warriors (1951-59)
- Career statistics of 19.4 PPG, 11.3 RPG, 44.4 FG%, 76.8 FT%
- Career playoff statistics of 15.0 PPG, 11.2 RPG, 39.0 FG%, 73.0 FT%
- 6 time NBA All Star (1953-58)
- Led the NBA in scoring three consecutive seasons (1952-55)
- Led the NBA in rebounding with 15.1 RPG (1954-55)
- 3 time NBA leader in FG% (1952-53, 1955-57)
- 4 time All-NBA 1st Team selection (1953-56)
- 1 time All-NBA 2nd Team selection (1956-57)
- Member of the NBA Champion Philadelphia Warriors (1956)
- Inducted into the Naismith Memorial Basketball Hall of Fame (1990)

Bill Conlin - Broadcaster

- Graduate of Temple University
- Sportswriter and longtime columnist for the Philadelphia Bulletin and Philadelphia Daily News
- Member of the Baseball Writers Association of America and is a voter for the National Baseball Hall of Fame
- One time regular contributor and guest on ESPN's The Sports Reporters program
- His direct style and wit have made him a staple of Philadelphia sports publications for many years

Tommy Lasorda - Baseball

- Signed as an undrafted free agent by the Phillies (1945)
- Pitched for the Montreal Royals of the International League for 8 seasons (1950-54, 1958-1960)
- 5 time winner of the Governors' Cup with the Royals (1951-54, 1958)
- Recipient of the International League's Most Valuable Pitcher Award (1958)
- Winningest pitcher in Montreal Royals history with a re cord of 107-57
- Has worked continuously for the Dodgers since signing as a scout (1961)
- MLB manager for 21 seasons for the Los Angeles Dodgers (1976-96)
- Lifetime record of 1599-1439 with a .526 winning percent age
- Led the Dodgers to 7 post season appearances
- Managed the Dodgers to 4 NL Pennants (1977, 1978, 1981, 1983)
- 2 World Series Champion with the Dodgers (1981, 1988)
- 2-time BWAA NL Manager of the Year (1983, 1988)
- His #2 was retired by the Dodgers (8/15/97)
- Inducted into the Canadian Baseball Hall of Fame (2006)
- Inducted into the National Baseball Hall of Fame (1997)

Pete Retzlaff - Football

- Played 11 seasons for the Philadelphia Eagles (1956-66)
- Career stats: 452 REC, 7412 YDS, 16.4 YDS/ REC, 47 TD
- 5 time Pro Bowl selection (1958, 1960, 1963-65)
- Retired as the Eagles all time leader in Receptions and Receiving Yards
- 1 time 1st Team AP All-Pro (1965), 2 time 2nd Team AP All-Pro (1958, 1964)
- 1 time 1st Team UPI All-Pro (1965), 2 time 2nd Team UPI All-Pro (1958, 1964)
- Set the Eagles single season record for Receptions and Receiving Yards (1965)
- Currently ranked 2nd on the Eagles all time leaders in Receptions and Receiving Yards
- Holds the Eagles record for most career 100 Yard Receiving Games with 23
- Recipient of the Maxwell Club's Bert Bell Award as NFL Player of the Year (1965)
- Member of the NFL Champion Philadelphia Eagles (1960)
- His uniform #44 jersey was retired by the Eagles
- Enshrined in the Eagles Honor Roll (1989)

Betty Shellenberger - Field Hockey/Lacrosse

- 21 Year National Team career is longest in USA Field Hockey history (1939-60)
- 3 time member of the USA IFWHA Tournament Team (1950, 1953, 1959)
- Outstanding lacrosse player as an attacker
- 11 time selection to the USA National Team & 5 time selection to the Reserve Team (1940-61)
- Received the first Golden Zebra Award for Philadelphia Field Hockey Umpiring
- Served as President of the United States Women's Lacrosse Association (1967-68)
- Honorary Secretary of the International Federation of Women's Lacrosse Associations (1983-86)
- Named a Distinguished Daughter of Pennsylvania for her contribution to sports (1987)
- Inducted into the National Lacrosse Hall of Fame (1994)
- Inducted as part of the Inaugural Class of the USA Field Hockey Hall of Fame (1988)

Mel Sheppard - Track & Field

- Arguably the greatest middle distance runner of his era
- First man to win Olympic gold medals in both the 800m and 1500m
- 5 time AAU 880 yd Outdoor Champion (1906-08, 1911-12)
- 2 time AAU 600 yd Indoor Champion (1908, 1909)
- 2 time AAU 1000 yd Indoor Champion (1906, 1907)
- AAU 1 Mile Relay champion (1909)
- Set four world records: 800m, 1500m, 600 yd (indoor), 1000 yd (indoor), and 1 Mile Relay
- 3 time Olympic Gold Medal winner at the Summer Games in London (1908)
  800m / 1500m / 1600m Relay
- Olympic Gold Medal winner in the 4x400m Relay at the Summer Games in Stockholm (1912)
- Olympic Silver Medal winner in the 800m at the Summer Games in Stockholm (1912)
- Inducted into the USA Track & Field Hall of Fame (1976)
- Inducted into the U.S. Olympic Hall of Fame (1989)

Emlen Tunnell - Football

- 13 year NFL career as DB/PR/KR with the NYG and GB (1948-1961)
- Finished his career with a then record 79 INT
- 9 time Pro Bowler including 8 straight (1950-1957, 1959)
- 4 time 1st Team AP All-Pro (1951, 1952, 1955, 1956)
- 2 time 2nd Team AP All-Pro (1954, 1957)
- 3 time 1st Team UPI All-Pro (1951, 1952, 1956)
- 2 time 2nd Team UPI All-Pro (1955, 1957)
- 2 time 1st Team The Sporting News All-NFL (1955, 1957)
- Member of the NFL Champion New York Giants (1956)
- Member of the NFL Champion Green Bay Packers (1961)
- First African-American elected into the Pro Football Hall of Fame (1967)

Merrill Reese - Legacy of Excellence

- Graduate of Temple University
- Philadelphia Eagles play-by-play announcer since 1977
- Hosts a radio interview show the day following Eagles games with current Eagles coaches, Eagles players and other guests
- His 30 years of service as the voice of the Eagles makes him the longest-serving current announcer in the NFL
- His signature voice, style and call "Its Gooooood!" have endeared him to a generation of Philadelphia Sports fans

Richard "Dick" Allen - Baseball

- Played 9 seasons with the Phillies as an IF/OF (1963-69, 1975-76)
- NL Rookie of the Year (1964)
- 3 time All Star (1965-67) with Phillies.
- Batted over .300 4 times with the Phillies, twice finishing in the Top 5 (1964, 1966)
- Leads NL in Triples, Runs, Total Bases and Extra Base Hits as a rookie (1964)
- 2 time runner up in NL HR (1966, 1968)
- Current rank on Phillies Career Leaders: 2nd in SLG% [.530]; 6th in HR [204}; 10th in 3B [64]
- Enshrined in the Phillies Wall of Fame (1994).

Elizabeth Becker - Diving

- 4-time winner of Middle Atlantic State Championship (first title at 15)
- 3-time U.S. 3m Springboard Champion (1922, 1923, 1926)
- U.S. 1m Springboard Champion (1924)
- Olympic Silver Medal winner in the 10m Platform at the Summer Games in Paris (1924)
- Olympic Gold Medal winner in the 3m Springboard at the Summer Games in Paris (1924)
- Olympic Gold Medal winner in the 10m Platform at the Summer Games in Amsterdam (1928)
- Member of International Swimming Hall of Fame (1967).

Hobey Baker - Hockey; Football

- Born in Bala Cynwyd.
- Captained Princeton's hockey and football teams
- Led Princeton to 1911 national football championship
- Led Princeton to 1912 & 1914 national Hockey championships.
- Known for exceptional athletic prowess and unmatched sportsmanship
- Served in World War I as a pilot, commanding the 103rd Aero Squadron.
- Received the Croix de Guerre, given by France for those who distinguish themselves by acts of heroism involving combat with enemy forces.
- Princeton's hockey rink named for him: Hobart Baker Rink
- The Hobey Baker Award (the "Heisman Trophy of Hockey") is awarded to the nations' best collegiate hockey player.
- First American inducted to the Hockey Hall of Fame (1945)
- Member of the College Football Hall of Fame (1975)
- Charter member of the US Hockey Hall of Fame (1973).

Tug McGraw - Baseball

- Played 10 seasons with the Phillies as a RP (1975-84)
- All Star appearance with the Phillies in 1975
- Finished 5th in the NL Cy Young Award voting(1980)
- Went 1-1 with 2 Saves including the Game 6 clincher in the 1980 World Series
- Phillies career saves leader at retirement (94)
- Ranks 3rd all time in games pitched for Phillies (463)
- 2 time NL Champion with the Phillies (1980, 1983)
- Member of the World Series Champion Phillies (1980)
- Enshrined in the Phillies Wall of Fame (1999)

Tom Brookshier - Football

- 7 seasons as D-Back for the Eagles (1953; 1956-1961)
- 20 career interceptions and 8 fumble recoveries.
- Key member on the 1960 World Championship team.
- Two time Pro-Bowl selection in 1959 and 1960
- Member of Eagles Honor Roll.
- One of only 7 Eagle players to have number (40) retired.
- CBS sports broadcaster/color analyst (1965-87); Paired with Pat Summerall as #1 NFL broadcast team 1974-81
- Founder of the all sports talk radio format at WIP 610 AM in 1989, hosting the Breakfast with Brookshier morning program.
- 2007 Inductee to Phila. Broadcast Pioneers Hall of Fame.
- Honors as a broadcaster include Washington Touchdown Club Outstanding Broadcaster award and multiple Emmys for live sports

Ron Hextall - Hockey

- Played 11 seasons as goalie for the Philadelphia Flyers.
- NHL Rookie of the Year (1986-87).
- 1987 Conn Smythe trophy as Stanley Cup Play off MVP
- 1986-87 Vezina trophy winner as top goaltender
- Holds the NHL record for Playoffs GP in one season with 26 (1987)
- NHL record for Combined Regular Season/Playoff GP with 92 (1986-87)
- All-time Flyers leader in games played (489); games won (240) and playoff wins (45).
- Team MVP for three consecutive years (1987 - 1989).
- Two time NHL All-Star (1987, 1988).
- Flyers record for most victories by a Rookie goalie (37)-(1986-87).
- Inducted into the Flyers Hall of Fame in 2008.

William Hyndman III - Golf

- One of the greatest U.S. amateur golfers of all time with a career spanning 50 years.
- 19 career tournament victories.
- 4-time runner up in major tournaments: U.S. Amateur (1955); British Amateur (1959, 1969, 1970).
- Two time US Senior Amateur Champion (1973 and 1983).
- Won 1983 US Senior Amateur, making him the oldest USGA winner ever at age 67.
- 5-time Walker Cup team member (1957, 1959, 1961, 1969 and 1971).
- Two time Eisenhower Trophy team member (1958 and 1960) (world amateur team golf championship).
- Three time winner of the Philadelphia Amateur Championship (1935, 1958 and 1965).
- Charter member of GAP Hall of Fame with J. Wood Platt and Jay Sigel. (2008)

Robert Clyde "Bobby" Jones - Basketball

- Played 8 NBA seasons as a F with the Philadelphia 76ers (1978-86)
- Career statistics with the 76ers 10.6 PPG, 4.7 RPG, 54.2 FG%, 1.13 BLK, 1.18 STL
- Career playoff statistics with the 76ers 11.1 PPG, 4.5 RPG, 53.4 FG%, 1.25 BLK,
- 2 time NBA All-Star (1981, 1982)
- Named NBA Sixth Man of the Year (1983)
- 6 time NBA All-Defense 1st Team with the 76ers (1979-84), NBA All-Defense 2nd Team (1985)
- 3 time NBA Eastern Conference Champion with the 76ers (1980, 1982, 1983)
- Member of the 1983 NBA Champion Philadelphia 76ers
- His #24 has been retired by the 76ers (11/7/86).

Phil Jasner - Legacy of Excellence

- Area Native and Temple Grad.
- Spent his early professional days at the Pottstown (Pa.) Mercury, Montgomery Newspapers (Fort Washington, Pa.), the Norristown (Pa.) Times-Herald and the Trentonian.
- Joined the staff of the Philadelphia Daily News in 1972.
- Covered 76ers and the NBA on a full-time basis since 1981.
- Past president of the Professional Basketball Writers Association and the Philadelphia College Basketball Writers Association.
- 1999 Pennsylvania Sports Writer of the Year for 1999
- 2001 lifetime achievement award from the Professional Basketball Writers Association.
- Also covered high school sports, the Philadelphia Big 5, the Eagles and the NFL, the World Football League, the North American Soccer League and what was then the Major Indoor Soccer League.
- 2004 Curt Gowdy Media Award, presented by the Naismith Basketball Hall Of Fame for outstanding contributions to the sport during his career.

Leroy Kelly - Football

- Starred as QB at Simon Gratz High School
- Four-year starter as a halfback at Morgan State.
- 10 seasons at RB for the Cleveland Browns (1964-73).
- Six time Pro-Bowl selection (1966 through 1971)
  - Five time All-Pro selection.
- 1968 Bert Bell Award winner.
- Member of 1960s NFL All-Decade team.
- Led the NFL in rushing yards, rushing attempts and yards from scrimmage in 1967 and 1968
- Led league in rushing TDs from 1966 through 1968.
- Retired 5th all-time in all-purpose yards (12,330) and TDs (90).
- Elected to the Pro Football Hall of Fame in 1994.

Lighthouse Boys/Soccer Club - Lifetime Commitment

- Established in 1897 as Lighthouse Boys Club.
- In the club's first month 350 boys joined; By 1924, the Club had19,000 members.
- Constant source of US Olympians including four former Lighthouse players on the 1936 Olympic Soccer Team
- Produced some of the greatest U.S. players of the early 20th century including Walter Bahr, Henry Fleming, Bob Gormley, Benny McLaughlin, Len Oliver, Francis Ryan & Dick Spalding
- Won 5 James P. McGuire Cups (Under 19 national champion ship) in 1938, 1948, 1949, 1957, and 1967
- Continues today as the Lighthouse Soccer Club.)

James J. Phelan - Basketball

- Area native; graduate of LaSalle High School (1947)
- 2 time All-Catholic selection (1946-47); All-City (1947)
- Played at LaSalle College (1948-51); 3-time All-Philadelphia selection (1949-51)
- Head Basketball Coach at Mount St. Mary's University for 49 seasons (1954-2003); career record of 830-524
- Led the Mountaineers 16 NCAA Division II Tournament appearances; 5 Final Fours; 2 Championship Games.
- Coached Mount St. Mary's to the NCAA College Division II Basketball Championship (1962)
- Led the Mountaineers to 2 NEC Championships (1995, 1999); NEC Coach of the Year (1993; 1996)
- 2-time Division II Coach of the Year (1962; 1981); 3-time District 2 Coach of the Year (1981, 1985, 1986)
- Clair Bee Coach of the Year award presented by the Basketball Hall of Fame (1998)
- Mt. St Mary's Knott Arena floor named "Coach Jim Phelan Court"; College Insider Coach-of-the-Year Award (2003) and Northeast Conference Coach of the Year Award both named after Jim Phelan.
- 1st in NCAA history for most games coached (1354); 2nd for most seasons coached (49) and Wins (830) - Most victories of any coach not in the National Basketball Hall of Fame
- Inducted into the LaSalle Hall of Athletes (1964)
- Inducted into National College Basketball Hall in 2008 with Nolan Richardson; Charles Barkley; Billy Packer & Dick Vitale.

Mike Quick - Football

- Played 9 seasons for the Philadelphia Eagles (1982-90).
- A first round pick (20th overall) in the 1982 NFL Draft.
- Five time Pro-Bowl selection (1983-87)
- Led NFL receivers in TDs (53) from 1983-87
- Led NFL in reception yards (1409) in 1983 (Eagles record).
- Two time AP All-Pro first team in 1983 and 1985.
- Finished Eagles career with 363 receptions (4th); 6,464 receiving yards (3rd); 61 TDs (3rd).
- Inducted into the Eagles Honor Roll in 1995.
- Member of the Eagles radio broadcast team since 1998.

Robert "Bobby" Shantz - Baseball

- Area native born in Pottstown, PA
- Played 16 years in the major leagues as a LHP primarily with the Athletics and Yankees
- 3 time All Star (1951, 1952, 1957)
- 8 time Gold Glove winner (1957-64)
- In 1952, led the AL in Wins; finished 3rd in ERA.
- 1952 AL MVP winner as a member of the Athletics
- Led the AL in ERA with a 2.45 mark (1957)
- 3 time AL Champion with the Yankees (1957-58, 1960)
- Member of the AL Champion Yankees (1958).

Marianne Crawford Stanley - Basketball

- Area native born in Yeadon.
- All-Catholic League at Archbishop Prendergast High
- Starred at Immaculata College under Coach Cathy Rush (1972-76)
- Career stats of 8.38 PPG, 6.11 APG, 41.2 FG%, and 65.9 FT%
- Holds Immaculata record for most career assists (544)
- 2 time Kodak All-American (1975, 1976)
- Reached the National Championship Final in all 4 years at Immaculata
- 2 time National Champion (1973, 1974)
- Head Coach at Old Dominion for 10 seasons (.820 w %
- Coached Woman's NIT Champion (1978), AIAW National Champions (1979, 1980)
- Coached NCAA National Champion (1985); 3-NCAA Final Fours; 5 Elite Eights and 10 NCAA Tournament berths.
- AIAW National Coach of the Year (1979); 5 time Virginia Collegiate Coach of the Year (1979-81, 1984, 1985); Mideast Region Coach of the Year (1984)
- Also coached at Penn, USC, California and in the WNBA
- Total of 21 collegiate coaching seasons (415-224 W-L)
- Inducted into the Woman's Basketball Hall of Fame (2002)

"Jersey" Joe Walcott - Boxing

- Born in Merchantville NJ, Arnold Raymond Cream, took the name Joe Walcott, Welterweight champ from his father's native Barbados
- Oldest man to win world Heavyweight title at age 37.
- Career record of 51-18-2 with 32 KO's
- At age 33 received his first title shot against Joe Louis and lost by split decision; Lost rematch by KO in the 11th.
- Beat Ezzard Charles for heavyweight title on July 18, 1951.
- 1951 Edward J. Neil Trophy for Fighter of the Year
- Retained title against Charles but lost it to Rocky Marciano in Sept1952 by KO, despite leading comfortably on points
- Co-starred with Humphrey Bogart and Max Baer in the boxing drama The Harder They Fall (1965)
- Refereed controversial world championship bout between Muhammad Ali and Sonny Liston (1965)
- Became Sheriff of Camden County in 1972; Chairman of the New Jersey State Athletic Commission in 1975 until 1984 (due to mandatory retirement age of 70)
- Member of NJ Boxing Hall of Fame; Ring Boxing Hall of Fame (1969);World Boxing Hall of Fame and Charter member of International Boxing Hall of Fame (1999)

ANSWER SECTIONS

EAGLES PASSING ANSWERS

1. Sonny Jurgenson

2. Bubby Brister - 1993; Randall Cunningham - 1994; Rodney Peete - 1995; Ty Detmer - 1996; Bobby Hoying - 1997; Koy Detmer - 1998; Doug Pederson - 1999; Donovan McNabb - 2000

3. Bruce Smith

4. Donovan McNabb - 29,320 yds

5. Adrian Burk

6. Donovan McNabb – 35

7. Ron Jaworski – 151

8. Kansas City Chiefs

9. 7

10. Jim McMahon, Pat Ryan, Brad Goebel and Jeff Kemp

11. 2 - Jim McMahon and Jeff Kemp

12. A.J. Feeley and Tim Hasselbeck

13. Yes. Randall beat the Redskins on September 22, 1985.

14. Donovan McNabb - 3,916 yds in 2008

15. Ty Detmer

16. Chad Lewis

17. Donovan McNabb - 571 in 2008

18. Roman Gabriel - 1973

19. Donovan McNabb - 194

20. Donovan McNabb - 464

21. 4 - Bobby Thompson, Sonny Jurgenson, Randall Cunningham & Donovan McNabb

22. Sonny Jurgenson - 32

23. 4 - Rams, Eagles, Dolphins and Chiefs

24. 5 – Packers, Eagles, 49ers, Browns and Lions

25. Yes

26. No

27. Joey Harrington

28. Donovan McNabb - 345 in 2008

29. 104

30. Roman Gabriel - 1973

EAGLES RUSHING ANSWERS

1. Heath Sherman

2. Wilbert Montgomery – 6,538

3. Keith Byars

4. Wilbert Montgomery - 1,465

5. Ernest Jackson in 1985

6. Brian Mitchell - 85 yards in 2000

7. Ricky Watters - 1,411 in 1996

8. Duce Staley in 2000

9. Steve Van Buren - 69

10. Correll Buckhalter - 134

11. Detroit Lions

12. Eagles

13. Wilbert Montgomery and Leroy Harris

14. Ernest Jackson – 1,028

15. Brian Westbrook - 613

16. Randall Cunningham – 32 (Ricky Watters had 31)

17. Wilbert Montgomery - 1979

18. Timmy Brown

19. Duce Staley

20. Steve Van Buren - 1949

21. Steve Van Buren

22. Ricky Watters - 353 in 1996

23. Duce Staley

24. Steve Van Buren - 15

25. Lesean McCoy - 637

26. 2

27. 3

28. Heath Sherman

29. Randall Cunningham

30. Dorsey Levens

EAGLES RECEIVING ANSWERS

1. Calvin Williams – 1993

2. Brian Westbrook – 90 in 2007

3. Irving Fryar and Jeff Graham

4. Brian Finneran

5. Harold Carmichael - 589

6. Keith Jackson - 81

7. Pete Retzlaff - 23

8. DeSean Jackson – 210 in 2010

9. Dan Looney and Brian Westbrook -14

10. Keith Byars

11. Donte Stallworth

12. Green Bay Packers

13. Terrell Owens – 7 in 2004

14. Charlie Smith - 825

15. Mike Quick - 1983

16. Terrell Owens – 14 in 2004

17. Yes – 11 in 1989

18. Rodney Parker and Scott Fitzkee

19. Jeff Graham - 600

20. Irving Fryar - 1996

21. 3

22. Harold Jackson and Harold Carmichael

23. 73

24. Charlie Young – 1974

25. Hershel Walker and Brian Westbrook

26. Harold Carmichael – 8,978

27. Tommy McDonald – 237

28. No

29. Terrell Owens – 5 in 2004

30. James Thrash - 49

EAGLES DEFENSE ANSWERS

1. Corey Simon, Rhett Hall and Andy Harmon

2. Wes Hopkins

3. Eric Allen

4. Trent Cole

5. James Willis and Troy Vincent

6. Eric Allen, Bill Bradley and Brian Dawkins - 34

7. William Thomas – 7 in 1995

8. 1981

9. 1996 – New York Giants

10. Nate Allem

11. Cincinnati Bengals

12. John Bunting

13. Michael Lewis – 129

14. 91

15. Eric Allen – 1992

16. Miami Dolphins

17. William Fuller – 13 in 1995

18. Ken Clarke, Jerome Brown, Andy Harmon and Corey Simon

19. Claude Humphrey

20. Brian Dawkins

21. Reggie White, William Fuller and Hugh Douglas

22. Russ Craft – 1950

23. Clyde Simmons and Hugh Douglas – 4.5

24. Jaiquawn Jarett

25. Sam Rayburn - 6

26. Memphis Showboats

27. Clyde Simmons – 19

28. Oakland Raiders

29. William Fuller – 7

30. Bill Bradley - 1971

EAGLES SPECIAL TEAMS ANSWERS

1. David Akers – 144 in 2008

2. Matt Dodge

3. Yes. David Akers

4. Vai Sikahema – 87 yards

5. Randall Cunningham

6. William Frizzell

7. David Akers

8. Tony Franklin and Paul McFadden

9. Jessie Small

10. Washington Redskins and San Francisco 49ers

11. Brian Westbrook

12. Tony Franklin

13. Brian Mitchell

14. David Akers – 154; from 2004 thru 2008

15. Bobby Watson – 1954

16. Timmy Brown

17. Quintin Demps

18. Brian Dawkins

19. David Akers - 294

20. Eddie Murray

21. Chris Boniol

22. Dave Meggett

23. Mike Vanderjagt

24. Clyde Simmons

25. Matt Bryant – 62 yards in 2006

26. Derrick Witherspoon - 1996

27. Tony Franklin – 59 yards versus Dallas in 1979

28. Brian Mitchell, Steve Van Buren, Brian Westrook and Desean Jackson

29. David Akers – 17 in 2001

30. Tom Dempsey - 6

EAGLES COACHING ANSWERS

1. Rich Kotite - 1992

2. 4

3. Yes – 29

4. Kotite – 1-0

5. Marion Campbell - 1985

6. Once

7. Cincinnati Bengals

8. Dallas Cowboys

9. Marion Campbell

10. Fred Bruney (finishing out the season when Marion Campbell was fired)

11. 1 – 2

12. New York Giants

13. Marion Campbell

14. UCLA

15. Jeff Fisher

16. Buddy Ryan

17. Danny Smith

18. Lud Wray

19. Bill Cowher

20. 7

21. Brad Childress and Leslie Frazier

22. Green Bay Packers

23. New York Jets

24. BYU

25. Jon Gruden

26. Kansas City Chiefs

27. Andy Reid - 10

28. Buddy Ryan

29. Offensive Coordinator

30. John Harbaugh

EAGLES COLLEGE ANSWERS

1. UNLV
2. University of Tennessee
3. Cal Poly
4. South Carolina
5. Syracuse
6. Youngstown State
7. Clemson
8. Mike Mamula
9. Louisville
10. Danny Watkins
11. Tennessee Chattanooga
12. Freddie Mitchell
13. Matt Ware
14. Michigan State
15. 20

16. University of Florida
17. North Carolina State
18. Trevor Laws and Victor Abiamiri
19. Michigan
20. Arkansas State
21. University of Miami
22. Florida State
23. Colorado
24. LSU
25. DeSean Jackson
26. Purdue
27. Penn State
28. Winston Justice
29. Houston
30. Tommy McDonald

EAGLES DRAFT ANSWERS

1. Lester Holmes and Leonard Renfro - 1993

2. Jerry Robinson

3. John Reaves – 1972

4. Mike Quick, Kenny Jackson, Freddie Mitchell and Jeremy Maclin

5. Mike Bellamy

6. Offensive Tackle – 5

7. Keith Jackson

8. Green Bay Packers

9. Barry Gardner

10. Kevin Allen

11. Trevor Laws and DeSean Jackson

12. Leroy Keyes

13. LeSean McCoy

14. Keith Byars

15. Third round – 1974 and 1978

16. 1987 Supplemental Draft – Fourth round

17. Keith Byars and Anthony Toney

18. Whit Marshall

19. Chuck Bednarik

20. Quinton Caver

21. Mike Mamula

22. Warren Sapp

23. Yes

24. Five – Davey O'Brien, Frank Tripucka, John Reeves, Donovan McNabb and Kevin Kolb

25. Tim Couch, Akili Smith, Daunte Culpepper and Cade McNown

26. Victor Bailey

27. Don McPherson

28. Ben Smith

29. Andy Harmon

30. Mark McMillian

EAGLES MEMORABLE MOMENTS ANSWERS

1. Herman Edwards

2. Tampa Bay Buccaneers

3. Reggie White and Randall Cunningham

4. Longest touchdown pass 99 yards

5. Jacksonville

6. Bryce Paup

7. Jimmie Giles

8. "They brought the house. We brought the pain."

9. Gary Cobb

10. "Bring It Home For Jerome"

11. Pickle juice

12. Roy Williams

13. Washington Redskins

14. Jim Brown and Emmitt Smith - 237 yards

15. Joe Montana - 1989

16. Will Smith

17. DeSean Jackson

18. Called for a fake kneel-down and a subsequent bomb by Randall Cunningham on what would have been the last play of the game. The fake kneel-down and pass resulted in a pass interference call against the Cowboys. The Eagles scored a touchdown on a one-yard run on the next play, which turned out to be the last play of the game.

19. Larry Csonka

20. Pittsburgh Steelers

21. Brian Mitchell and Duce Staley

22. Arizona Cardinals

23. Eric Allen

24. Brandon Whiting

25. Tokyo

26. Pam Oliver

27. Wilbert Montgomery

28. Brooklyn Dodgers

29. "This f------ game is over!"

30. Most coaching victories in an NFL career

EAGLES PLAYOFF ANSWERS

1. Rob Carpenter

2. Keith Krepfle

3. Mike Michel

4. 58 – 12/30/95 vs. Detroit

5. Reggie White

6. Atlanta Falcons

7. Chad Lewis - 38

8. Yes

9. San Francisco 49ers

10. Tampa Bay Buccaneers

11. Chicago Cardinals

12. Pittsburgh Steelers

13. Had the team buses drive around Soilder Field with their horns honking to announce the Eagles presence in Chicago

14. Max Runager – 49ers

15. Jeff Blake

16. Three times -1993,1996 and 2010

17. 20 – 17

18. Randall Cunningham

19. Yes

20. Tony Franklin and David Akers

21. Rodney Parker

22. Los Angeles Rams

23. Damon Moore

24. Brian Dawkins, Jermaine Mayberry and Hollis Thomas

25. Chicago Bears, Los Angeles Rams and Washington Redskins

26. Donovan McNabb – 3,522

27. Harold Carmichael

28. Donovan McNabb – 30

29. 0

30. Brian Westbrook - 591

EAGLES JERSEY NUMBERS ANSWERS

1970	1975	1980	1985
1. D	1. F	1. O	1. B
2. I	2. A	2. L	2. D
3. J	3. K	3. I	3. F
4. L	4. G	4. F	4. H
5. B	5. B	5. C	5. J
6. H	6. L	6. N	6. L
7. A	7. H	7. K	7. N
8. E	8. C	8. H	8. A
9. K	9. M	9. E	9. C
10. M	10. N	10. B	10. E
11. C	11. I	11. M	11. G
12. O	12. D	12. J	12. I
13. F	13. O	13. G	13. K
14. G	14. J	14. D	14. M
15. N	15. E	15. A	15. O

1990	1995	2000	2005
1. H	1. C	1. I	1. C
2. A	2. F	2. F	2. H
3. N	3. I	3. C	3. G
4. D	4. L	4. O	4. A
5. O	5. O	5. L	5. K
6. E	6. A	6. N	6. B
7. I	7. D	7. H	7. I
8. L	8. G	8. E	8. J
9. C	9. J	9. B	9. N
10. M	10. M	10. K	10. O
11. B	11. B	11. M	11. D
12. K	12. E	12. J	12. E
13. J	13. H	13. G	13. L
14. G	14. K	14. D	14. M
15. F	15. N	15. A	15. F

PHILLIES AWARDS ANSWERS

1. Robin Roberts

2. Ryan Howard, 2005

3. John Denny

4. Al Holland (1983), Steve Bedrosian (1987) and Brad Lidge (2008)

5. By Saam

6. Zero

7. Ten

8. Eight

9. Napoleon "Nap" Lajoie, 1896-1900. Selected in 1937

10. Steve Bedrosian, 1987

11. Steve Carlton in 1982 and John Denny in 1983

12. Jim Konstanty

13. Richie Allen, 1964

14. Curt Schilling

15. B - Willie Hernandez (who won with the Tigers in 1984)

16. B - Mike Schmidt

17. D - Gary Matthews

18. Five. (Chuck Klein (1932), Jim Konstanty (1950), Mike Schmidt (1980, 1981, 1986), Ryan Howard (2006), Jimmy Rollins (2007)

PHILLIES ALL-STARS ANSWERS

1. Mike Schmidt, 12

2. Greg Luzinski

3. Larry Bowa, Schmidt, Luzinski, Bob Boone, Dave Cash

4. Schmidt, Pete Rose, Boone, Bowa, Steve Carlton

5. Chuck Klein, outfield and Dick Bartell, shortstop

6. Curt Schilling, Andy Ashby, Paul Byrd

7. D – Ricky Bottalico

8. 1976 at Veterans Stadium and 1952 at Shibe Park

9. Shane Victorino, 2009

10. Johnny Callison

PHILLIES TWO-BASE ERRORS ANSWERS

1. Tony Taylor, 2,195

2. Troy Glaus

3. Hank Aaron

4. Al Kaline

5. Carl Yastrzemski

6. A – 1920's (566-962-6)

7. Pat Corrales

8. A – Kevin Gross

9. Frank Thomas

10. C – 6 ½

11. Jerry Martin

12. Kyle Abbott

13. Ron Jones

14. Jim Bunning and Chris Short

15. Cinncinati Reds and St. Louis Cardinals

16. 23 games

17. Ferguson Jenkins

18. Boston Red Sox

19. New York Yankees

PHILLIES REGULAR SEASON ANSWERS

1. Robert Person

2. Steve Carlton

3. Connie Ryan with four singles, two doubles vs. Pittsburgh on April 16, 1953

4. Rawley Eastwick

5. Pinch-hitter John Stephenson

6. B - Houston

7. B - Dick Sisler

8. D - Bobby Abreu

9. A - Darren Daulton

10. D - Kim Batiste

11. B - Charlie Hayes

12. C - Tommy Greene, who fielded a comebacker off the bat of Tim Wallach

PHILLIES REGULAR SEASON ANSWERS (CONT.)

13. B - Doug Glanville

14. B - 26-7

15. A - Von Hayes

16. Mariano Duncan

17. Lee Smith of St. Louis and Denny Neagle of Pittsburgh

18. Sil Campusano

19. Todd Pratt

20. Steve Jeltz

21. 13

22. Jim Eisenreich and Wes Chamberlain

23. Curt Schilling

24. Pete Incaviglia

25. Bob Dernier

26. Ronnie Paulino (perfect game) & Brandon Phillips (playoff no-hitter)

PHILLIES CLINCHERS ANSWERS

1. Don McCormack

2. B – Manny Trillo

3. Garry Maddox

4. Frank White

5. Willie Wilson

6. Steve Carlton

7. Los Angeles Dodgers

8. Al "Mr. T." Holland

9. Cal Ripken, Jr.

10. B – Donn Pall

11. Greg Maddux

12. Tommy Greene

13. Bill Pecota

14. Washington Nationals

PHILLIES FIRSTS, LASTS & MOSTS ANSWERS

1. Gene Mauch – 1,331

2. David Bell – June 28, 2004

3. Mike Schmidt – 18 seasons

4. Richie Ashburn – 730

5. Chuck Klein – 44 in 1930

6. 170 - Chuck Klein

7. Robin Roberts – 272 complete games and 3739 1/3 innings pitched

8. Chuck Klein, in 1933

9. Jim Bunning, on April 10, 1971

10. Pat Burrell

11. Ryan Howard, 58 in 2006

12. D – Robin Roberts, 199

13. A - 158, set in 1930

14. 2000s (850)

15. Jimmy Rollins (212 in 2007)

16. Chuck Klein, 107

17. Juan Samuel, 72 in 1984

18. Larry Christenson and Rick Wise with 11

19. Jim Thome, a home run in an exhibition game

20. San Diego

21. Robin Roberts

22. Ed Delahanty

23. Steve Carlton (241)

24. Kent Tekulve (90 in 1987)

25. Jose Mesa (112)

26. Jose Mesa, 45 in 2002

27. Curt Schilling, 319 in 1997

LEFTY & MICHAEL JACK ANSWERS

1. Dayton, Ohio

2. Minnesota Twins

3. Eighteen (1972-89)

4. Six

5. Pittsburgh's Three Rivers Stadium

6. C – 77

7. D – 1.97

8. D – Eight

9. Don Robinson

10. 13 (Nine with the Phillies)

11. Jim Kaat

12. Two – One with St. Louis in 1967 and one with Cleveland in 1987

13. B – 11

14. One, in 1973 (13-20)

15. Less – 174

PHILLIES PLAYOFF ANSWERS

1. A - Two (1915 and 1950)

2. Three

3. Four

4. D – '76 Reds, '77 and '78 Dodgers

5. C – Four

6. Greg Luzinski, in Game 1

7. Montreal Expos

8. Otis Nixon, Mark Lemke, Fred McGriff, David Justice, Ron Gant

9. C – Kim Batiste

10. Mitch Williams

11. Carlos Ruiz

12. Jimmy Rollins with four

PHILLIES CHAMPIONSHIP SEASONS ANSWERS

1. Dallas Green

2. First base

3. Mike Schmidt (48), Greg Luzinski (19) and Garry Maddox (11)

4. Lonnie "Skates" Smith (.339)

5. Frank

6. 20

7. Bake McBride

8. 5-0

9. 13

10. Tug McGraw – 1.46 ERA

11. Bob Walk

12. Dickie Noles

13. Dick Ruthven

14. Lonnie Smith (won the Fall Classic with Kansas City after being released by the Cardinals earlier in the season)

15. Terry Mulholland – 3.25

16. David West

17. Johnny Podres

18. Tommy Greene, at Mile High Stadium

19. Curt Schilling and Tommy Greene

20. 4.02

21. Greene, Schilling, Danny Jackson, Mulholland and Ben Rivera

22. Ron Reed

23. Joe Morgan

24. Zero

25. C – Jim Eisenreich

26. Juan Bell

27. B – One (1915)

PHILLIES 2008 WORLD CHAMP ANSWERS

1. Three (Ryan Howard with 48, Chase Utley and Pat Burrell both with 33)

2. Pat Burrell – 102

3. Joe Blanton

4. Seven

5. Six (Chad Durbin, Ryan Madson, J.C. Romero, Clay Condrey, Tom Gordon and Brad Lidge)

6. 149

7. 251

8. 2004

9. 177

10. 2000

11. Fabio Castro

12. Montreal Expos

13. Jimmy Rollins, in 2007

14. Second base

15. First and second base

16. 1986

17. Chicago Cubs and Philadelphia Phillies

18. Minnesota Twins and Los Angeles Dodgers

19. Four

20. Yakult Swallows and Kintetsu Buffaloes

PHILLIES 2008 WORLD CHAMP (POSTSEASON) ANSWERS

1. Ryan Zimmerman

2. 7-0

3. Carlos Ruiz

4. Los Angeles Dodgers

5. Jonathan Broxton

6. Nomar Garciaparra

7. Chase Utley

8. Jayson Werth

9. Utley, Ryan Howard, Werth, Joe Blanton, Ruiz, Eric Bruntlett

PHILLIES 2008 WORLD CHAMP (POSTSEASON) ANSWERS (CONT.)

10. J.C. Romero

11. Ryan Madson

12. Nine

13. Chris Coste and Matt Stairs

14. Brett Myers

15. Geoff Jenkins

16. Eric Bruntlett

17. Eric Hinske

2009 PHILLIES ANSWERS

1. Matt Stairs

2. Washington, DC

3. D – Cincinnati

4. Unassisted triple play

5. One - the final out of the contest

6. Miguel Cairo

7. Four – Ryan Howard, Chase Utley, Raul Ibanez and Jayson Werth

8. D - J.A. Happ with a .750 winning percentage (12-4)

9. Huston Street

10. Curt Schilling in Game 5 of the 1993 World Series

11. Eric Bruntlett, Carlos Ruiz

12. Three – Jayson Werth (2), Shane Victorino and Pedro Feliz

13. Chase Utley

14. Cliff Lee

15. Shane Victorino

PHILLIES TRULY TRIVIAL ANSWERS

1. Mike Schmidt

2. Pat Burrell, 1998

3. Jon Leiber, 2006

4. Desi Relaford

5. Richie Ashburn-1, Jim Bunning-14, Mike Schmidt-20, Steve Carlton-32, Robin Roberts-36, and Jackie Robinson-42

6. Don Money

7. Eddie Sawyer

8. Burgundy

9. Ron Reed, Frankie Baumholtz, Gene Conley, Dick Groat

10. Brooklyn/LA Dodgers

11. Dave Cross, Sam Thompson, Cy Williams, Chuck Klein, Johnny Callison, Gregg Jeffries and David Bell

12. 1964

13. Detroit Tigers

14. San Francisco Giants

15. Dave Cash

16. Richie Ashburn

17. Pittsburgh Pirates

18. Grover Cleveland Alexander

19. Grover Cleveland Alexander

20. Went over Niagara Falls

21. New York Mets

22. 51 minutes, in a loss to the New York Giants in 1919

23. John Kennedy in 1957

24. 8 (From latest to earliest: Roy Halladay (2),Kevin Millwood, Tommy Greene, Terry Mulholland, Rick Wise, John Lush, Chick Fraser)

25. D - 60 (The two hits were separated by the players' strike.)

26. 15th and Huntingdon Streets

27. 1967

28. Mayor James Tate

29. 28

30. C - Glenn Wilson

31. C - Chicago Cubs

338

32. 5 (Manny Trillo, Jay Baller, Julio Franco, George Vukovich, Jerry Willard)

33. Ivan DeJesus

34. Grover Cleveland Alexander

35. Father's Day

36. Chase Utley

37. C - Greg Luzinski

38. C - Bo Diaz

39. B - John Kruk

40. C - A wig

41. Jim Fregosi in 1991

42. Dale Murphy

43. D - Yankee Stadium

44. Todd Zeile and Benito Santiago

45. Frank Lucchesi

46. Jim Lonborg

47. Yellow

48. Chicago White Sox

49. 0

50. Phillies, Mets, Cubs

51. Pittsburgh Pirates

52. Eddie Sawyer

53. Broad Street and Pattison Avenue

54. The Bull Blast

55. "We the People 200"

56. Rich Ashburn

57. Blue Jays (1943, 1944)

58. 3

59. Pete Rose

60. New York Yankees

PHILLIES "PHAN GROUP" ANSWERS

Pat Burrell	Girls
Jose Mesa	Faces
Brandon Duckworth	Pond
Robert Person	People
Randy Wolf	Pack
Vicente Padilla	Flotilla
Chase Utley	Chicks
Sal Fasano	Pals
Cole Hamels	Train
Chris Coste	Guard
Jim Thome	Homies
Jeremy Giambi	Zombies

PHILLIES "OTHER" NUMBERS ANSWERS

Ryan Howard	12
Jimmy Rollins	29, 11
Mike Schmidt	22
Pat Burrell	33
Shane Victorino	18
Brett Myers	39
Garry Maddox	31
Mitch Williams	99
John Kruk	11, 19

PHILADELPHIA WARRIORS ANSWERS

1. Paul Arizin

2. Neil Johnston

3. Tom Gola

4. The Fort Wayne Pistons

5. 37.6 Points and 27 Rebounds

6. Syracuse Nationals

7. 1961-62

8. Hershey, PA / New York Knicks

9. Bill Campbell

10. Sam Jones

11. Eddie Gottlieb

12. One season

SYRACUSE NATIONALS ANSWERS

1. 1946

2. Danny Biasone

3. 1954-55

4. Dolph Schayes (2/1/59 v. Boston)

5. Philadelphia Warriors

6. Ike Richman and Irv Kosloff

76ERS RECORDS ANSWERS

REGULAR SEASON GAME RECORDS

1. Wilt Chamberlain – 68 points (12/16/67 v. Chicago)

2. Wilt Chamberlain – 43 rebounds (3/6/65 v. Boston)

3. Wilt Chamberlain – 21 assists (2/2/68 v. Detroit) and Maurice Cheeks (10/30/82 v. New Jersey)

4. Maurice Cheeks – 9 steals (1/5/87 v. Los Angles Clippers), Hersey Hawkins (1/25/91 v. Boston) and Allen Iverson (twice: 3/19/00 v. Orlando and 12/20/02 v. Los Angeles Lakers)

5. Harvey Catchings – 10 blocks (3/21/75 v.Atlanta),Manute Bol (2/14/91 v. Sacramento) and Dikembe Mutombo (12/1/02 v. Chicago)

6. Dana Barros - 9 three-pointers made (1/27/95 v. Phoenix)

REGULAR SEASON SEASON RECORDS

1. Wilt Chamberlain – 33.5 points per game (1965-66)

2. Allen Iverson – 225 steals (2002-03)

3. Kyle Kover – 226 three-pointers made (2004-05)

4. Shawn Bradley – 18 disqualifications (1994-95)

REGULAR SEASON CAREER RECORDS

1. Allen Iverson – 28.1 points per game [Wilt averaged only 27.6 points per game]

2. Maurice Cheeks – 6,212 assists

3. Charles Barkley – 2,688 offensive rebounds

4. Maurice Cheeks –1,942 steals

5. Julius Erving – 1,293 blocked shots

6. Allen Iverson – 877 three-pointers made

7. Allen Iverson – 2,605 turnovers

76ERS DRAFT ANSWERS

1. Two: Doug Collins – 1973 and Allen Iverson – 1996

2. 1975 / 5th overall pick

3. Leon Wood (Charles Barkley went 5th overall)

4. Charles Smith

5. Clarence Weatherspoon

6. Jerry Stackhouse

7. 1996

8. San Antonio Spurs

76ERS TRADE ANSWERS

1. Paul Neumann, Lee Shaffer & Connie Dierking

2. Jerry Chambers, Archie Clark & Darrall Imhoff

3. 1976

4. Roy Hinson

5. Terry Catledge

6. Jeff Hornacek, Tim Perry and Andrew Lang

7. Jerry Stackhouse & Eric Montross

8. Andre Miller, Joe Smith and 2 first-round draft picks

9. Gordan Giricek and a first-round draft pick

10. Rodney Carney

76ERS COACHING ANSWERS

1. Billy Cunningham – almost eight full seasons (close to the beginning of the 1977-78 season through 1984-85)

2. Dolph Schayes

3. Gene Shue

4. Billy Cunningham – 454 wins

5. Larry Brown – 205 loses

6. Alex Hannum – .798 winning percentage

7. Roy Rubin – .078 winning percentage (4 - 47)

8. Billy Cunningham – 66 wins

9. Billy Cunningham – 39 losses

10. Dr. Jack Ramsay in 1977 with the Portland Trailblazers

11. Matt Goukas

12. John Lucas

13. Johnny Davis

14. Six

15. Randy Ayers and Chris Ford

76ERS PLAYOFFS ANSWERS

1. Miami Heat

2. Orlando Magic

3. Detroit Pistons

4. Detroit Pistons

5. Detroit Pistons

6. Boston Celtics

7. Los Angeles Lakers

8. Indiana Pacers

9. Indiana Pacers

10. Chicago Bulls

11. Chicago Bulls

12. New York Knicks

13. Milwaukee Bucks

14. Milwaukee Bucks

15. Boston Celtics

16. New Jersey Nets

17. Los Angeles Lakers

18. Boston Celtics

76ERS PLAYOFF ANSWERS
continued

19. Los Angeles Lakers

20. San Antonio Spurs

21. Washington Bullets

22. Portland Trail Blazers

23. Games 3, 4, 5 and 6

24. 113 – 112

25. Boston Celtics

26. When John Havlicek stole the ball off a Sixers inbounds pass and the Celtics ran out the clock to end the game.

27. Six: 1967, 1977, 1980, 1982, 1983 and 2001

INDIVIDUAL GAME PLAYER PLAYOFF RECORDS

1. Allen Iverson – 55 points (4/20/03 v. New Orleans)

2. Wilt Chamberlain – 41 rebounds (4/5/67 v. Boston)

3. Wilt Chamberlain – 19 assists (3/24/67 v. Cincinnati)

4. Allen Iverson – 10 steals (5/13/99 v. Orlando)

5. Darryl Dawkins – 8 blocks (4/21/82 v. Atlanta) and Caldwell Jones (5/3/82 v. Washington)

6. Allen Iverson – 8 three-pointers (5/16/01 – v. Toronto)

CAREER PLAYER PLAYOFF RECORDS

1. Julius Erving – 141 games

2. Julius Erving – 3,088 points

3. Wilt Chamberlain – 1,208 rebounds

4. Maurice Cheeks – 807 assists

5. Maurice Cheeks – 269 steals

6. Julius Erving – 239 blocks

7. Allen Iverson – 115 three-pointers

8. Julius Erving – 396 turnovers

9. 0-5

10. Two (0 in '99; 2 in '00)

11. Matt Geiger

12. Indiana, Toronto and Milwaukee

13. Scott Williams

14. Jumaine Jones

15. Raja Bell

16. 48 points

17. Rick Carlisle (2003); Jim O'Brien (2002); Phil Jackson (2001) ; Larry Bird (2000)

18. Four times (1999, 2000, 2001 & 2003)

19. 6th seed

20. Samuel Dalembert

CHAMPIONSHIP YEARS ANSWERS

THE CHAMPIONSHIP YEARS: 1967-68 & 1982-83

1. 68-13

2. Alex Hannum

3. Six (Wilt Chamberlain, Hal Greer, Chet Walker, Billy Cunningham, Wali Jones and Luke Jackson)

4. San Francisco Warriors

5. Philadelphia Civic Center

6. PHILA

7. Pat Williams

8. 65-17

9. Mo Cheeks, Andrew Toney, Julius Erving, Marc Iavaroni and Moses Malone

10. Mo Cheeks, Andrew Toney, Julius Erving and Moses Malone. All 4 started (Larry Bird was the other starter)

11. Milwaukee Bucks

12. Los Angeles Lakers

13. Dick Stockton & Bill Russell

14. 115-108

15. The Forum

16. 12-1

17. Billy Cunningham

AWARDS & HONORS
ANSWERS

1. Julius Erving – 6; Maurice Cheeks – 10; Wilt Chamberlain – 13; Hal Greer – 15; Bobby Jones – 24; Billy Cunningham – 32; Charles Barkley – 34

2. Wilt Chamberlain (1965-66, 1966-67 and 1967-68), Julius Erving (1980-81), Moses Malone (1982-83) & Allen Iverson (2000-01)

3. Allen Iverson (1996-97)

4. Dolph Schayes (1965-66) and Larry Brown (2000-01)

5. Dikembe Mutombo (2000-2001)

6. Bobby Jones (1982-83) and Aaron McKie (2000 – 2001)

7. Allen Iverson – MVP; Larry Brown – Coach of the Year; Dikembe Mutombo – Defensive Player of the Year; Aaron McKie – Sixth Man of the Year

8. Julius Erving – 5 times

9. Doug Collins

10. Charles Barkley

11. Hal Greer (1968), Julius Erving (1977 and 1983), Charles Barkley (1991) and Allen Iverson (2001 & 2005)

12. Dana Barros (1995)

NICKNAME ANSWERS

1. Darryl Dawkins

2. Charles Barkley

3. Billy Cunningham

4. Charles Barkley & Rick Mahorn

5. Armon Gilliam

6. Wilt Chamberlain

7. Rodney Bufford

8. Andrew Toney

9. Mike Gminski

10. "Dr. J," "The Doctor" & "Doc"

UNIFORM NUMBERS ANSWERS

1. Orlando Woolridge
2. Benoit Benjamin
3. Tim Thomas
4. Greg Grant
5. Keith Van Horn
6. Marc Iavaroni
7. George Lynch
8. Manute Bol
9. Charles Shackleford
10. Ron Anderson
11. Larry Hughes
12. Lou Williams
13. Andrew Lang
14. George McGinnis
15. Kenny Durrett
16. Clarence Weatherspoon
17. Theo Ratliff
18. Todd MacCulloch
19. Shawn Bradley

NAME THE COLLEGE ANSWERS

Name the college or university for the following players?

1. Marshall
2. North Carolina
3. Illinois State
4. Providence
5. West Texas State
6. Detroit
7. SW Louisiana
8. Syracuse
9. Auburn
10. Washington
11. Louisville
12. Clemson
13. St. Louis
14. Hofstra
15. Georgia Tech

348

RANDOM HISTORY BY DECADE ANSWERS

1960's

1. 1963

2. A Philadelphia sports fan named Walter Stahlberg won a contest with his submission of the name "76ers"

3. Dolph Schayes

4. 34-46

5. Hal Greer

6. Chet Walker

7. Oscar Robertson

8. 1967

9. 1965

10. 1965-66

11. 1967-68

12. Hal Greer

13. Matt Guokas

14. Only time in NBA history a player has recorded a "double triple-double" (22 points/25 rebounds/21 assists)

15. 1968

16. Billy Cunningham

1970's

1. 1973-74

2. Billy Cunningham

3. 1972-73

4. Doug Collins & Bobby Jones

5. 9-73 (worst in NBA history)

6. 2 (2-35)

7. Fred Carter (20.0 points per game)

8. John Block (17.9 points per game)

9. Steve Mix

10. Lloyd

11. Henry Bibby and Joe Bryant

12. 1976-77

13. Darryl Dawkins

14. Fitz Dixon

15. 1977-78

16. Kevin Loughery

17. Henry Bibby, Doug Collins, Julius Erving, George McGinnis and Bobby Jones

18. George McGinnis

19. Clint Richardson

1980's

1. Moses Malone (51 points v. Detroit 11/14/84)

2. Harold Katz

3. "Beat LA. Beat LA."

4. Caldwell Jones

5. Michael Cooper

6. Mo Cheeks

7. Five (1982-83 through 1985-86 and 1993-94)

8. Grover Washington

9. Dave Zinkoff

10. Billy Cunningham

11. Roy Hinson and Jeff Ruland. Two games

12. Eleven

13. Mo Cheeks

14. Mike Gminski

15. Dave Zinkoff

16. Bobby Jones

17. John Nash

18. Johnny Dawkins

350

1990's

1. Jimmy Lynam

2. Detroit Pistons

3. Derek Smith

4. Gene Shue

5. Jeff Ruland

6. 32 - In honor of Magic Johnson who had announced he tested HIV-Positive

7. Six

8. Jerry Stackhouse (19.2 points per game in 1995-96)

9. Eight

10. Jimmy Lynam

11. Doug Moe

12. Manute Bol (Bol is 7'7"; Bradley is 7'6")

13. Hersey Hawkins (20.3 points per game)

14. Marc Zumoff

15. Dana Barros

16. Dana Barros (50 points 3/14/95 v. Houston)

17. Vernon Maxwell

18. First club in league history to lose more games in a season than the team had the year before for the sixth consecutive season

19. Brad Greenberg

20. Eric Montross

21. 28 – 22

22. Matt Geiger

23. PCOM (Philadelphia College of Osteopathic Medicine)

24. 1996

25. Lost

26. 20,318

27. Core States Center, First Union Center and Wachovia Center

28. John Lucas, Johnny Davis and Larry Brown

29. Hip Hop; replaced Big Shot

30. Brad Greenberg

2000's

1. Pat Croce
2. "Are you kidding me?!"
3. Ten
4. Vince Carter
5. Tyronn Lue
6. Marv Albert and Doug Collins
7. Speedy Claxton and Raja Bell
8. Tyrone Hill
9. Kyle Korver
10. Allen Iverson, Glenn Robinson and Derrick Coleman
11. Orlando Magic
12. Marc Jackson
13. Theo Ratliff
14. Miami Heat
15. Andre Miller
16. Andre Iguodala
17. "The Philly Max"
18. Torn Achilles
19. Willie Green
20. World B. Free
21. Maurice Speights
22. Senior Vice President and Assistant General Manager
23. Andre Iguodala
24. Theo Ratliff

FLYERS DECADE ANSWERS
1960's

1. Pittsburgh Penguins, St. Louis Blues, Minnesota North Stars, Oakland Seals and Los Angeles Kings

2. Less than a year

3. Philadelphia Eagles

4. Lou Angotti

5. West Division

6. Keith Allen

7. Bud Poile

8. St. Louis on October 18, 1967

9. Pittsburgh on October 19, 1967

10. Losing – 31-32-11

11. Doug Favell and Bernie Parent

12. B – Leon Rochefort November 4, 1967 at Montreal

13. Madison Square Garden and Maple Leaf Gardens

14. St. Louis Blues

15. 6

16. Chicago Blackhawks

17. Bernie Parent and Ed Van Impe

18. St. Louis

19. Vic Stasiuk

20. Bobby Clarke

1970's

1. Fred Shero

2. Bruce Gamble

3. St. Louis Blues

4. C – Buffalo Sabres

5. Doug Favell

6. Chicago Blackhawks

7. A – Dave Schultz

8. Bill "Cowboy" Flett

9. Rick MacLeish

10. Ken Hodge

11. D – California Golden Seals

12. Bob Kelly

13. Bill Clement

14. Four

15. Mel Bridgman

16. Wayne Stephenson

17. Marv Albert and Gene Hart

18. Joe Watson

1970's Continued

19. LCB Line: Leach, Clark & Barber
20. Boston Bruins
21. Hat Trick in '76
22. Los Angeles Kings
23. Terry Crisp
24. Al Hill
25. Tom Bladon
26. Skate
27. Colorado Rockies
28. Three (1973, 1975, 1976)
29. Atlanta Flames
30. D – Boston

1980's

1. Minnesota North Stars
2. Paul Holmgren
3. B – Eight (seven wins, one tie)
4. Ilkka Sinisalo
5. Pete Peeters
6. Bobby Clarke
7. Edmonton Oilers
8. Len Hachborn
9. B – 1985-86 (October 19-November 17, 1985)
10. Pelle Eklund
11. Four (1983-84 through 1986-87)
12. New York Rangers
13. Dave Poulin
14. C – Todd Bergen
15. Ted Sator
16. Guffaw
17. D – Brad Marsh
18. Tim Kerr (58)
19. Ed Hospodar
20. Rick Tocchet
21. Brad McCrimmon
22. J.J. Daigneault
23. B – Jari Kurri
24. D – Rick Tocchet
25. Dale Hunter
26. Mark Laforest
27. Washington Capitals
28. Ken Wregget
29. Mike Bullard
30. Chris Chelios

1990's

1. Russ Farwell

2. Boston Bruins

3. Bill and Kevin Dineen

4. Rod Brind'Amour

5. C – Eric Lindros, Mark Recchi and Brent Fedyk

6. Win, 5-4

7. Los Angeles Kings

8. Josef Beranek

9. Mikael Renberg (38 goals, 44 assists, 82 points)

10. Quebec Nordiques

11. John LeClair, Eric Desjardins and Gilbert Dionne

12. New Jersey Devils

13. Karl Dykhuis

14. Petr Svoboda

15. Craig MacTavish

16. Dominic Roussel

17. Loss, 3-1 to Florida, on October 5, 1996

18. Tampa Bay Lightning

19. Montreal Canadiens

20. Garth Snow (Philly) and Steve Shields (Buffalo)

21. A – Rod Brind'Amour with three

22. Daniel Lacroix

23. Dan Kordic, Lacroix and Scott Daniels.

24. New Jersey Devils

25. Vancouver Canucks

26. Detroit Red Wings – March 14, 1998

27. Dominik Hasek

28. A – Toronto Maple Leafs

29. B – Twelve (0-8-4 from February 24-March 16, 1999)

30. Adam Burt

2000's

1. C – New York Islanders

2. Rod Brind'Amour and Jean-Marc Pelletier

3. Craig Ramsay

4. 2-1

5. Ron Tugnutt

6. John LeClair

7. Keith Jones

8. Brian Boucher

9. Rick Tocchet

10. Chris Gratton

2000's Continued

11. Ruslan Fedotenko and Dan McGillis

12. B – Jeff Hackett

13. Antero Niittymaki

14. His skate

15. Ruslan Fedotenko

16. Lost, 5-3

17. Lost

18. R.J. Umberger

19. Thirteen

20. Scottie Upshall, Ryan Parent, Kimmo Timonen and Scott Hartnell

21. Joffrey Lupul and R.J. Umberger

22. Bust

23. Vaclav "Vinny" Prospal

24. New Jersey and Pittsburgh

25. Joffrey Lupul (son of ex-Canuck Gary Lupul)

26. R.J. Umberger – 10

27. Danny Briere – 9

28. Mike Richards

29. Jeff Carter – 46

30. New York Rangers

2010 ANSWERS

1. B – Jeff Hackett, in a 2-0 win over Buffalo on October 9, 2003

2. D – Mike Richards

3. C – Fenway Park

4. A – James Taylor

5. Bobby Clarke and Bobby Orr

6. B – Carcillo and Thornton, decision by knockdown to Carcillo

7. D – Danny Syvret, who scored his first career goal outdoors

8. Mark Recchi

9. C – Marco Sturm

10. C – Claude Giroux

11. Olli Jokinen

12. Simon Gagne

13. C – New York Islanders

14. Bernie Parent

15. Mike Richards

16. A – Ben Eager

17. Scott Hartnell

18. D – Dino Ciccarelli (with Minnesota in 1981)

19. A – Brian Propp (28 points)

20. 14-9

FLYERS NUMBERS ANSWERS

1. Four (Bernie Parent – 1; Barry Ashbee – 4; Bill Barber – 7; Bobby Clarke – 16)

2. 24

3. Reach the 50-goal mark

4. D – 1975-76

5. A – 2006-07

6. 472

7. 420

8. Thirteen (March 22, 1984 vs. Pittsburgh; October 18, 1984 vs. Vancouver)

9. D – Eight

10. B – 34 (in 1985-86)

11. A – 1992-93

12. B – 1993-94

13. 123

14. Eleven – because Jody Hull had taken 8

15. One, in 1995-96

16. Four – one vs. Buffalo, two vs. the Rangers, one vs. the Devils

17. 10-7

18. 122 games

19. 80 (61 in regular season, 19 in playoffs)

20. 45-24-13

21. 118

22. 350

23. B – Six (five losses, one tie)

24. 115

25. Seven

FLYERS UNIFORMS ANSWERS

1. 1, 30
2. 36
3. Long pants
4. 1997-98
5. 2002-03
6. 2003-04
7. 9
8. 77
9. 117
10. Stanley Cup patches
11. Thomas Eriksson
12. 1983-84 (orange and black at home, white and black on the road)
13. Pumpkins
14. Eleven
15. Halloween
16. Klatt, Otto and Podein; King of Prussia
17. Five
18. D – Jeremy Roenick (97 from 2001-04)
19. 21 and 12
20. On the shoulder
21. Stanley Cup 100th anniversary
22. Orange
23. America's Bicentennial
24. Reebok
25. Orange Third Jerseys

PELLE LINDBERGH ANSWERS

1. Swedish
2. Stockholm
3. United States (which tied Sweden, 2-2)
4. 31
5. 1981-82
6. Maine Mariners
7. Bernie Parent
8. Bob Froese
9. Bob McCammon
10. D – 40
11. Three
12. D – Chicago Blackhawks on November 7, 1985
13. Boston Bruins
14. D – Porsche Carrera 930
15. Edmonton Oilers
16. Wearing small "31" patches on shoulder, above the player's number.
17. John Vanbiesbrouck
18. More – 87
19. Less – Seven
20. 1994

RON HEXTALL ANSWERS

1. D – Brandon Wheat Kings
2. Hershey Bears
3. Edmonton Oilers
4. October and November
5. More – 104
6. 37
7. Kent Nilsson
8. Conn Smythe Trophy
9. Boston Bruins and Washington Capitals
10. Twelve
11. Quebec Nordiques and New York Islanders
12. Tommy Soderstrom
13. Rob Pearson
14. A – 1994-95 and 1995-96
15. 5
16. Los Angeles Kings
17. John Vanbiesbrouck
18. New York Rangers
19. Less – 296
20. Los Angeles Kings

ERIC LINDROS ANSWERS

1. Quebec Nordiques
2. New York Rangers
3. Six – Mike Ricci, Ron Hextall, Kerry Huffman, Steve Duchesne, Peter Forsberg and Chris Simon
4. Carl and Bonnie
5. D – Oshawa Generals
6. A – Pittsburgh Penguins on October 6, 1992
7. Ottawa Senators
8. 3 (1992-93, 1993-94, 1995-96)
9. New York Rangers
10. Jaromir Jagr
11. Martin Brodeur
12. Cried
13. D – Hartford Whalers
14. Bob Clarke
15. D – Igor Ulanov
16. D – Ed Jovanovski
17. Hangover
18. Darius Kasparaitis
19. Collapsed Lung
20. D – Colorado Avalanche
21. Less – 290
22. Toronto Maple Leafs
23. Kim Johnsson, Jan Hlavac, Pavel Brendl
24. Roman Cechmanek and Brian Boucher
25. Dallas Stars

MINOR LEAGUE ANSWERS

1. Philadelphia Civic Center
2. Jersey Devils
3. Firebirds
4. Maine Mariners
5. Bears
6. 1996-97
7. Bill Barber
8. Colorado Avalanche
9. "The Animal"
10. Jim Montgomery
11. Son-in-Law
12. B – Saint John Flames
13. Brian Boucher and Neil Little
14. D - Chicago Wolves
15. John Stevens
16. Jeff Carter and Mike Richards
17. 23
18. Tony Voce
19. John Paddock
20. Hershey Bears

FLYERS COLLEGE ANSWERS

1. Michigan Tech
2. Western Michigan
3. Boston University
4. Princeton
5. University of New Hampshire
6. University of Michigan
7. University of Vermont
8. Providence
9. University of Maine
10. Spartan of Michigan State
11. Boston College
12. Notre Dame
13. University of Pennsylvania
14. Ohio State
15. University of Denver

FLYERS NICKNAMES ANSWERS

1. Ed Hospodar
2. Eric Desjardins
3. Bob Kelly
4. Jeremy Roenick
5. Murray Craven
6. Peter Forsberg
7. Larry Goodenough
8. Ken Linseman
9. Lasse Kukkonen
10. F-1; L-2; Y-3; E-4; R-5; S-6

A'S THE EARLY YEARS ANSWERS

1. The Boston Braves

2. 1910 and 1911

3. True

4. Chicago Cubs

5. 1902

6. 349 strikeouts

7. 1905

8. 36-117

9. True - Their .235 winning percentage was the worst in the 20th century in all of baseball.

10. Chief Bender

A'S IN THE 20'S & 30'S ANSWERS

1. Bill Lamar – 29 games in 1925

2. Lefty Grove

3. Mickey Cochrane

4. 104

5. True – for two seasons at the age of 40 and 41 Cobb batted .327 with the As

6. Lefty Grove (31 wins), George Earnshaw (21 wins) and Rube Walberg (20 wins)

7. Boston Red Sox

8. False – The A's were the first AL club, but not the first MLB club

9. Mickey Cochrane, Pinky Higgins and Jimmie Foxx

10. Lefty Grove (1931) and Jimmie Foxx (1932 and 1933)

A'S IN THE 40'S & 50'S ANSWERS

1. Only full-time catcher to not make an error for an entire season. Rosar played in 117 games and had 532 putouts and 73 assists without making an error.

2. 1943

3. Bill McCahan on September 3, 1947

4. 1954

5. Ferris Fain

6. Bobby Shantz

7. Jackie Robinson and Stan Musial

8. The game was rained out

9. Bob Trice played his first game with the As on September 13, 1953

10. Kansas City.

ALL-TIME A'S ANSWERS

1. Eddie Collins

2. 96

3. Nap Lajoie (1901) and Jimmy Foxx (1933)

4. Al Simmons – 152 runs in 1930

5. George

6. Harry Byrd in 1952

7. 31 in 1931

8. Eddie Plank – 284 wins

9. By Saam

10. True

MISCELLANEOUS A'S ANSWERS

1. 50 years (1901-1950)

2. Jimmy Dykes (1951-1953) and Eddie Joost (1954). Earl Mack also served as interim manager on occasions when Connie Mack's health would not allow him to coach.

3. 1909

4. 468 feet

5. None

6. 21st and Lehigh Avenue

7. Robert

8. Five – 1910, 1911, 1913, 1929 and 1930.

9. 88.

10. Cornelius McGillicuddy

PENN BIG FIVE TRIVIA ANSWERS

1. Ernie Beck – 1,827 points

2. Ernie Beck – 1,557 rebounds

3. Jerome Allen – 505 assists

4. Geoff Owens – 195 blocks

5. Ibby Jabber – 303 steals

6. Stan Pawlak

7. Matt Maloney and Jerome Allen

8. Bob Weinhauer

9. Dick Harter

10. Corky Calhoun

11. Dave Wohl

12. Bob Morse

13. Michigan State

14. Jerome Allen

15. Three

16. Jack McCloskey

17. Brian Seltzer and Vince Curran

18. True – he won an awesome 83.1 percentage

19. Ibby Jabber

20. Michael Jordan

21. Ten times

22. Texas

23. Ira Bowman

24. Tim Begley

25. Ugonna Onyekwe

ST. JOSEPHS BIG FIVE TRIVIA ANSWERS

1. Jameer Nelson – 2,094 points
2. Cliff Anderson – 1,228 rebounds
3. Jameer Nelson – 713 assists
4. Rodney Blake – 419 blocks
5. Jameer Nelson – 256 steals
6. Cliff Anderson
7. Denver Nuggets
8. John Smith
9. Mike Bantom
10. Jim Lynam
11. Xavier and Oklahoma State
12. James "Bruiser" Flint
13. Denver Nuggets
14. #1
15. Tyrone Barley
16. Jim Boyle
17. Marty Blake
18. Matt Goukas, Jr.
19. Marvin O'Connor
20. Bernard Blunt and Rap Curry
21. Pat Carroll
22. Ahmad Nivins
23. Dr. Jack Ramsey
24. Widener
25. Kentucky

TEMPLE BIG FIVE
TRIVIA ANSWERS

1. Mark Macon – 2,609 points

2. John Baum – 1,042 rebounds

3. Howie Evans – 748 assists

4. Tim Perry – 392 blocks

5. Pepe Sanchez – 365 steals

6. Guy Rodgers

7. Howard Evans, Mark Macon, Mike Vreeswyk, Tim Perry and Ramon Rivas

8. Phoenix Suns

9. Hal Lear

10. Harry Litwack

11. Lamar Odom

12. UNLV and Duke

13. Terence Stansbury

14. McGonigle Hall

15. Cincinnati

16. 2001 – as an 11th seed they lost to Michigan State in South Regional Final

17. Guy Rodgers and Hal Lear

18. Rick Brunson, Eddie Jones and Aaron McKie

19. SMU

20. Cheyney State

21. Don Casey

22. Denver Nuggets

23. Sacramento Kings

24. John Calipari

25. Pepe Sanchez

LA SALLE TRIVIA ANSWERS

1. Lionel Simmons – 3,217 points
2. Tom Gola – 2,201 rebounds
3. Doug Overton – 671 assists
4. Lionel Simmons – 248 blocks
5. Doug Overton – 277 steals
6. Larry Cannon
7. Steve Black
8. Michael Brooks & Lionel Simmons
9. Tom Gola
10. Dick Harter
11. Larry Cannon
12. Kenny Durrett – 46 games
13. Convention Hall
14. Randy Woods
15. Sacramento Kings
16. Donnie Carr
17. Rasual Butler
18. Speedy Morris
19. Tim Legler
20. 15
21. Rowen
22. Billy Hahn
23. Lefty Ervin
24. 33
25. 22

VILLANOVA TRIVIA ANSWERS

1. Kerry Kittles – 2,243 points
2. Howard Porter – 1,325 rebounds
3. Kenny Wilson – 627 assists
4. Jason Lawson – 375 blocks
5. Kerry Kittles – 277 steals
6. Wali Jones
7. Dwayne McClain, Harold Pressley and Ed Pinckney
8. Sacramento Kings
9. Atlanta Hawks
10. UCLA
11. Memphis State
12. Howard Porter and Ed Pinckney
13. George Raveling
14. Howard Porter
15. An eight seed
16. Nevin Fieldhouse
17. Chuck Everson
18. Allen Iverson
19. Harold Jensen
20. Lexington, KY
21. Al Severance
22. 1973
23. True
24. UNLV
25. Scottie Reynolds

367

MISCELLANEOUS BIG FIVE TRIVIA ANSWERS

1. Chuck Daly

2. Michael Brooks

3. Dr. Jack Ramsay, Paul Westhead and Chuck Daly

4. John Nash

5. Temple

6. Jim Williams – Temple

7. John Chaney

8. 1955

9. The Palestra

10. St. Joe's over Villanova 83-70

11. St. Joe's

12. Penn

13. 1991-92

14. 1999-2000

15. John Chaney – Temple; Speedy Morris – LaSalle; Fran Dunphy – Penn; Steve Lappas – Villanova; Phil Martelli – St. Joe's

16. LaSalle

17. Penn

18. Tom Ingelsby

19. 1927

20. LaSalle – only four

21. Temple

22. Villanova and St. Joe's

23. Temple and St. Joe's

24. 0

25. Once – 1980-81

368

PHILADELPHIA GOLF
ANSWERS
Courses

1. Pine Valley Golf Club

2. Huntingdon Valley Country Club

3. Merion Country Club

4. Sandy Run Country Club

5. Waynesborough Country Club

6. Whitemarsh Valley

7. The Walker Cup

8. Merion Country Club

9. TPC at Jasna Polana

10. Huntingdon Valley Country Club

11. Chester Valley Golf Course,
    White Manor Country Club,
    Hartefeld National Country Club

12. Lancaster Country Club

13. Cobb's Creek

14. 19
    (Aronimink Golf Course.,
    Atlantic City Country Club,
    Bala Country Club,
    Blue Heron Pines Golf Course,
    Centre Square Golf Course,
    Cobbs Creek Golf Course,
    Gulph Mills Golf Course,
    Hershey Golf Course,
    Manufacturer's Golf & Country Club,
    Merion Golf Course,
    Moselem Springs Golf Course,
    Philadelphia Country Club,
    Philadelphia Cricket Club,
    Rolling Green Golf Course,
    Saucon Valley Golf Course,
    Shawnee Country Club,
    Sunnybrook Golf Course,
    Whitemarsh Valley Country Club,
    Wilmington Country Club)

THE MAJORS ANSWERS

1. 1938 - Shawnee Country Club,
    1940 - Country Club of Hershey,
    1942 - Seaview Resort,
    1958 - Llanerch Country Club,
    1962 - Aronimink Golf Course

2. Aronimink Golf Course / John Jacobs

3. Ben Hogan / One Iron

4. Lee Trevino tossed a rubber snake at Jack Nicklaus

5. Lee Trevino

6. George Burns

7. Byron Nelson

8. PGA Championship

9. Jim Furyk

10. Merion Country Club's 11th hole

11. U.S. Open

12. Merion Country Club

13. Art Wall

THE WINNERS ANSWERS

1. Tom Kite

2. Jack Nicklaus

3. Jay Sigel

4. Dale Douglass and Lee Trevino

5. Don January, Dave Hill and Tom Jenkins

6. Jim Masserio

7. Chris DiMarco

8. Ed Dougherty

9. Dick Smith, Sr.

10. Pete Oakley

11. Ski Regal

12. Arnold Palmer

13. Buddy Marucci

14. Billy Maxwell

15. Jimmy McHale, William Hyndman III, Micheal Brown and Chris Lang

16. Ed Dougherty

17. Jack Connelly

18. Gary Deetscreek

19. George Griffin Sr. and Jr.

20. Jim Booros

21. Mike Nilon

THE WINNERS ANSWERS CONT.

22. Andy Thompson

23. John Appleget

24. Bud Lewis

25. Gene Sauers

LPGA ANSWERS

1. Rolling Green Golf Course

2. Dupont Country Club

3. Laura Davies, Juli Inkster, Se Ri Pak and Annika Sorenstam

4. Bala Golf Course

5. Dorothy Porter

6. Joanne Carner

7. Ten

MISCELLANEOUS GOLF ANSWERS

1. The U.S. Open was played at Merion and the PGA Tour did not want two events in Philadelphia in the same year

2. Jack Nicklaus

3. C-52

4. Stu Ingraham

5. Six

6. J. Wood Platt

7. US Senior Amateur

8. University of Arizona

9. The Nye Family and the Reilly Family

10. John Carson

11. Will Reilly

BOXING TRIVIA ANSWERS
Famous Fights, Fighters and Firsts

1. Lew Tendler vs. Mickey Walker in 1924 for the welterweight crown. Won by Walker

2. 1918. In November, Dempsey defeated Battling Levinsky at the Olympia Athletic Club.

3. Sesquicentennial Stadium (later JFK).

4. More - 120,757.

5. Charles Dawes.

6. Tunney won a 10 round decision over Dempsey to capture the Heavyweight title.

7. Gus Lesnevich knocked out Fox in a light heavyweight title bout on 2/8/47 in New York.

8. Jersey Joe Walcott won a decision over Ezzard Charles 6/5/52, Kid Gavilan won by TKO over Gil Turner in 11 rounds in July, and Rocky Marciano KO'd Joe Walcott on 9/23/52.

9. All fights were at Municipal Stadium, a.k.a. JFK stadium.

10. 1958.

11. Connie Mack Stadium, (previously called Shibe Park).

12. Kid Gavilan.

13. Thirteenth round

14. Benny Bass.

15. Marvin Hagler

16. Hagler won a 10-round decision.

17. Jimmy Young

18. Meldrick Taylor

19. Jimmy Ellis

20. George Foreman

21. On January 22, 1973, at Kingston, Jamaica, Frazier, a 3-1 favorite, was floored six times by Foreman before referee Arthur Mercante stopped the action at 1:35 of the second round

22. True. Between 1892 and 1908, Walcott never lost a fight in Philadelphia.

23. Danny Dougherty, in 1900

BOXING NICKNAME ANSWERS

1. "Two Ton" Tony Galento

2. Bob Montgomery, of North Philly. He was the lightweight champion of the world in the 1940's

3. The Iceman, or The Wyalusing Iceman. Adgie lived on Wyalusing Ave in Philly

4. "Gypsy" Joe Harris

5. Boogaloo

6. The Worm

7. Kitten

8. The Executioner

TRAINERS, PROMOTERS & VENUE ANSWERS

1. Champs

2. Kensington Avenue and Somerset Street

3. 11th and and Catherine Streets

4. The Blue Horizon

5. 1314 North Broad Street

6. A penny a round. Starting at 40 cents admission for forty rounds of boxing, it eventually increased to 52 cents for 52 rounds

7. Boo Boo

8. Herman Taylor

9. Angelo Dundee

10. J. Russell Peltz

11. September 30, 1969 - Bennie Briscoe vs. Tito Marshall

MISCELLANOUS PHILADELPHIA SPORTS TRIVIA ANSWERS

1. Philadelphia Bell (WFL), Philadelphia Stars (USFL)

2. Six (1989-90, 1994-95, 1998, 2001)

3. Sean Landeta

4. One:1984. The other title came the following season as the Baltimore Stars

5. Eric Heiden (five Gold medals at the 1980 Winter Games at Lake Placid)

6. Philadelphia Atoms/ Philadelphia Fury

7. Bulldogs

8. Rich Gannon

9. Frankford Yellow Jackets

10. Brendan Hansen

11. The Philadelphia Fury

12. Atlantic City Seagulls

13. Gino's

14. Jim Mora, Sr.

15. Villanova Stadium

16. Dad Vail Regatta

17. Buster Mathis, Jr.

18. Gary and Paul Gait

19. New Orleans Voodoo

20. Miami Heat

MISCELLANOUS COLLEGE SPORTS TRIVIA ANSWERS

1. Immaculata College

2. Duke and Kentucky

3. Yale

4. Two (1982 and 1986)

5. Paul Palmer

6. Steve Goodrich

7. Mark Plansky

8. Oklahoma State

9. John Lucas, III (son of John Lucas, Jr. who coached the Sixers from 1994-96)

10. Ron Dickerson, who resigned after losing a 53-52 game at Pitt which Temple led by as much as 30 points

11. Curtis Enis

12. La Salle University

13. Cheyney State

14. UCLA

15. Atlantic City's Boardwalk Hall (then called Convention Hall)

16. 27 wins, no losses

17. Jerry Berndt

18. Colgate University

19. Syracuse

20. Indiana University, 1976 and 1981

21. McGonigle Hall

22. Hagan Arena

MISCELLANEOUS HIGH SCHOOL SPORTS TRIVIA ANSWERS

1. Anthony Becht (Monsignor Bonner) and Victor Hobson (St. Joseph's Prep)

2. Simon Gratz

3. Overbrook High

4. Cheltenham High

5. Lower Merion High School, graduated in 1996

6. Roman Catholic High School, St. Joseph's Prep

7. Eric "Hank" Gathers and Bo Kimble

8. Roman Catholic

9. Malvern Prep

10. Camden High School

REALLY RANDOM TRIVIA ANSWERS

1. Sesquicentennial Stadium

2. Tom Brookshier

3. Rowing

4. John Service

5. "Honk For Herschel"

6. 97.5-FM The Fanatic

7. Stu Nahan, Don Earle, Mike Emrick, Marc Zumoff

8. Nicolette Sheridan

9. Jim Barniak

10. Birdstone

11. Phillies cap and Flyers jersey

12. The Rhode Island Ram

13. Ear Flaps

14. Union

15. Passion

16. Greasing the poles

17. Chinatown

18. Chester

19. 330 feet to left and right field, 408 to center, 371 in the power alleys

20. Camera

21. Glens Falls, New York

22. Laser pointer

23. Bit his finger

PHOTO CREDITS

Harry Kalas pg. 3, courtesy The P.A.S.T. staff

The Philadelphia Association of Sports Trivia Member - pgs, 8 & 9, courtesy The P.A.S.T. staff

Lincoln Financial Field - pg. 22, courtesy The P.A.S.T. staff

Chuck Bednarik - pg. 28, courtesy Chuck Bednarik Family

Kicker statue located in the Philadelphia Sports Complex - pg. 37, courtesy The P.A.S.T. staff

Chuck Bednarik - pg. 47, courtesy Chuck Bednarik Family

Phillies game 2009, pg. 59, courtesy Sean Cronin

Carlos Ruiz - pg. 65, courtesy Sean Cronin

Charlie Manuel - pg. 68, courtesy Sean Cronin

Brad Lidge - pg. 71, courtesy Sean Cronin

1980 Phillies ticket - pg. 77, courtesy Sean Cronin

Broad Street Sign - pg. 78, courtesy Sean Cronin

Phillies Parade - pg. 80, courtesy Sean Cronin

Jimmy Rollins - pg. 82, courtesy Sean Cronin

Phillie Uniforms - pg. 87, picture taken by The P.A.S.T. staff with permission by the Philadelphia Athletics Historical Society, Hatboro, PA

Phillies Pennant - pg. 90, picture taken by The P.A.S.T. staff with permission by the Philadelphia Athletics Historical Society, Hatboro, PA

Chase Utley World Series Speech - pg. 91, courtesy Sean Cronin

Andre Igodula - pg. 102, courtesy The P.A.S.T. Staff

Sixers computer stats - pg. 107, courtesy The P.A.S.T. Staff

Allen Iverson - pg.108, courtesy The P.A.S.T. Staff

Hanging banners - pg. 111, courtesy The P.A.S.T. Staff

Sixers floor logo - pg. 120, courtesy The P.A.S.T. Staff

Sixers game action shot - pg. 126, courtesy The P.A.S.T. Staff

Eddie Jordan - pg. 127, courtesy The P.A.S.T. Staff

Flyers banners - pg. 137, courtesy The P.A.S.T. Staff

Spectrum - pg. 143, courtsey The P.A.S.T. Staff

Flyers Statue in the Philadelphia Sports Complex - pg. 145, courtesy The P.A.S.T. Staff

A's Team Photo - pg. 173, picture taken by The P.A.S.T. staff with permission by the Philadelphia Athletics Historical Society, Hatboro, PA

A's Uniforms - pg. 174, picture taken by The P.A.S.T. staff with permission by the Philadelphia Athletics Historical Society, Hatboro, PA

Connie Mack - pg. 176, picture taken by The P.A.S.T. staff with permission by the Philadelphia Athletics Historical Society, Hatboro, PA

Gate to Penn University stadium - pg. 184, courtesy The P.A.S.T. Staff

Villanova Basketball Team - pg. 194, courtesy Villanova University

Philadelphia Cricket Club, Militia Hill Course hole #3, pg. 213, courtesy The P.A.S.T. Staff

"Jersey" Joe Walcott - pg. 223, courtesy The P.A.S.T. Staff

Philadelphia Hall of Fame logo - pg. 235, courtesy Philadelphia Sports Hall of Fame

All Hall of Fame Inductees photos and artwork - pgs. 240-315 as well as all chapter header artwork, Front and Back Cover Hall of Fame Inductees artwork were provided by the Philadelphia Sports Hall of Fame.

Thank you to all the *wonderful* people who supplied us with photos from their personal photo archives!!